W9-CQO-124

Bay Area Houses

(Overleaf) ESHERICK, *San Francisco townhouse, 1951, entrance hall* (Baer)

Bay Area Houses

NEW EDITION

Edited by
SALLY WOODBRIDGE

Introduction and Foreword by
DAVID GEBHARD

Photographs by
MORLEY BAER, ROGER STURTEVANT,
and
OTHERS

Architectural drawings by
RANDOLPH MEADORS
and
FLOYD CAMPBELL

PEREGRINE SMITH BOOKS
SALT LAKE CITY

This is a Peregrine Smith Book
Copyright ©1988 by Gibbs M. Smith, Inc.

Published by Gibbs M. Smith, Inc., P.O. Box 667,
Layton, Utah 84041

Manufactured in the United States of America

92 91 90 89 88 5 4 3 2 1

First Edition

New Edition cover and final chapter designed by J. Scott Knudsen

Front cover photographs:
Back cover photograph:

Library of Congress Cataloging-in-Publication Data

Bay area houses / edited by Sally Woodbridge; introduction by
    David Gebhard; photographs by Morley Baer, Roger
    Sturtevant, and others; architectural drawings by Randolph
    Meadors and Floyd Campbell. – New ed.
    p. cm.
Bibliography: p.
Includes index.
ISBN 0-87905-306-2 : $35.00
    1. Architecture, Domestic – California – San Francisco Bay Area.
I.Woodbridge, Sally Byrne.
NA7235.C11S353 1988
728'.09794'6 – dc19   87-27802
                                              CIP

Preface

The classic observation that the most zealous in a cause are often the converts aptly applies to the five authors of this volume. At least in part each of us was drawn to the San Francisco Bay Area because of a regional architectural phenomenon which, by the time we arrived, had become known as the Bay Area Tradition. All of us were impressed or perhaps we should say beguiled by what we found. Here was a warm and winsome woodsy architecture which seemed to successfully straddle all sorts of ideological fences. These late 1940's and 1950's houses of Wurster, Dailey, Esherick, and others allowed us to retain our firm belief in the Modern (upward and onward). At the same time we did not have to feel too guilty about responding to a broad array of traditional architectural values. Having once experienced these contemporary Bay Area Tradition houses we were of course intrigued by the question of the roots of this movement, and equally curious about where the movement was going. Along with others who had preceded us we "discovered" the regional native genius of Bernard Maybeck, Julia Morgan, Ernest Coxhead, and John Hudson Thomas. Those of us who were historians plunged into this highly stimulating regional past, while those who were practicing architects took up the theme and participated in the development of the Third Bay Area Tradition, a tradition which is still very much

with us. In our self-conscious involvement with the past we have become increasingly aware that to touch it is to transform it. Having, Midas-like, transformed the past, we are sensitive to the fact that we may, in turn, affect the present and future.

Those who have inspired and contributed to this volume are:

> Joseph Baird
> Mary Ann Beach
> Kenneth Cardwell
> Esther McCoy
> Richard Longstreth
> Thomas Gordon Smith
> William L. C. Wheaton
> Robert Winter
> Diana Woodbridge

and the many architects and members of their staffs who furnished us with necessary information and documents.

April 1976   S. W.
                                              D. G.

To make the comparison of buildings easier, Randolph Meadors and Floyd Campbell drew all the plans for the first edition to the same scale: one-eighth inch equals five feet. Axonometric drawings, site plans for housing developments, and plans in the final chapter in the New Edition are not drawn to scale.

Contents

DAVID GEBHARD
Foreword to the New Edition, ix

DAVID GEBHARD
Introduction: The Bay Area Tradition, 3

JOHN BEACH
1. The Bay Area Tradition 1890-1918, 23

DAVID GEBHARD
2. Life in the Dollhouse, 99

RICHARD C. PETERS
3. William Wilson Wurster: An Architect of Homes, 121

SALLY WOODBRIDGE
4. From the Large-Small House to the Large-Large House, 155

ROGER MONTGOMERY
5. Mass Producing Bay Area Architecture, 229

CHARLES MOORE
6. The End of Arcadia, 265

SALLY WOODBRIDGE
7. Arcadia Revisited, 313

NOTES, 357
Architect's Biographies, 361
Index, 369

Foreword to the New Edition

DAVID GEBHARD

Some years have passed since the first publication of *Bay Area Houses*. At the time of its publication, there was a growing interest on the part of practicing architects and of architectural historians in the turn-of-the-century California designs of Ernest Coxhead, Willis Polk, Bernard Maybeck and others whose adventurous, and often startling, combination of historic details and images with a woodsy, natural style has come to be known as San Francisco's Bay Area Tradition. Obviously, the approach these architects had used fit in quite comfortably with what was then being called Post Modernism.

The richness of this first phase of San Francisco's Bay Area Tradition has been revealing itself, step by step, through recent articles and books. Kenneth Cardwell's *Bernard Maybeck: Artisan, Architect, Artist* (Salt Lake City: Peregrine Smith Books, 1977) and Richard Longstreth's *On the Edge of the World, Four Architects in San Francisco at the Turn of the Century* (Cambridge: M.I.T., 1983), are both major contributions to our understanding of the Bay Tradition and to American architecture in the first decades of this century. In addition, Richard Longstreth has provided us with a wonderful exposition of Willis Polk's thoughts about architecture in his Introduction and editing of *A Matter of Taste: Willis Polk's Writings on Architecture for the Wave* (San Francisco: The Book Club of California, 1979); and he has furthered our appreciation of Julia Morgan with his article, "Julia Morgan: Some Introductory Notes," in *Perspecta 15*, (Yale Papers on Architecture, 1975, pp.74-86). Other studies

are currently being written on the work of Julia Morgan and John Hudson Thomas; and it is to be hoped that the notes and unfinished writings of John Beach on Ernest Coxhead will be brought together to form a monograph on the work of this architect.

But while our knowledge and understanding of a number of aspects of the first phase of the Bay Area Tradition has been expanding in the past decade, such has not been the case with the Tradition's later phases. In recent writings on twentieth-century architecture, treatment of the later phases of the Bay Area Tradition has either been omitted entirely or generally dealt with in a fragmentary and cursory manner.

The reason for this lack of interest has to do with the current fashion in architectural design, in historiography, and in criticism. Post Modernist interest in the first phase work of Coxhead, Polk, and Maybeck, revolves around these architects' manipulation of Classical elements, not in their approach to the Medieval. And yet, as we are aware, references to the Medieval were often seminal in their designs. At present, Medieval forms are, at best, only a marginal part of Post Modernism.

In the second phase of the Bay Area Tradition, the playfulness and delight expressed in so much of the work of John Hudson Thomas, Henry Gutterson, W. R. Yelland, and Carr Jones is (with few exceptions, Charles Moore being one of them) contrary to the high and oft times pretentious seriousness of most Post Modernists. Also foreign to the mood of Post Modernism in the 1980s is much of the work in the thirties and forties of William W. Wurster and Gardner Dailey. Their approach to designs and use of traditional and modern imagery was simply too gentle and quiet for the egocentric assertiveness of either the Post Modernists or the latter-day exponents of the Modern.

Recently published histories of twentieth-century architecture illustrate the current view of the Bay Area Tradition. Kenneth Frampton, in his *Modern Architecture: A Critical History* (New York: Oxford, 1980) essentially updates the traditional Giedion/Pevsner view of twentieth century architecture: namely that the only meaningful architectural tradition in this century is that represented by the imagery and ideology of the European Modernists. Frampton disposes of the Bay Area Tradition, and, for that matter, historic traditionalism in general, by the simple device of basically leaving it out. William J. R. Curtis, in his *Modern Architecture Since 1900* (Englewood Cliffs: Prentice Hall, 1983), adheres to a similar line. Curtis does mention Bernard Maybeck and his First Christian Science Church in Berkeley, but it is mentioned as a latter-day example of the American Arts and Crafts Movement—a design by a somewhat confused pioneer of the Modern. William Wurster briefly enters the text as a West Coast regionalist who "attempted" (one assumes the implication that he did not succeed) to merge regionalism with the Modern.

In Marcus Whitten and Frederick Koeper's *American Architecture 1607-1976* (Cambridge: M. I. T., 1981), the first phase and the late aspect of the second phase are discussed. Omitted is the romantic work of the twenties and on into the thirties. (This latter omission may well be a result of what appears to be these authors' general lack of sympathy with traditional historic imagery from these two decades).

These and other recent views of the Bay Area Tradition carry on into the present several prevalent twentieth-century interpretations of architectural history. In reading through much of the current literature devoted to the history of twentieth-century architecture, it is quite apparent that the Modernist view still prevails. In fact, the ideology of Modernism has shown itself to be more tenacious in its hold than has the architecture itself. A second factor still in evidence is the contradictory manner in which Europe and the American "East Coast" continue to react to the West Coast scene. On one hand, through the decades of this century, the architecture of California and the West Coast has held a strong fascination for Europeans and "Easterners"; sometimes on the order of a perverse but delicious fruit. In contrast, the West Coast has often been seen as a distant provincial place, one that needs to be considered only marginally when thinking about the national or international scene.

Since interest (or lack of interest) in the history of the Bay Area Tradition is so closely tied to current architectural fashion, changing fashions will undoubtedly alter perceptions of the various phases of the Tradition. It is not unlikely that designers of the near future will turn their attention to the Tradition's second phase, finding a new source of inspiration in the open romanticism and easy-going quality of the work of the later thirties and forties.

It is equally apparent that the history of the Bay Area Tradition will be undergoing significant changes, not only through the addition of major biographies devoted to the Tradition's principal figures, but also through our perception of what the tradition was and is about, the sources upon which it has drawn, and its interchanges with other architectural approaches present at different times.

A case in point would be the publication and exhibition presented in 1979 of the nineteenth-century California architecture of Samuel and Joseph Cather Newsom.[1] The delightful and at times outrageous buildings designed by these two architects provide us with clues which help explain the approach to design taken at the turn of the century by Coxhead, Polk, and others. Additionally, recent studies of California's Mission Revival, the Monterey Revival, and the twentieth-century California Ranch House help to explain the work of the thirties and forties of William W. Wurster, Gardner Dailey, and others.[2]

California's self-conscious involvement with its own regional past (part fact and even more myth) is a continual source of inspiration for the proponents of the Bay Area Tradition. It is obvious that as our knowledge of the Tradition expands, so too will its influence, within California and without.

David Gebhard
Santa Barbara, California

Bay Area Houses

Introduction:
The Bay Area Tradition

DAVID GEBHARD

A DISTINCT REGIONAL TRADITION

The public became conscious that there was a Bay Area tradition of architecture towards the end of the 1940's. Lewis Mumford pointed to a "Bay Region Style" in a symposium held at the Museum of Modern Art in 1948.[1] Early the following year, nine Bay Area architects were asked by the editors of the *Architectural Record* whether there was indeed such a style.[2] All nine of these practitioners squirmed a bit, were vague and evasive, and ended up answering no. But the illustrations accompanying their comments indicated that these buildings represented a reasonable example of just what historians generally mean when they talk about style in architecture. Their rejection of the idea that a style existed was simply "prompted by a concern lest the term become so widely accepted that they would find themselves prematurely forced into a style. . . ."[3]

A somewhat more objective presentation of what the post–World War II Bay Area Tradition, as it will be called in this book, was about was contained in the catalogue accompanying the exhibition "Domestic Architecture of the San Francisco Bay Region," which was presented in late 1949 at the San Francisco Museum of Art. In his introduction to that catalogue Lewis Mumford emphasized the fact that here we were indeed dealing with "the existence of a vigorous tradition of modern building, which took root in California some half century ago."[4] And he went on

to gently slap the hands of the Bay Area practitioners and others for their childish unwillingness to realize that self-awareness, self-consciousness, and critical evaluation (i.e., the awareness of a style) are the prices which any movement must pay for its maturity.[5] By the beginning of the fifties the phrase "the Bay Area Style" had become nationally and internationally accepted.

If we look back, we can see that there actually had been a strong self-consciousness in the architecture of the San Francisco area for a long time. As early as 1906 Herbert D. Croly, the associate editor of the New York–based *Architectural Record*, looked beneath the surface of the Mission Revival and Craftsman houses then being built in California and concluded that a unique architecture was slowly coming to the fore there—an architecture which he felt represented a radically new approach to design.[6] He looked back into California's nineteenth-century past and discerned what he felt to be the sources of this new architecture—the Hispanic adobe houses and the later Anglo board-and-batten and clapboard houses. "Rudimentary as these buildings [the adobes] were and simple to the verge of attenuation, they reached, both by what they avoided and by what they effected, the essentials of good domestic architecture." And the rural wooden board-and-batten houses of the mid to later nineteenth century were such "that the easiest

WURSTER, *Grover house, San Francisco, 1939 (Sturtevant)*

and most economical way to build happened to make a tolerably pleasing building, and by the same happy chance, even the barns thrown together as they were in the hastiest flimsiest way frequently had a good curve or angle to their big roofs and a certain symmetry in the arrangement of their fronts."[7] Croly argued that the new regional architecture was drawing on these two nineteenth-century traditions.

There was a surge of awareness of the architecture of the Bay Area during the thirties and at the beginning of the forties. One of the effects of the Depres-

sion was a renewed nationalism which sparked a resurgence of Colonial revival architecture throughout the U.S., and California was no exception. The Monterey Style was an architecture which was national (based upon the Federal and Greek Revival styles) and at the same time unique to California. The "American Scene" of the thirties was staunchly rural and anti-urban; for the West Coast this meant that the untutored architecture of the mid nineteenth century could most accurately reflect the virtue of the simple, honest life, firmly attached to the soil. Bay

DAILEY, *house in Woodside, 1940 (Baer)*

MAYBECK, *Boke house, Berkeley, 1902 (Baer)*

DINWIDDIE, *Roos house, San Francisco, 1938* (Baer)

Area architects tended to emphasize the "Anglo-ness" of this nineteenth-century rural California tradition much more than their Southern California counterparts. And one of the hallmarks of the Anglo was wood—board-and-batten and clapboard walls, shingle roofs, long porches supported by simple thin square wood columns, wood-framed double-hung windows and other details.

The dominant Bay Area figure in this borrowing was William W. Wurster. Like Coxhead, Polk, and Maybeck before him, Wurster used the nineteenth-century visual language in a soft and really urbane fashion—somewhat like the poems of the thirties by Carl Sandburg. Wurster was not rural and untutored—he simply used the visual language of the rural vernacular to create his specifically American forms

of the thirties. The editors of *Pencil Points* in 1938 wrote well of the Gregory farmhouse, "Forms natural to materials and uses, undistorted by any faint suggestion of 'artiness,' give this house the charm of honesty that might have been produced by a carpenter endowed with good taste."[8]

During the thirties the work of the Bay Area designers was illustrated more and more frequently in the national home magazines and the national professional architectural journals. By the late 1930's no discussion in them could be complete without reference to the work of Wurster, Dailey, Dinwiddie, Funk, Goodman, McCarthy, and others.

In 1940 Henry-Russell Hitchcock visited the West Coast and in looking at the work of these designers, especially that of John Dinwiddie, sensed "a pro-

6

nouncedly regional quality."[9] As an apologist for the Modern, Hitchcock had some serious reservations about Wurster's and Dailey's continued use of historic imagery, and being a European-oriented urbanist he was continually disturbed by the "unexpected harshness" of Wurster's buildings.[10] In 1939 and again in 1941 another Easterner, Talbot F. Hamlin, focused attention on San Francisco and particularly the domestic architecture of the Bay Area in a series of articles published in *Pencil Points*.[11] In his article "California Fair Houses," Hamlin pointedly emphasized that what was occurring in the Bay Area was the continuation of a regional tradition derived from the nineteenth-century California Ranch House and the turn-of-the-century California Bungalow.[12] And he went on to observe that although many of the houses were modern they succumbed to "International Style clichés."[13] By 1941 the regional professional journals (*The Architect and Engineer* and *California's Arts and Architecture*) were fully aware that the Bay Area architects were creating something out of the normal.[14]

In a review of a local exhibition of residential architecture, the San Francisco architect Ernest Born noted that the Bay Area had the "extraordinary good luck of having a highly talented group of architects living here to interpret and to give life to a regional viewpoint."[15] This mood filtered down to popular magazines—*Sunset* in its March 1941 issue, for example, illustrated two woodsy houses, one by Wurster, the other by Dailey, under the title "More Sources in Western Living"—the source in this case being the California board-and-batten barn, illustrations of which accompanied those of the two houses.[16]

In 1944 Wurster published an illustrative article, "San Francisco Bay Portfolio," in the *Magazine of Art*.[17] Through his brief text and above all through his selection of illustrations he sought to show how he and his contemporaries were carrying on the earlier Bay Area Tradition of Polk and Maybeck.[18] Later in the same year New York's Museum of Modern Art organized its highly influential exhibition "Built in USA, 1932-44," which included a hefty sampling of

WURSTER, *Le Hane house, Palo Alto, 1937* (Sturtevant)

Bay Area buildings designed by Wurster, Dailey, Funk, and others.[19] Elizabeth Mock (Wurster's sister-in-law), who had organized the exhibition, noted in her introduction to the accompanying catalogue that "it was suddenly discovered that California had been enjoying a continuous but curiously unpublished tradition of building. . . ."[20]

Though the Museum of Modern Art in its 1952 architectural exhibition "Built in the USA: Post-War Architecture" pretty well turned its back on the Bay Area Tradition, the Tradition continued to be discussed and written about both in the U.S. and abroad.[21] The *Architect's Yearbook* of London (1949) contained an article by Walter Landor in which he wrote about the "California School" of architecture; and other English and Continental journals discussed the work of the Bay Area architects as if everyone was fully aware that a separate distinct school had been and was in existence.[22]

GENERAL CHARACTERISTICS

What did these writers of the late 1940's really mean when they employed the term "Bay Area Tradition"? As with most descriptive architectural terms it is not at all easy to pin down what it meant, either as an abstract concept or descriptively in relation to an aesthetic style. Though the term is imprecise, we do tend to conjure up certain specific images when we are confronted with it—perhaps a narrow high-pitched gable-roofed house in the Berkeley hills, designed in the early 1900's by Bernard Maybeck, or a boxy wood-sheathed city or suburban house of the late thirties produced by William W. Wurster. Whenever we think of these characteristic buildings we end up with certain common denominators—they are always houses, they are almost always small in scale, they are above all woodsy, sheathed in redwood (often inside as well as outside), they suggest a visual mode which is vernacular and anti-urban, they seem to be related to their respective "place" in the landscape (urban or suburban), and they are generally filled with visual and ideological contradictions.

The national and international impact of houses such as these has—since 1945—been immense and long lasting. On the popular level, features of this tradi-

tion were amalgamated in the turn-of-the-century California Craftsman bungalow, one of the first "great" exports from the West Coast, and later in that second resounding export, the post–World War II California Ranch House.[23] Among architects the products of the Bay Area Tradition have served as a source for borrowing for almost three-quarters of a century.

Ironically those buildings which most accurately reflect the Bay Area Tradition have never been the characteristic buildings of the urban environment of the Bay Area. Only in suburbia—the residential section of the East Bay communities, in parts of Marin County and in a few residential portions of San Francisco—will one discover a predominance of buildings which reflect this woodsy tradition. The usual urban buildings which one encounters in and around San Francisco and Oakland have been, especially since the mid 1890's, reasonably sophisticated interpretations of national architectural styles. San Francisco versions of turn-of-the-century City Beautiful government buildings, Gothic Revival churches, or "New Brutalist" buildings of the late fifties and sixties are basically no different from Boston and Minneapolis versions. The *dominant* architecture of the Bay Area from the 1890's through the mid 1970's has not been regional. If the general architecture of San Francisco or Oakland has exhibited a local tendency, it has been in its up-to-date, "correct," and somewhat dry interpretation of the latest national fashion. The typical Bay Area client and architect would seem to have been more concerned with reserve and respectability than with the formation of a local tradition.

So the term "Bay Area Tradition" represents an elitist view of the architecture of the region. It is closely associated with two segments in Bay Area society—the intelligentsia (would-be or otherwise) and a segment of the area's upper middle class. Bay Area Tradition architecture has never been really popular, even though in their homes the middle-middle and lower-middle classes have been perfectly willing to accept and adopt certain of its features. In this it is not unique. Like all of the other major twentieth-century traditions of European and American architecture, the Bay Area Tradition has been the province of an exclusive and small but dominant segment of society, and in the long run this is just as it should be. The do-it-yourself houses of the "Wood-Butchers" in the late sixties and the seventies are as much an expression of exclusiveness (they being, almost to the last woman and man, products of the upper middle class) as the early Maybeck houses of 1900 were for academicians and camp followers of the University of California.

Bay Area Tradition buildings, whether they are to function as firehouses, churches, schools, or houses, always end up being domestic, anti-urban, and often picturesque. The buildings are inevitably woodsy in atmosphere; they express a self-conscious delight in using "natural material"; traditional materials—redwood, brick, stone, even stucco and plaster—are lovingly manipulated as both texture and structure. Architects and their clients appear to have appreciated these materials for their unique qualities. And because the materials and the structural forms tend to be traditional, old-fashioned, and earthy, the buildings convey a sense of belonging to their respective sites.

Self-conscious contradiction is another long-enduring quality found in these Bay Area Tradition buildings. The ordinary day-to-day builder's vernacular is purposely played off against highly sophisticated spatial arrangements, surfaces, and details of design, and against a learned understanding of past historic architectural history. Interior spaces which are open and flowing at one moment become closed and boxy at the next; and plans which appear logical, simple, and direct turn out to be highly complex and even in some cases idiosyncratic.

Fragments from the past and even from the present are yanked from their traditional places in the hierarchy of a building and are presented in new and unlikely contexts. The scale of these fragments is often bizarre: gigantic columns placed in the small-scaled world of a dwarf, or windows placed and designed so that it becomes difficult or even impossible to "read" what the building is all about. The proponents of the Bay Area Tradition seem to have taken a continual and almost perverse delight in creating volumes, surfaces, spaces, and details which are just plain ugly or ungainly, then ranging them alongside elements which are refined, delicate, and sophisticated.

Most vernacular and high art architecture is deadly serious, but the Bay Area Tradition designers have obviously enjoyed countering this prevalent attitude with humor and satire—sometimes in a manner very subtle and light, at other times more directly. Elements of humor and satire have often helped to suggest the world of romance, of the storybook, as opposed to the realities of the present, even of the past; and they have helped to suggest the images of our childhood. For, as these architects realized, the conceptual reality of the world of the child can make the down-to-earth reality of the adult world appear ridiculous, even unreal.

Behind these many elements which make up the Bay Area Tradition has been an awareness upon the part of the architect of whom he is addressing. To "misuse" historic detail, to employ the out-and-out uncultured vernacular, would hardly appeal to the normal red-blooded San Franciscan, let alone American. For this new and complex language to work, i.e., to be read and understood, demanded that the architect and his client both know what the "correct" architectural verbiage is for the Classical, Medieval, or Renaissance; and equally they must be aware of the vagrancies of the uncouth vernacular world of low art. Only after he has acquired a familiarity with the historic language of architecture (including all of its traditional value judgment) has it been possible for the artist (in this case the architect) to extract here and there these historic elements, refine them, and then constitute a composite whole which lends itself to a new subtle reading.

HISTORY

A rather artificial ordering suggests that this tradition has three expressive phases.

The First Phase

The suburban shingle architecture of Ernest Coxhead, Willis Polk, A. C. Schweinfurt, John Galen Howard, and others.

The Bay Area's version of the Craftsman building; the early work of Bernard Maybeck, Julia Morgan, Louis Christian Mullgardt, Henry Gutterson, and John Hudson Thomas.

The Second Phase

The Hansel and Gretel cottage world of the twenties; the work of John Hudson Thomas, W. R. Yelland, Henry Gutterson, W. H. Ratcliff, Jr., Carr Jones, and Clarence Tantau.

The thirties wood imagery of rural California; William W. Wurster, Gardner Dailey, John Funk, and Francis Joseph McCarthy and others.

Carry-over of approach from the late thirties, the redwood post and beam box; Wurster, Bernardi & Emmons, Gardner Dailey, Henry Hill, Joseph Esherick, Mario Corbett, and others.

The new self-conscious historicism of the later fifties and the sixties; Charles W. Callister, William W. Wurster, and others.

The Third Phase

The wood-sheathed vertical box—Charles W. Moore, William Turnbull, Donlyn Lyndon, Richard Peters, Joseph Esherick, George Homsey, and Dmitri Vedensky. A new borrowing from the vernacular, this time from the builder.

COXHEAD, *St. John's Episcopal, San Francisco, 1890* (*California Historical Society, San Francisco*)

THE FIRST PHASE

The English expatriate Ernest Coxhead reduced his various churches in Northern California to a size and scale which is barely believable. One could easily believe that his Byzantine/Romanesque St. John's Episcopal Church in San Francisco (1890), with miniature entrance and side isles and a peculiar, almost sinister, tower of immense bulk pressing down, had emerged from the pages of a late Victorian volume of fairy tales. His St. John's Episcopal Church in Monterey (1891) carries its surface pattern of straight and wavy shingles down over the roof and the eaves onto the walls, and, like the bark of a tree, right down to the ground. In his St. John's Episcopal Church in Petaluma (c. 1890) he created an entrance screen composed of a pair of tiny Ionic columns, set on a single one below, and above the arched entrance is a curved broken pediment (Baroque?) in the middle of which he set a Mission Revival quatrefoil window. Now all of these historic rummagings which Coxhead used

were being used elsewhere in the East and Midwest, in the early work of Ralph Adams Cram in and around Boston, or in the Midwestern work of Cass Gilbert. But what separates Coxhead's work from the others is the open contradiction of these elements, a contradiction which constitutes the building's basic visual statement.

Though generally more staid and "respectable," Coxhead's contemporaries Willis Polk and A. C. Schweinfurt often used a similar rich and contradictory visual vocabulary in their buildings of the late 1890's. Polk's own house in Russian Hill in San Francisco (1892, actually a double house) represented another case of miniaturization. In his 1893 Rey house on Belvedere Island, Polk evoked a complex miniaturized interior space organized around an open vertical staircase core. Arches and other historical interior details hinted that the Rey house was of appropriate manorial dignity; externally his stucco walls, arched openings, and quatrefoil windows lightly suggested the Mission heritage of California.

The sources which Polk, Coxhead, and others of this generation drew upon were quite catholic. In the early nineties the late Shingle Style, with a heavy overlay of Classical details (in wood) derived in part from the then-popular Colonial Revival (and also from the English Queen Anne), was their usual fare.

COXHEAD, *St. John's Episcopal, Monterey, 1891*

COXHEAD, *Holy Innocents, San Francisco, 1890 (David Gebhard)*

COXHEAD, *St. John's, Petaluma, 1890 (David Gebhard)*

POLK, *Polk-Williams house, San Francisco, 1892* (Baer)

But very early they began to mix these elements with Medieval fragments and with surface and volume reminiscent of Medieval town houses and rural Medieval cottages. Before 1900 specific Hispanic elements crept in—Mission Revival, and then Mexican and Spanish; and finally these Bay Area designers, like their counterparts elsewhere in the country, became enamored of the Neo-Classic forms of the City Beautiful Movement.

Coxhead's younger contemporary, the Beaux-Arts–trained Bernard Maybeck, had a similarly catholic taste. On the surface Maybeck's Berkeley houses of the early 1900's might be thought of simply as idiosyncratic examples of the last gasp of the Shingle Tradition, or of the newly developing version of the American Craftsman Movement. And yet they do not really represent either one of these modes—though he certainly freely used their vocabulary.

Maybeck's exposed wood structure, board-and-batten walls, and enormous rough brick fireplaces never seem to end up as being either within the late Shingle Style or within the confines of the Craftsman movement.

Their space is abbreviated and condensed—tending to denote the unreal; and, both internally and externally, these houses strongly suggest a storybook illusion (the romance of the past, not scholarly historicism). The high peak hall of the Faculty Club of the University of California at Berkeley (1902; 1903-4) creates the sense of a Viking hall. Like the turn-of-the-century English architect Charles F. A. Voysey Maybeck brought the "realism" of our childhood experience into the physical environment of our adult world. Maybeck transformed the wood surface and structural vernacular of Northern California into an illusion of a distant mythical Golden Age—suggestive of a Medieval past in the Keeler house (Berkeley, 1894) and in the 1913 Chick house (Berkeley) with its quatrefoil balcony and pointed elliptical arch, or suggesting the Classical past in his 1915 Palace of Fine

MAYBECK, *Kellog house, Palo Alto, 1899 (Baer)*

Arts. Like Coxhead's, Maybeck's visual language of contradictions ran the full gamut—playing one historicism off against another: finely crafted windows and staircases situated next to rough exposed floor joists and rafters; axial sequences of space ending (or starting) in a maze of seemingly confused, mysterious space. Maybeck's language was even more varied and erudite than Coxhead's and Polk's before him; he added new ingredients, among which were a highly selective version of Swiss architecture and a highly selective version of the California rural vernacular, especially that characterized by redwood board-and-batten construction. But Maybeck's work differed from that of his older contemporaries in two marked ways—first, he was much more open and inventive in his willingness to mix new and older materials and structural forms; and second, his brilliant inventiveness as a designer made it possible for him to evoke the dreamy romanticism of a Classical or Medieval past—not through historic fragments which are experienced as separately removed elements, but through the integration of all these elements into a total composition.

The third generation of Bay Area designers continued the tradition, some with really deep and intense conviction, like John Hudson Thomas. Others, like Julia Morgan, Henry T. Gutterson, Clarence Tantau, or W. H. Ratcliff, dabbled in the tradition, but eventually settled down to a more traditional use of the then-popular architectural idioms. Thomas' early buildings (pre-1915) are in several instances the most unbelievable designs to be produced within the Bay Area Tradition. We have only to look at his Locke house (1911), his Dungan house (1915), or the Peters house (1915) to sense the oddity of his designs. He attempted to create forms and spaces that should never have been. He seems to have gathered on his drafting table a Sweets catalogue of samples of every avant-garde movement which was then being practiced in Europe and America; Austrian and German Secessionist forms and details; a hint of Voysey's Alice in Wonderland cottages; MacIntosh's personal version of the Art Nouveau; Wright's Midwestern Prairie Style; the American Craftsman interest in North American Indian art (especially America's own indigenous Pueblo art); the forms and details of the turn-of-the-century Mission Revival; and

elements of Maybeck's rich and varied work available right at his doorstep. The strength and fascination of these early buildings of Thomas lie in the fact that by the time he had finished manipulating these sources they ended up as a strange and unusual parody (of a sort) on the original. Maybeck's visions succeeded because of his ability to capture the romance of the past—as a childhood experience—in the completeness and totality of each of his buildings. Thomas succeeded for just the opposite reason—his buildings give the appearance that they never should have been; they are purposely left incomplete, abrupt, awkward, fragmented—impossible.

MAYBECK, *detail of Goslinsky house, San Francisco, 1909 (Baer)*

THOMAS, *Peters house, Berkeley, 1907* (Baer)

THOMAS, *plan of Dungan house, Berkeley, 1915*

 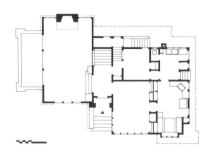

15

THE SECOND PHASE

The Bay Area Tradition of the twenties tended to employ a more limited historical architectural imagery and to refrain from emphasizing a variety of past historical fragments in one single building. Polk, Coxhead, and Maybeck—all of whom continued to work during the twenties—employed the prevalent Spanish Colonial Revival images, but they also used historical styles which were loosely Medieval—usually English or French Norman. The younger designers, Thomas, Gutterson, Ratcliff, W. R. Yelland, Carr Jones, and Hugh Comstock, were almost exclusively committed to suggesting the Medieval, especially in the image of the Cotswold cottage or the Norman French farmhouse. The styles in which these architects clothed their buildings did not differ from those being used in the Southland of California and throughout the U.S., though the Colonial Revival enjoyed only a marginal popularity on the West Coast. What set the work of these men apart was their peculiar way of using these historical forms and details; the complexity of their forms and spaces; their desire to miniaturize; and their desire fully to exploit the site as a major ingredient in creating a romantic aura. One's traditional sense of scale is denied in such buildings as Thomas' Hume house in Berkeley (1928); it appears to be a distant, not quite believable stone castle (it is actually built of exposed concrete blocks) high on a mountainous crag; its walled courtyard and great hall should resound to the sounds of armor and knights and ladies of the court (the twenties Hollywood variety). But all has been so reduced in scale that we feel we are outsiders peering into a child's vision of the past.

Thomas' contemporary W. R. Yelland created in his Thornberg Village (Berkeley, 1928) a stage-set version of a whole French Norman village which even today suggests that this vision of the past has more meaning than the day-to-day reality of the present. And Henry H. Gutterson and others sprinkled the Berkeley hills with numerous highly fanciful small-scaled Hansel and Gretel cottages hidden away from the trespassing eyes of the modern world in their dense thickets of trees, shrubs, and flowers.

While the use of Medieval imagery was by no means abandoned by Thomas, Maybeck, and others in the thirties, Bay Area Tradition architects looked elsewhere for their visual sources—at first to the Monterey Revival style, then to the wooden board-and-batten and clapboard California rural ranch house and barn, later to a stripped version of the Regency, and finally to a domesticated and much softened interpretation of the Modern (the International Style). By the early thirties William W. Wurster had emerged as the major figure of this aspect of the Second Phase. Wurster's typical buildings, like Polk's and Gutterson's, were purposely low-keyed. On first encounter they seem anonymous, even pedestrian, and in some cases just plain dull. Actually, these very qualities of anonymity and blandness were highly important elements of his visual language; and

THOMAS, *drawing of Hume house, Berkeley, 1928*

THOMAS, *Hume house* (*Baer*)

if we are patient we will find that his spaces and forms represent a concoction of traditional, modern, and builder's vernacular elements which no well-trained, self-respecting architect would ever have thought of using.

From his 1928 Gregory farmhouse, or ranch house, as it is so often called, near Santa Cruz to his 1938 Van Deusen house in Berkeley, he contrasted and played off everything imaginable—space which conveys a Classical order is juxtaposed with space which ap-

pears casual, placement of windows and doors seems to deny the hand of the architect, and so on. By the late thirties Gardner Dailey (and to a considerable degree the younger designers in his office such as Joseph Esherick), John Funk, Clarence Mayhew, John Dinwiddie, Hervey Clark, Michael Goodman, and Joseph McCarthy had taken up and begun to play the game of countering the modern with the traditional and the vernacular.

After the Second World War the Second Phase

Hume house, interior of court (Baer)

18

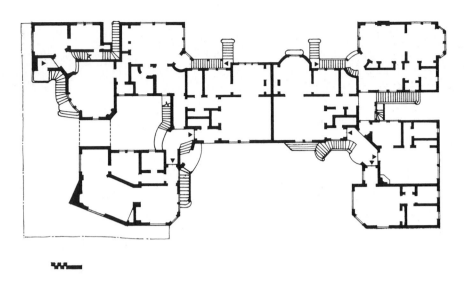

YELLAND, *plan of Thornberg Village, Berkeley, 1928*

WURSTER, *Gregory farmhouse, Santa Cruz, 1926-27* (*Sturtevant*)

CORBETT, *house on Wolfback Ridge, 1948 (Baer)*

continued in the hands of Wurster, Dailey, and Funk, who were joined by Joseph Esherick (now on his own), Mario Corbett, Roger Lee, and Henry Hill. The Second Phase was now both at its weakest (within the tradition) and at its strongest in terms of popular and professional acceptance. By the late fifties it was evident that the practitioners of the tradition were groping for new images which could revitalize what had become tired. Formalism with a tinge of structural exoticism came to the fore in the elegant designs of Jack Hillmer and others, but this proved to be, as far as the Bay Area Tradition was concerned, a dead end. Another possibility which presented itself was to go back to the styles of the First Phase and rework the imagery of Maybeck and others. Although several designers, including Charles W. Callister, tried it, occasionally creating beautiful details, this self-conscious artsy craftism seldom produced really convincing buildings.

THE THIRD PHASE

The major turning point came in the early sixties with the emergence of Charles W. Moore, William Turnbull, Donlyn Lyndon, Richard Peters, and George Homsey, and with the changes which took place in the designs of the Esherick office.[24] From the contemporary world these designers plagiarized (in the best sense of the term) the work of the Philadelphian Louis Kahn and of the Finnish designer Alvar Aalto. They countered these new high-art images by borrowing from the California rural tradition, especially the wood sheathed outbuildings and barns, with a renewed pop art appreciation of the constructor/builder's vernacular. In their buildings they tended to turn the horizontal Second Phase buildings on end and to introduce vertical spatial complexity. Picturesqueness once again entered the scene—internal as well as external picturesqueness.

The buildings of Moore and his contemporaries

M/L/T/W, *Talbert house, Oakland, 1962 (Baer)*

21

were from the beginning as exclusive in their language as were the buildings of Coxhead, Maybeck, Thomas, and Wurster. It could well be argued that the Bay Area Tradition had at last arrived at a point where its visual language must be accompanied by written language. Even the erudite needed help in "reading" and responding to the sophisticated vagaries of this visual language.

The critical reactions to the Third Phase changed radically during the sixties. To a marked degree this was due to the major shift occurring worldwide in the rejection of the precepts and imagery of the International Style. It was equally an outcome of two local changes: the emergence of a new imagery, the vertical "mine-shaft" box; and the coupling together of visual and verbal ideas in the writings of several Bay Area designers, especially those of Charles W. Moore. By the late sixties the vertical shed-roofed box, generally sheathed in wood, had caught on as *the* new fashion, and by the mid seventies variations on the shed-roofed vertical box were to be found all over the U.S., some designed by architects, most produced by designers working for builders and developers on condominium projects. So the Third Phase has become as popular an export from its natural habitat as the Second Phase was. Only, once again, the richness of language—of contradiction and conflicts—has been smoothed over and disguised. What is left is a mellow "style"—occasionally striving toward the pretense of High Art; generally, though, of a low-art nature. Also cast aside has been the rich verbal imagery (the wealth of caption material) which is an essential element in a Moore, Esherick, or Turnbull product. The packaging of this exported product has thus become pure Style, totally devoid of its other implications.

1

The Bay Area Tradition 1890-1918

JOHN BEACH

California's architecture is the record of a series of responses, some of them unconscious but many self-conscious to an extreme degree, to a certain set of myths and realities. There is the myth of a Spanish California devoted to luxuries and fiestas. There is the myth of instant riches for all. There has been an aura of almost Tibetan exoticism fostered by California's early remoteness and the perils of the journey there. The realities are those of the climate (which is mild and generally benign) and the landscape (which is spectacular and, when adequately watered, fantastically fertile). In the late 1880's the realities also included a frontier society just beginning to transform itself into something else. The population of this society had been brought here primarily by the gold rush. The gold fever infected equally all social, cultural, and economic classes, and the society which resulted was uniquely rich and varied: it was simultaneously cultured and ignorant, brawling and refined.

A nearly legendary California was created, an idyllic land where anything was possible and where the rules of conventional society did not necessarily apply. It was a place where man's mark on the environment demanded the emphatic, the extravagant, the fabulous. This challenge was, of course, not always met: the architecture of California, like the architecture of other places, ranges largely from the negligible to the dreadful. In fact, the generation of archi-

tects brought to California by the gold rush did not seem to recognize the challenge at all; they built, as closely as frontier technology would allow, the buildings they would have built had they stayed in St. Louis, Manchester, or Stuttgart.

But at the end of the 1880's and the beginning of the nineties a group of designers appeared in California who were attracted by both the opportunity and the challenge. Arriving at the perfect moment, Ernest Coxhead, Willis Polk, Bernard Maybeck, A. C. Schweinfurth, and A. Page Brown encountered a situation exactly suited to their talents and ambitions: a society with adequate means just beginning to realize a desire for more permanent buildings, a clientele with aspirations but without esthetic prejudices. These designers brought with them stylistic and philosophical luggage from a wide range of backgrounds. They used fragments of the past as well as fragments of the present and juxtaposed them in a manner which expressed the complexities, the myths, and the realities of the California experience. The local building vernacular, the straightforwardly utilitarian wood frame buildings of the mining and boom towns of the second half of the nineteenth century, provided the ideal neutral base upon which to impose preferences of space, style, and form.

The Bay Area Tradition represents not a style, but a process of synthesis and transformation: a design approach with trademarks and no rules. This has created some confusion for critics who have tried to define what the Bay Area Tradition is all about. The confusion has been compounded by the fact that there have been designers not directly related to the tradition who have used some of the trademarks some of the time, and by the fact that even the major practitioners have not used all the trademarks all of the time. But there is a definable body of work which shares an easily discernible continuity of thought. This thought evolved in two places: the office of Ernest Coxhead, and the office of A. Page Brown.

Coxhead was an Englishman who had established himself in Los Angeles in the mid-1880's (where Willis Polk had worked for him for a short time); he moved his office to San Francisco in 1890. Coxhead's early study of English ecclesiastical architecture had developed in him a keen appreciation of the residues of change. In such designs as his 1890 St. John the Evangelist Episcopal Church in San Francisco, the juxtaposition of seemingly unrelated components is an exploitation of the visual qualities of buildings which have undergone successive alterations over a period of centuries. The contradictory elements in Coxhead's designs create implications of a non-specified history for the building. There is a strong strain of parody in Coxhead's work which is unusual in architecture (traditionally the most self-consciously serious of the arts). It is a risky business to judge the past by the attitudes of the present, but it is impossible not to feel that in the 1895 Earl house Coxhead satirized, as well as satisfied, the client's cultural pretensions.

One of Coxhead's interests was the English manor house. His first buildings in Northern California display half timbering, neo-Elizabethan window mullion patterns, and other quaint, period-revival details. These he soon shed. But he had a continuing interest in certain traditional spatial concepts: he frequently integrated into his California houses variations of the Great Hall and Long Gallery of the English country house. In his own house, built in 1893 on a narrow lot in urban San Francisco, the entrance hall is a miniature Long Gallery. The living room, dining room, kitchen, and stairs are all strung along this hall: it functions as a spine, a corridor, and a room. It is many times longer than its width and boasts two fire-

places. The first, in the narrow end wall, near the entrance to the house, performs a symbolic function of welcome. The other, placed in the long wall near the opposite end, faces a square bay which widens the hall enough for a comfortable seating area, providing a pleasant, light place for tea on San Francisco's fog-bound afternoons. This bay overlooks the garden of a small house next door, also designed by Coxhead. The two houses form an ell around the shared open space. The master bedroom upstairs has a high vaulted ceiling with roof-bracing trusses near the top. All details of the room are scaled to increase its apparent size. The windows are small-paned, and closer to the floor than one expects: in one corner at an angle is the entrance to the room with a fireplace on one side and a seat on the other. As long as the door is open it, the fireplace, and the seat remain separate elements; but when the door is closed, these elements are joined to form a cozy inglenook. That the door must be closed to create this private place reinforces the intimate feeling of separation from the world outside.

COXHEAD, *Earl house, Los Angeles (destroyed; early photo)*, *1895*

COXHEAD, *Coxhead house (early photo), San Francisco, 1893*

Coxhead house (early photo), San Francisco, side elevation

26

Coxhead house, San Francisco, bedroom (Baer)

Many of the nineties houses of both Coxhead and Polk have spatial qualities which seem derived specifically from the stairwell spaces of some of the grander Queen Anne/Shingle Style houses of the East Coast. It is as if the house had been trimmed away, leaving only the circulation space. Then a step here and a landing there are extruded horizontally, expanded from a small space to a larger one. By this curious process the stair sequence ceases to be simply an element of a larger building, but is transformed into the building itself.

This is clearly seen in two of Coxhead's houses from the early 1890's which are essentially expanded stairways: Coxhead's own second house in San Mateo

and the Greenlease house in Alameda. The Greenlease house is a more ample version than Coxhead's own, but they are basically identical in spatial concept. Each is entered through a low enclosed space which is in fact tucked beneath a stair landing (a frequent device of Coxhead's). From there a series of steps leads through a brightly lit, open space to a landing which is extended to become the main living space. Then the stair turns and continues its interrupted flight to the platform which defines the ceiling of the low entrance space. In Coxhead's house this landing is simply that; a landing. In the Greenlease house the platform is again expanded, into a sitting area and gallery overlooking the main space.

Coxhead house, San Mateo, entrance (Baer)

Coxhead house (early photo), San Mateo, c. 1893

Coxhead house, San Mateo, interior with stair (Baer)

Coxhead house, San Mateo, plan

Coxhead house, San Mateo, section

COXHEAD, *Greenlease house, Alameda, 1892-94* (Baer)

In both cases the stair continues its journey from this second platform to the second floor.

The 3200 and 3300 blocks of San Francisco's Pacific Avenue are a superb showcase of the urban phase of the Bay Area Tradition. There are buildings by Maybeck, Polk, and Coxhead, as well as work by lesser designers and anonymous contractors. These houses, mostly of redwood shingles, create that distinctive San Francisco ambience resulting from the union of urban form and rustic materials. The most fascinating group is the row of five houses lining the north side of the 3200 block. The steeply sloping triangular site is forty-five feet deep at the upper end. The top house, which is the widest, is by an anonymous builder. The next two houses are by Ernest Coxhead, and the remaining two are by William F. Knowles. The lowest of the Knowles houses, occupying the very end of the triangle, is only three and one-half feet wide at its narrowest point. From just below this house it is possible to look up and see the entire complex cascading down the hill like Duchamp's *Nude Descending a Staircase*. Although the front facades maintain a reasonably precise plane, the backs are an amazing collection of bays and boxes extruded into space bootlegged from the Army Presidio, whose wall defines the property line. Of the five buildings, the two Coxhead houses are architecturally the most sophisticated.

One of these was built in 1904 for the San Francisco artist/craftsman/dilletante Bruce Porter. The other, the more interesting of the two, had been built two years earlier for Porter's sister and her husband, Julian Waybur. Both facades present simple shingle planes which serve as a backdrop for careful concen-

Greenlease house, stairway (Baer)

COXHEAD AND KNOWLES, *3200 block of Pacific Avenue,
San Francisco* (Baer)

trations of Georgian-derived ornament. The Porter house is rather straightforward, but the Waybur house is Coxhead at his most playful. Above a squat, heavily pedimented entrance, the treads and risers of the circulation stair are pulled through the facade, distorting, in a mannerist fashion, the expected form of the Palladian window which lights the stair hall.

Coxhead seems to have had a thorough understanding of both the possibilities and limitations of urban life: of all the Bay Area designers he was probably the only one to whom these cramped and impossible sites were a congenial problem. Even on less cramped sites, Coxhead's buildings do not expand into the out-of-doors. If there is a garden, the house is carefully designed to take maximum advantage of its views, but sometimes actual access is not really provided for

3200 block of Pacific Avenue,
view from Presidio side (Baer)

(in at least one case it is necessary for the gardener to get to the garden through the window of a service room). But it is interesting to compare Coxhead's straightforward acceptance of the limitations of the sites on Pacific Avenue with Maybeck's very fine Goslinsky house of 1909, across the street. On a similarly cramped but slightly deeper lot, Maybeck adroitly deceives the observer. The house is entered at street level from a tiny entrance court notched out of the front of the building. The entry hall is a high, narrow volume filled with a spiral cascade of steps leading to the main floor half a story above. Although

Goslinsky house, original plan

34

MAYBECK, *Goslinsky house, Pacific Avenue, San Francisco, 1909* (Baer)

35

this space is brightly lit, there are no eye-level openings to the front: this successfully isolates the visitor from the world of the street. From the top of the steps, at the door into the living room, there is an unbroken diagonal vista, through the glass doors which separate the living and dining room, and through french doors at the rear of the dining room to a small garden. This unexpected glimpse of seemingly distant greenery creates a convincing illusion that the house has been magically transported to suburban Berkeley.

Except for Coxhead, all the major figures worked at one time or another in the office of A. Page Brown. Brown's office attracted talented, ambitious, but unestablished young architects; it had a reputation for being one of those places where designers were pretty much left on their own to develop their own ideas. Much of the work from the office was either Colonial Revival or in the Shingle Style idiom which Brown brought with him from the East Coast, where he had built up a fashionable practice (both Polk and Schweinfurth had been associated with the Brown office before the move to California). Such buildings as the Mary Ann Crocker Old People's Home (1890)

were an important influence on subsequent Bay Area designs.

It was Brown's office which produced, in 1894, one of the Bay Area's most popular minor monuments, the Church of the New Jerusalem (Swedenborgian). The pastor, Joseph Worcester, was an influential member of a circle of intellectuals involved in the visual arts, and he had considerable say in the design process of the church. Who else was involved, and who was responsible for what, is not possible to determine, but the question continues to provide material for endless speculation by historians and critics. Bruce Porter sketched the Italian chapel upon which the church design is supposedly based. There is a presentation drawing of the building by Bernard Maybeck, and the simplified detailing of parts of the interior is quite similar to his later work. The use of madrone trees in their natural state for roof beams suggests Schweinfurth and his interest in the imagery of primitive building modes. Polk, as a member of the Worcester circle, may have contributed something to the work, at least as a kibitzer (he was not at this time connected with Brown's office). It could be argued (and has been by writers with various axes to

BROWN, *Old People's Home* (*early photo*), *San Francisco, 1890*
(*California Historical Society, San Francisco*)

BROWN, *Church of the New Jerusalem (Swedenborgian)*,
San Francisco, 1894 (Baer)

grind) that any of these was the major figure in the design of the building. But it seems likely, given the nature of the situation, and the fact that none of the designers who was or may have been involved ever claimed it as his own work, that the church was the cooperative effort of a group of men with closely shared views. The Swedenborgian Church is a milestone—not, as is often stated, the starting point for the Bay Area Tradition. The combination of the rustic and the urban, the primitive and the sophisticated, the European and the American, the historic and the new, which so firmly places the church in the tradition, had already been stated by Coxhead, Polk, and others, from 1890 on. But despite the confusion and conjecture the fact of the building remains untouched. It is a serene place. Entrance is first into a loggia, and then to a walled garden which gives access to the church itself. This interweaving of nature and architecture reflects the profound love of natural things embodied in Swedenborgian tenets, and is echoed inside the sanctuary by the madrone trunk roof beams and by murals of the four seasons by

Church of the New Jerusalem (Swedenborgian), interior (Baer)

Worcester's friend, the San Francisco painter William Keith. Bruce Porter designed two stained glass windows for the church. Maybeck designed the starkly simple chairs, credited by Gustave Stickley as the source for Mission Style furniture.

Maybeck's father was a wood-carver and Maybeck himself had trained briefly in that craft before attending the Ecole des Beaux-Arts; he was always to have the craftsman's feel for his own buildings. He carved, painted, and tinkered on them; he was involved in the construction process in a way that neither Polk nor Coxhead ever was (or wished to be). Thus his buildings were closer to the hand-built imagery of the American Craftsman Movement than were the buildings of other Bay Area Tradition practitioners. In such designs as the 1902 Boke house in Berkeley, there is a hint of Swiss folk art in the carved decorative motifs. Apart from the superficial Swiss influences the Boke house boasts a modular plan which appears to derive from Oriental sources and an exterior wall treatment which could have popped right out of the pages of a nineteenth-century Stick-Style pattern book. As in many early Coxhead and Polk houses the stair/circulation space is treated grandly

*Church of the New Jerusalem (Swedenborgian),
interior (Baer)*

Boke house, living room (Baer)

MAYBECK, *Boke house, Berkeley, 1902 (Baer)*

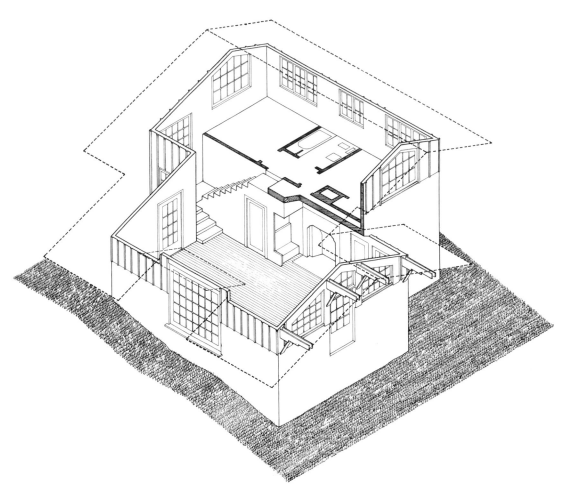

MAYBECK, *Mathewson house, Berkeley, 1916, axonometric*

enough to lend visual expansiveness to what is essentially a cottage. The problem of the small, inexpensive house intrigued and occupied Maybeck to the end of his career. The Mathewson house of 1916 is a replay of the same problem, but the image is different, the solution smoother, the means more efficiently used, and the sources more completely absorbed and transformed. The Mathewson house is small but perfect, quiet but distinctively Maybeckian. One-third of the floor space and most of the spatial excitement are concentrated on the large living room; the remaining functions are efficiently packed into a two-story space to one side. The basic structure consists of a series of beams perpendicular to the gable ends and their supports and braces. The living room is defined by carefully unobtrusive sheathing and glazing which showcases the structural system for the maximum visual drama. In 1909, about midway chronologically between the Boke and Mathewson houses, Maybeck executed a commission which proved that he was adept not only at the design of small-scale structures, but that he could turn to large lavish projects with no loss of confidence or skill. His house for Leon Roos was outrageously dramatic. Where Coxhead and Polk were interested in Georgian and Baroque design sources, Maybeck was always intrigued by the Medieval productions of France and Germany. The Roos living room, with its double-height

Mathewson house (Baer)

MAYBECK, *Roos house, San Francisco, 1909 and 1926*
(Sally Woodbridge)

ceiling hung with heraldic pennants and its more than baronial fireplace, was more Medieval than any actual Medieval building is likely to have been.

The Senger house of 1907 is more typical of the Maybeck houses scattered through the upper-middle-class suburbs of Berkeley, Oakland, and Marin County. Although much more domestic in scale, the Senger house does have certain features in common with the Roos house: the split gable end, which is almost a Maybeck trademark; the use of brilliant color to delineate carved detail; freely adapted Gothic ornament; complex spaces which expand vertically in one place and horizontally in another; and an unorthodox mixture of formal and informal elements.

The house has two entrances which give access, at different levels, to the same space. One, punched rather undramatically into the wall at street level, is the prosaic entrance for everyday use. The other, reached by a short but grand set of steps, opens into an area used for music performances. The entry and

Roos house, living room (Rob Super)

MAYBECK, *Senger house, Berkeley, 1907 (Baer)*

music area are simply portions of a large, multi-level space which also includes stairs, the living and dining areas, and a breakfast area, all arranged along a series of successively raised platforms; the stair, again, with landings expanded to become living areas. To define the separate functional areas a series of pairs of drapery panels (since removed) were used. These did not actually partition off the space; each panel was a couple of feet wide and they were hung at the outside edges of the space. But they symbolized quite clearly changes in function from area to area and they imposed an impressive (if rather theatrical) formality upon the rambling, variegated space. Besides the contrast between the formal and the casual, there is a contrast between the decorative and the utilitarian. The main space is lit by low-wattage bulbs left

Senger house, plan

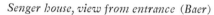

Senger house, view from entrance (Baer)

Senger house, fireplace (Rob Super)

unshaded. The sockets are mounted behind the red-wood boards which sheath the walls, and the bulbs are screwed in through an unrimmed hole punched unceremoniously into the wood. Around each hole is painted an abstracted floral motif of dull gold. The effect is of many small flowers whose blossoms are light. Gold patterns, similar to those in Celtic manuscripts, are also twined about the ceiling beams. The simply detailed, almost severe paneling system of the room is contrasted to a large and flamboyantly elaborate fireplace and mantel.

MAYBECK, *Chick house, Berkeley, 1913* (Baer)

Maybeck's 1913 Chick house, laid along the edge of a wooded Oakland hillside, shows interesting contrasts with the Senger house. While both are two-story buildings, the Chick house has none of the vertical qualities of the Senger house; it is emphatically horizontal both in its exterior massing and in its interior spatial disposition. The upper and lower floors are separate horizontal slices of space, and the only intermediate level is the stair landing, which extends through the wall to form a small balcony. The Chick house is an amazing combination of the prophetic and the backward-looking. Sheathed in wood, the exterior surface could have come from the 1890's. This is particularly true of the lower floor, where the shingle sheathing flares at the base line and terminates in a series of superimposed sawtooths which could have come from any of Coxhead's churches of 1890-91, as could the treatment around the arch of the kitchen porch where the shingle courses have been pulled up in the center like a curtain on a string. The sheathing of the upper floor makes reference to, but does not copy, the board-and-batten buildings of early California. Here there are two different batten types: a regular, lath-like batten and a rounded, high-relief one which creates a much deeper shadow line. This is a solid, flattened version of the effect created by a series of stacked-stick trellises which project from the gable ends. These trellises are in turn a man-made echo of the way the light filters irregularly through the leaves and branches of the live oaks which cover the site. But if the exterior is in some ways backward-looking, the interior is an astonishing forecast of the

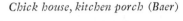

Chick house, kitchen porch (Baer)

Chick house, trellis with garden seat (Baer)

48

Chick house, living room (Baer)

taste of four decades later. Looking at the severely simple detailing and indirect lighting of the main rooms, the squared block pattern of the library fireplace, and the large-paned glass doors which open great areas of wall to outdoor terraces and walks, it is difficult to believe that the Chick house was designed at any time before the late 1940's or early fifties. In fact, the Chick house, carefully groomed and pre-sented, was a crucial link in the chain of argument which convinced the purists of the 1950's to accept Maybeck as a step-greatgrandfather (twice removed) of the Modern Movement.

The clincher to the argument was Maybeck's mas-terpiece and best-known building, the 1910 Christian Science church in Berkeley. The church is a demon-stration piece of all the components which made

MAYBECK, *First Church of Christ Scientist, Berkeley, 1910 (Baer)*

Maybeck's work, residential and otherwise, significant; and it is prodigal enough of ideas to keep most architects busy for a lifetime. It is full of elegant makeshifts and sturdy sophistications. It is simultaneously Oriental, Gothic, Byzantine, and Californian. It is an open, welcoming gesture surrounding a quiet, private place. It is serene and flamboyant, enormous and unobtrusive. Its main space is defined by and glorifies its dramatically stated structural system (which the sensibilities of the 1950's applauded); yet

the structure is lovingly coated with brilliant, intricate ornament (which the sensibilities of the 1950's opted simply to ignore). It poses hand-blown glass against catalogue factory sash and asbestos industrial paneling against hand-carved redwood. It has timber members which state structure with the clarity of a Miesian steel box, and Romanesque capitals executed in reinforced concrete. It has high spaces and low, light spaces and dark, graceful elements and clumsy ones, simplicity and complexity—and wisteria which

First Church of Christ Scientist, interior (Baer)

is as important as any of the purely architectural components.

While other designers were interested in the picturesque qualities of vernacular building modes, or in the surprises of scale or unexpected formal juxtapositions, A. C. Schweinfurth was most intrigued with the visual evidence of primitive materials and technology. Although he was one of the early champions of the Mission Revival, many aspects of his work appear to derive not from the missions but from pueblos and other native American buildings. Schweinfurth died very young, and of his few completed buildings only a couple survive in a condition which approximates their original form. His 1898 Moody house, today extensively altered, was widely published in local and national architectural periodicals. Loosely patterned on the South African Dutch Colonial house, it is a massive box built of irregular brick unevenly laid; the visual qualities of primitivism are here fully exploited. The living room, dining room,

First Church of Christ Scientist, interior column (Baer)

Moody house, axonometric

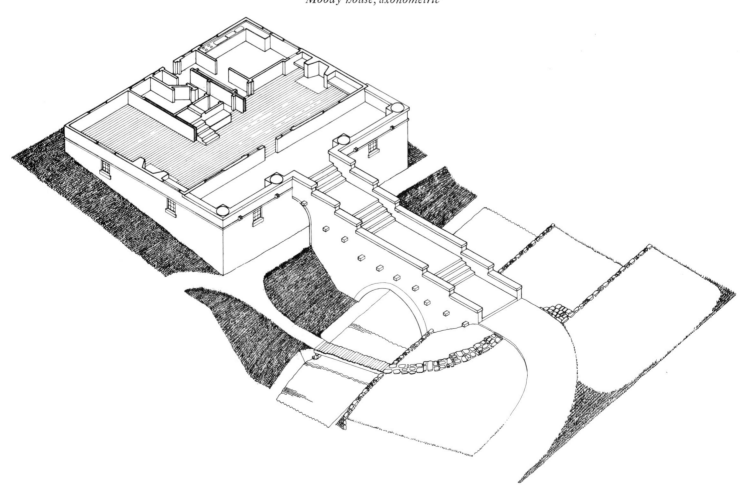

First Church of Christ Scientist, exterior column (Baer)

SCHWEINFURTH, *Moody house, Berkeley, 1898*
(California Historical Society, San Francisco)

SCHWEINFURTH, *Unitarian Church* (early photo), *Berkeley, 1898*)
(*California Historical Society, San Francisco*)

Unitarian Church, detail of window (*Baer*)

Unitarian Church, porch column (Baer)

and stair hall of the main floor are separated by sliding doors almost half the width of the house, which can be slid back to create a single space. This space opens through the main entrance to a veranda. The house is placed on the steep bank of a small stream, and the entrance is along a walled brick pathway which becomes a bridge to the veranda and the house. This extension of the structure and material of the house into the landscape simultaneously accentuates the wildness of the site and domesticates it, claiming it for the architecture. The veranda itself is not treated as a conventional porch shed attached to the front of the house, but occupies a void carved from the massive block of the building itself. This configuration emphasizes the cavelike qualities of the outdoor space, increasing the building's sense of shelter and protection.

Schweinfurth's finest shingle building is his 1898 Unitarian Church in Berkeley. Its most exciting aspect is the street facade, where an array of visual devices has been used to give dignity and presence to a building of no great size.

The facade is a symmetrical gable end; the ample gable embraces two entrance porches which have been placed at the side, rather than on the front, to increase the street frontage by almost one-half. Every element of the facade is in a single plane, which creates a surface like a cardboard cutout, with clues of scale deliberately withheld. At one moment the round window which is centered in the facade seems of enormous size; at another it appears normal, which implies that the eaves must come very close to the ground. But if the eaves come very close to the ground then no one could stand up on the porches. The observer is teased; the problem remains unresolved.

The other elements of the facade are scaled to reinforce the ambiguity. Certain elements which are far away from the observer are underscaled: the sawtooth shingle pattern and the trellis which extends from the gable edge, for instance, seem, when isolated, to be fussy or flimsy; but in their context these very qualities cause the facade to appear that much more substantial. Details which come into near contact with the observer, however, are heavily scaled and give an impression of extreme massiveness to anyone entering the building; the lintels of the entrance

POLK, *Batten house, San Francisco, 1891* (Baer)

Batten house, plan

Batten house, section

porches are large-dimension timber, and the support posts are bulky sections of redwood trunks with the bark still on them. There is a further contrast between the elegantly proportioned long-dimensional shingles in which the building is sheathed, and these primitive, rugged logs (like the ones from which the shingles were themselves made).

The most flamboyant personality of the local architectural scene in the 1890's was undoubtedly Willis Polk. Polk, the son of a Midwestern designer/builder, was quite ambitious and early grasped the values of publicity; it is clear that he took great pleasure in being something of a character, and newspapers of the period frequently refer to his latest escapade or practical joke. Polk was perhaps too sensitive to changes in prevailing fashion; his later work tends to be correct rather than interesting. But in the early 1890's he did a handful of superb houses which were quite important to the developing Bay Area sensibility.

One of Polk's earliest buildings in the Bay Area is the 1891 Batten house. The image, like that of two houses which Polk worked on while in Coxhead's office in Los Angeles, is strongly Queen Anne/Colonial Revival. But the elements have been played with, distorted. The tiny dormer in the large, slightly splayed roof plane and the non-corresponding sizes of the su-

perimposed bays foretell mannerist tendencies which Polk would soon explore. Spatially too, the house is prophetic: the circulation and stair areas are combined in a slice of space which pierces all levels of the house, creating a spatial variety which would normally be associated with a house of considerably larger scope.

In 1892 Polk built a double house for Mrs. Virgil Williams. Mrs. Williams, a San Francisco artist, had her studio and living quarters in one half of the building; Polk and his family lived in the other half. The house climbs an impossibly steep site on Russian Hill: it is three stories high in the front; six at the back. The street facade is respectable enough: "quaint," in the language of the time, with elements rather loosely adapted from the medieval vernacular. The rear shows a playful, joyous acceptance of the visual and material elements of San Francisco's hillside shacks. It is difficult to reconstruct its original interior configurations exactly; it has been altered considerably through the years. But in the upper levels of the house it is still possible to experience the complex vertical interlocking of the living spaces.

An 1893 Polk house and one of Coxhead's designs of 1892 present an interesting series of similarities and contrasts. Coxhead's Murdock house is a San Francisco townhouse clothed in the form and materials of

POLK, *Polk-Williams house, San Francisco, 1892* (Baer)

58

Polk-Williams house, rear view (Baer)

Polk-Williams house, living room (Baer)

a rustic vernacular. Polk's Rey house climbs a wooded hill in suburban Belvedere but is as tightly packed and introspective as an urban house. Both houses use a vernacular mode as a background for and contrast to specific pieces adapted from high-art European architectural history: but where Coxhead chose the carpenter's wood-frame vernacular, the Rey house references the wood and adobe buildings of early Anglo Monterey. Each house is a series of staggered-level platforms stacked around a stairwell. But where the Rey house is an open, constantly changing spatial progression (a perfect example of the stair-become-a-

house), the Murdock house is a series of separate compartments.

There are a number of Bay Area architects who have generally been grouped with the first-generation innovators, although their intentions and their products were actually quite different. Despite close personal association and occasional architectural collaboration with Coxhead, Polk, or Maybeck, and the fact that their work, too, was primarily executed in redwood, such designers as William Knowles, Edgar Mathews, and Albert Farr were essentially eclectics. The difference in approach can be made quite clear.

Polk-Williams house, gallery (Baer)

61

COXHEAD, *Murdock house, San Francisco, 1892 (Baer)*

POLK, *Rey house, (original Polk drawing), Belvedere, 1893*

All of these designers were interested in a specific vernacular: anonymous English residential work from the Medieval period through the Jacobean. In the case of Coxhead, Maybeck, and Polk, this English work was one component of a design repertoire; in the case of Knowles, Mathews, and Farr, it was pretty much the only component. Where the synthesists found in the haphazard and clumsy qualities of vernacular work ideas for expressive distortion of scale and decorative device, the straight eclectics were interested almost exclusively in a "roses 'round the door" picturesqueness. This is immediately seen by comparing the Coxhead and Knowles houses in the 3200 block of San Francisco's Pacific Avenue. The operative attitude on the part of Knowles, Mathews, and Farr is that an architectural style is a design mode rather than a design resource. This is not to say that they were not fine designers; although their design philosophy seldom, if ever, allowed them to commit the playful outrages against correct taste of which Coxhead, Polk, and Maybeck were so fond, their work forms an undeniably important part of the Bay Area architectural scene. Less concerned with experimentation than with competence, each of these eclectics developed a personalized standard idiom to which he remained reasonably faithful and which he

63

Rey house, entrance (Baer)

refined through the years. Still it is obvious that without its redwood overcoat, the work of any of the Bay Region eclectics would fit comfortably into the commonplace residential neighborhoods of Portland, Oregon, Kansas City, Missouri, or Cincinnati, Ohio.

Certain buildings of Edgar Mathews would not need even this change of clothing to feel at home in other places. Mathews developed two standard de-

sign types, each, again, derived from the English residential vernacular. One of these, a half timber and stucco mode, bears little relationship to the special qualities of the Bay Area Tradition. The other, a steep-roofed shingled box with foundations, retaining walls, and porch elements of clinker brick, and sometimes sporting windows of small, diamond-shaped panes, is quite convincingly Medieval in feel-

Rey house, stair hall (Baer)

COXHEAD, *Murdock house, stair hall toward entrance* (*Baer*)

POLK, *Rey house, living room* (*Baer*)

COXHEAD, *Murdock house, living room* (*Rob Super*)

MATHEWS, *San Francisco apartment house, c. 1900* (Baer)

ing, and quite compatible with the Bay Area Tradition image. Mathews apparently found this redwood shingle mode both congenial and adaptable, for he applied it to residential commissions ranging from single-family to multiple-unit. Mathews came from a family heavily involved in the visual arts: his father and one brother were well-established architects. Another brother was the San Francisco painter/furniture-maker Arthur Mathews, and Edgar's work is often finished and furnished in the local Arts and Crafts/Art Nouveau idiom of which Arthur was a leading proponent and practitioner. Edgar Mathews' shingle designs have been in large part responsible for creating the image of the Pacific Heights area of San Francisco as a preserve of the redwood shingle townhouse. They establish that atmosphere by the frequency of their occurrence in the Pacific Heights landscape, despite the fact that the discreet quality of the individual designs is such that they do not usually attract specific attention. Mathews designs are background buildings in the best sense of that term.

Perhaps the most versatile and accomplished of the local eclectic practitioners (at least until Willis Polk went respectable) was Albert Farr. Farr ran a highly successful, fashionable practice, and his clients' tastes, aspirations, and budgets frequently tended towards the baronial. His work included rather ponderous Georgian Revival townhouses at one end of the scale and Jack London's rustic but luxurious country house in Sonoma County at the other. Farr's most characteristic work, however, consists of a large number of wooden houses erected from the 1890's through the mid-teens. Located in urban, suburban, and country situations, these houses almost always have redwood shingle exteriors and are artfully devoid of decorative detail. If ornament is at all present, it is restrained and of Georgian derivation. Care-

fully massed and proportioned, his buildings often have an at least superficial resemblance to the work of Ernest Coxhead. A comparison of Coxhead's Waybur and Porter houses with some designs of Farr's in the next block of Pacific will show both the resemblances and the differences. The clean-cut window openings with no obvious exterior moldings and the large areas of unbroken shingled wall seen in both Coxhead's and Farr's designs would appear to derive from vernacular sources. Coxhead uses this vernacular element as a backdrop against which various ele-

FARR, *townhouses, San Francisco, c. 1900* (Baer)

FARR, *Belvedere Land Company building (early photo)*, *1905 (Belvedere Land Co.)*

70

MORGAN, *house in Berkeley* (*Mary Ann Beach*)

ments (Georgian details manipulated in unorthodox ways; giant windows for light and the views; unexpected contrasts of scale) create a complex series of cultural and esthetic cross-references. The Farr houses, which share with each other such devices as projecting upper floors and small windows glazed with diamond-shaped panes (the standard architectural shorthand used to evoke medieval England or early America), seem knowledgeable, polished efforts to recreate the past. Farr was given the opportunity to explore this evocation of the past on a large scale (and with superb results) in a series of commissions obtained either from or through the Belvedere Land Company. Apart from a large number of fine houses for various clients, Farr created, for the Belvedere Land Company, a complex of shop and flat structures which tiptoe along what was at that time a very narrow spit of land. The rear of some of these structures hung over the water, resting on piles rising directly out of the Bay; it was a peculiar mixture of California life-style and ye olde Englishe imagery which seemed to work together in a very special way.

One architect who has been strongly identified with the innovative strand of the Bay Area Tradition is Julia Morgan. But despite her relationship at various periods as student, friend, employee, and collaborator with Bernard Maybeck, the work of Julia Morgan sits firmly on the eclectic side of the esthetic fence. Miss Morgan, whose cult in the Berkeley/Oakland area is a strong one indeed, was a careful designer, more interested in workability and livability than visual drama or spatial exploration. The plans of her residences, seldom unusual, are thoroughly thought out, thoroughly functional. Morgan consistently refused to have her buildings published, and most of them do not attract attention; the observer must make the first contact. She seems to have altered Vitruvius in some subtle way: firmness, commodity, and propriety were her watchwords. She believed that the architect should remain an anonymous craftsman in the tradition of the medieval builder; in fact, the aspect of vernacular design which appealed most to Morgan was its anonymity. All the Bay Area practitioners seem to have had a fascination with the vernacular to some degree, but of them all, only Morgan produced buildings which in their straightforwardness and suppression of decorative qualities

71

MORGAN, *Livermore house, San Francisco, 1917 (Baer)*

were actually indistinguishable from those of an earnest carpetect (in Walter Steilberg's apt term). The majority of Morgan's work, however, was styled to a certain extent. She developed a residential type which usually had an exterior of stucco or half timber and brick; windows leaded in various geometric patterns; and restrained touches of decorative carving derived from Gothic sources.

On a few occasions, however, Morgan was capable of producing surprises: work which shows that her low profile was a conscious and deliberate choice and that had she desired she could have been a different sort of designer altogether. Besides her amazing act as a juggler of artifacts for William Randolph Hearst at San Simeon, there are two Morgan buildings of the teens which provide opportunities to speculate about other directions her work might have taken. In the Livermore house of 1917 it becomes clear that Morgan was aware not only of the anonymous qualities of vernacular design, but also of that awkwardness which sometimes informs vernacular buildings with such forcefulness. The Livermore house could be a building block dropped on a hillside by a careless child. Tucked in behind Willis Polk's house on Russian

72

Hill, it is a small house providing the accommodations of a large apartment. The main floor originally contained a large living room and a bedroom and bath, the floor below a dining room and kitchen. The house is now somewhat larger than originally; it was altered slightly by Morgan in 1927 and again in 1930. With its casual placement on a steep hillside, its pronounced vertical organization, its hillside-to-house entrance bridge, its exploitation of the forceful clumsiness of some vernacular designs, and its almost total suppression of decorative devices, the Livermore house comes closer to fulfilling the requirements for Keeler's "Simple Home" than the work of Maybeck, Coxhead, or Polk.

St. John's Presbyterian Church, designed in 1910 and probably Morgan's best-known building after San Simeon, is a piece of lightly sheathed engineering, a glorious combination of barn and bungalow, utility and grace. The bare-bone budget allowed few frills, and the drama of the interior derives from the careful arrangement and display of structural elements: every functioning member is visible and every visible member functions. Even the Craftsman/constructivist lighting fixtures of the Social Hall seem

Livermore house, axonometric

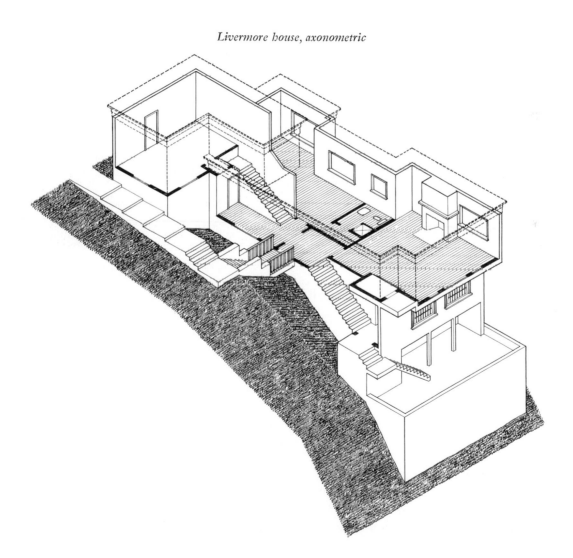

MORGAN, *St. John's Presbyterian Church, Berkeley, 1910 (Baer)*

extensions of the structural system. The nave roof is raised above the rest of the building, providing a clerestory which runs around all four sides of the space, creating a cage of light above the heads of worshippers (the clerestory above the altar end of the church has since been filled in). Lighting is handled quite subtly throughout the building, and it is chiefly this element which creates, in the passage from social hall to sanctuary, a transition from cheerful radiance to mystery. Much of the credit for the accomplishment at St. John's, particularly the interior, belongs to Walter Steilberg, a resourceful designer/engineer who was Morgan's structure man for many years. Morgan's primary concern, charac-

teristically, was that the exterior not be obtrusive; that the church fit quietly into the residential neighborhood which is its setting. Consequently both scale and imagery are residential; except for the cross perched on top of the primary roof structure, the building could be a rather extensive bungalow. The original intention was not to have even this reference to the building's religious function; instead, there is a cross outlined in the window dividers of the central section of the front clerestory. While this may have seemed adequate identification to Morgan, it did not seem so to the congregation, at whose continued insistence the rooftop cross was eventually added.

There is one other work of Morgan's which relates

74

St. John's Presbyterian Church, interior (Baer)

quite strongly to St. John's although it is considerably more modest in scope. But like St. John's it cloaks a dramatic interior space in a quiet, almost anonymous exterior; and like St. John's interior, the drama is created by a visual exploitation of an engineering idea. It also clearly states Morgan's design philosophy: there is a primary concern that the new work should provide continuity with its immediate surroundings, in this case John Galen Howard's own house, to which she was making additions.

Howard was an Easterner trained at MIT and at the Ecole des Beaux-Arts, who had worked for the most fashionable offices of the day: H. H. Richardson, Richardson's successors, Shepley, Rutan & Coolidge, and McKim, Mead & White. Infected by the California myth while living briefly in Los Angeles in the late 1880's (he had hoped at the time to be employed by Ernest Coxhead, but Coxhead's office was low on work), he was impatient for an opportunity to settle permanently on the West Coast. That opportunity occurred when Emile Bénard, winner of the international competition for a plan for the University of California, Berkeley campus, declined to come to California to supervise the execution of his plan. Howard, whose entry placed fourth in the competition, was offered the commission instead. (The final product was more Howard than Bénard.) California, the Lotusland of Opportunity, exerted a continuing but intermittent influence upon Howard, as his buildings show.

Most of Howard's domestic work is unexceptional; but when it is good, it is very good indeed, and three wooden residences commissioned by the Gregory family are among the finest. These houses are located near one another in a wooded section of the Berkeley hills; despite the rustic setting these designs avoid the hearty folksiness of the American Craftsman Movement, although in the Frances Gregory house there is a hint of the Maybeckian chalet. The house for Warren Gregory was begun in 1904 and became a sort of process house, with periodic additions over a number of years. But perhaps the most interesting of these, and the most instructive in terms of Howard's split loyalties as a designer, is the house he designed for himself. Actually commissioned and built by the Gregorys, who then rented it to Howard for a nominal sum, it is a grand gesture of architectural patron-

St. John's Presbyterian Church, lighting fixture (Brooks Harrison)

HOWARD, *Howard house, Berkeley, 1912 (Baer)*

age. The house is sited in a particularly fortunate place: a hillside corner lot with unobstructed views downhill to the Bay. A small area was cut out of the slope for a paved terrace, around two sides of which the house is tightly wrapped. Beyond that the hill rises steeply to the top of the property. Originally left in its unaltered state, the hill has since been developed as a sequence of lawn and garden areas. The relationship between the building and the later gardens gives the house much of its special character. A pair of french doors from the living room and a pair from the dining room open to the terrace one step above the paving. This unites living room, terrace, dining room, and entrance/stair hall in a single changing space which leads back upon itself. The stair rises through an angled bay in the inner corner of the building so that anyone using the stairs in either direction is in constant visual contact with the garden. Each level of the house corresponds to a specific area of the grounds; thus there is not a single, static-object-seen-from-different-views relationship with the garden, but a constantly changing spatial/visual relationship. The house becomes a shelter from which to enjoy the seasonal drama of the garden. The views of the Bay are still there, but the house does not focus on them; they form a subliminal background which relates this private and protected place to the world beyond. The exterior of the build-

Howard house, garden side (Baer)

ing gives an impression of informality, but the individual rooms are unexpectedly formal in both their layout and their detailing.

The plan of the house, though rambling and complex in detail, has a simple source: the standard, formal, central hall format with a living room and a library/reception room on one side, and a dining room and kitchen on the other. The visual clarity of this scheme, however, is compromised and distorted (or enriched) by polygonal facade elements lifted straight out of the Queen Anne Revival. These are used to transform the reception room and the dining room into pivot points upon which the whole scheme swings around the corner in pursuit of the street (Howard's house is one of the most ingenious passages in the whole literature of corner-turning). These polygonal elements protrude as bays doubled by corresponding forms above. The strong verticals of the double-story projection make a strong statement of tower, but they do not project, as any proper Queen Anne tower would, above the roof line. Also, a strong horizontal element, a balcony, spans the space between them at the second floor. Are they bays or are they towers? The ambiguity is never resolved. But as twin landmarks in an otherwise uneventful facade, they create a fleeting image of the formal and symmetrical; flanking the main door reached by a wide flight of wandering steps, they mark the entrance in a way which is partly forceful, partly restrained, and totally elegant.

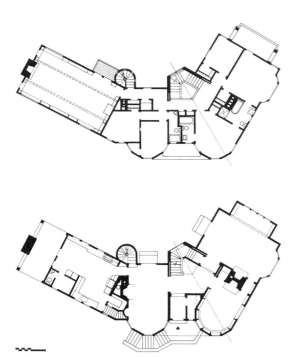

Howard house, plan

The house was sold in the 1920's. The new owner, the head of UC's English department, had more books than could be accommodated in the room which had housed Howard's library. Julia Morgan was commissioned to add a new library and perform other alterations (one bedroom was enlarged, a sleeping porch enclosed, a bath added, etc.). The library is a remarkable room; it is much longer than it is wide, and its gabled ceiling is supported by two exposed trusses which perversely span the long, rather than the short, direction. The trusses themselves are a contradictory combination of the decorative and the utilitarian: there are squat, elaborately profiled baluster forms which act as connectors between the upper and lower chords of the truss; these in turn are fastened with heavy duty nuts and bolts, clearly industrial in nature, with their specifications and manufacturer's name stamped into the metal. The library is entered from a door located in the extreme corner

MORGAN, *library addition to Howard residence, Berkeley, 1927* (Baer)

79

of the room. This door is approached either up a special stair or along a jogged corridor so that the space is not glimpsed until it is actually entered. This secretive approach heightens the contrast between the drama of the library and the straightlaced spatial configuration of the rest of the house. Again, the library maintains a special relationship with the garden through two sets of french doors leading to a balcony tucked into the angle between the library and the wall of the stair tower. This tower, also a Morgan addition, houses a tight spiral stair allowing direct circulation between the library and the dining room. The form of the tower is curvilinear and it is the perfect counterpoint to Howard's polygonally housed main stair. In fact, having seen the terrace side of the house with Morgan's additions, it is difficult to believe that they were not always there. It is necessary to consider her alterations not in the nature of an addition, but as part of a process of completion.

Julia Morgan was not the only participant in this process of completion. There is a lovely spot at the top of the Howard garden: a small, level area of shaded lawn. From here there is a view down across the now-matured landscaping, the brick-paved terrace, across the segmented arc of the house to the Bay, the ocean, and beyond. It is as if momentarily one could glimpse that myth of California's potential which so continuously fascinated and escaped John Galen Howard. The sky, the Bay, a myth, a couple of generations of anonymous gardeners, and two architects have collaborated to create one of the Bay Area's finest moments and most special places.

The particular line of esthetic enquiry followed by the Bay Area woodsy mannerists was cut off abruptly and prematurely before the complete possibilities of this approach could be exhausted. Circumstance and a change of public tastes altered preferences in materials, imagery, and approach. After the turn of the century there was a general feeling that while those flimsy and sometimes funny-looking buildings designed by Coxhead and others might have been well and good for an almost frontier situation, they were inadequately pretentious for what was becoming one of America's major cities. The area's periodicals began to publish historic European architecture and examples of the work of Eastern firms as if to provide the locals with a yardstick by which to measure their

own achievement. There was an increased interest in Beaux-Arts Classicism, in architectural respectability. But this changed attitude would no doubt have taken much longer to develop fully had it not been for the disastrous 1906 earthquake and fire. The 490 square blocks in the heart of San Francisco which were swept clear by fire became, in reconstruction, a dramatic and conspicuous showcase for changed tastes and aspirations. Of the first generation of Bay Area innovators, only Willis Polk had any appreciable role in the rebuilding of the city. His commercial work, polished, classically derived, and slightly dull, has nothing to do with the manipulation and synthesis which had made the domestic design of the 1890's unique.

The disaster and its aftermath not only revealed certain trends in fashion; they also created a tremendous prejudice against timber construction (or at least its image). Potential clients had seen all too dramatically how rapidly redwood burned, and had reservations about building with such easily flammable materials. There was, of course, a strong California design precedent for stucco and masonry buildings: the missions dating from California's greatly romanticized Spanish past. The largely fabricated Mission Revival mode was loosely derived from them.

The Mission Revival was launched with impeccable architectural sponsorship. Coxhead, Polk, Schweinfurth, Howard, and others had sketched the remains of missions and adobe houses; some of them did so as early as the 1880's. Polk's 1890 *Architectural News* ran an article on the missions which appeared in installments through the three issues of that short-lived periodical. The first monument of the Mission Revival which attracted national attention was produced by the A. Page Brown office: the California Building at Chicago's World Columbian Exposition of 1892. Polk's 1893 Rey house was influenced to a great extent, particularly in its exterior composition, by early California sources. There has been a persistent local legend that before designing the gatehouse for the Coryell estate, Polk was sent, at his client's expense, to study the architectural monuments of Spain. There is no evidence, however, that Polk was in Europe during this period, and the finished building, with its stocky proportions and star-shaped window, hints that if Coryell sent Polk anywhere, it

POLK, *Coryell gatehouse, Atherton, c. 1912 (Sally Woodbridge)*

was to Carmel for a quick once-over of San Carlos Borromeo, the obvious design source for the building.

Of the people associated with Brown's office who worked within the Mission Revival, A. C. Schweinfurth seems to have been most deeply committed to it. It was Schweinfurth who created the grandest gesture of all Mission Revival designs: the Hacienda del Pozo de Verona, Phoebe Apperson Hearst's country house located in a warm, dry valley to the east of Berkeley. It was a romantic, not a real, hacienda, one that could only exist inside the California myth. The image of the fortified outpost is so convincing that the lack of attacking marauders seems somehow an oversight on Schweinfurth's part.

But if the Mission Revival began as the darling of the High-Arters, it did not hold that honor for long. There were from the beginning critics who pointed out that perhaps an essentially ecclesiastic mode made an inappropriate pattern for residences, shops, and warehouses, and who further observed that the temporary never-never land of an exposition was the

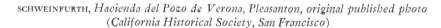

SCHWEINFURTH, *Hacienda del Pozo de Verona, Pleasanton, original published photo (California Historical Society, San Francisco)*

proper locale for such a spurious style. It was in an attempt to reproduce those same exotic, exciting overtones of an exposition that developers, railroaders, hotel owners, and others with a piece of California to exploit grabbed on to the Mission Revival; Mission Revival became the official style of Eden-as-a-commodity. It was also a cheap, easy style to use: for the developer a single plaster arch and a row of Spanish tile perched on the front parapet of a flat-roofed box became the standard shorthand for a romantic and largely mythical past.

Thus, by the middle of the first decade of the century, the Mission Revival was held in low esteem by most serious designers; and just at the time that the first-generation pathfinders needed a new input to rejuvenate their approach, the Mission Revival was felt to be unworthy of serious consideration. In fact, it seemed that none of the surviving old guard was able to make the transition in stylistic and structural vocabulary. Schweinfurth and A. Page Brown were both dead; Polk had emphatically rejected his early adventurous unorthodoxy; and Coxhead's attempts to embrace the new sensibility were at best embarrassing. Maybeck carried on the tradition to some extent: the Christian Science Church, after all, was not designed until 1910. But his work, especially after the

STORCH, *Park Congregational Church, Berkeley, 1910 (Baer)*

Park Congregational Church, sanctuary (Baer)

1915 Pan Pacific International Exposition, became ever more grandly eclectic and scenographic. If designers who attempted to reclaim the Mission Revival for High Art are to be found they must be sought, not among the established old-line architects, but either among those designers who were out of the mainstream and so impervious to the unfashionable stigma attached to the Mission Revival, or among young designers who, with fresh eyes, were able to treat the Mission Revival with the same serious playfulness to which their elders had subjected various wooden vernaculars.

Of the first group, the most intriguing figure is the obscure Oakland designer Hugo Storch. Storch was not so much an architect as an inspired tinkerer who occasionally tinkered in architecture. His career was erratic; he was more in demand as an engineer than a designer; and he died when still in his forties. Consequently, he did not create a very large body of work. Most of that work consists of a series of modest residences in the Arts and Crafts mode, pleasant enough, but not remarkable. However, between 1908 and 1911 Storch designed two buildings which are remarkable in every way. Both Congregational churches, they are both pure Mission Revival on the exterior and pure engineering on the interior. The interior of Julia Morgan's St. John's Presbyterian is the immediate and obvious comparison. But in St. John's the engineering is made elegant, decorative; in Storch's buildings it is simply exposed. And just as there is no attempt on Storch's part to prettify the structure, there is no attempt to impose superficial unity upon the various parts of the building: space abuts space, structural system abuts structural system, without a single gesture of transition or accommodation. Park Congregational Church, built in 1910, is remarkable for the flexibility of its interior. A series of vertically sliding partitions can be used to enclose the central portion of the sanctuary, transforming it into an intimate space for small groups. As successive dividers are

Park Congregational Church, Sunday school (Rob Super)

raised out of the way, the sanctuary gathers to itself several subsidiary spaces culminating in an eight-segmented fan-shaped Sunday School auditorium which is wider than the sanctuary itself. The separate identity of these successive spaces is clearly echoed in the exterior of the building, creating a composition of superimposed surprises.

There were other designers, of primarily Crafts-man tendencies, who were strongly influenced by elements of the Mission Revival although their work itself was not specifically Mission Revival. Two of these, Louis Christian Mullgardt and John Hudson Thomas, seem, in the breadth of their influences and the nature of their design process, to embody many of the principles and techniques of the woodsy man-nerists.

Mullgardt was essentially a Craftsman designer who appears to have borrowed certain visual effects from the Mission Revival (or from the missions themselves). Even many of his wooden buildings

have the battered walls, the wide-eaved shallow ga-bles, and the hefty roof substructure associated with adobe construction. The Evans house, built in Mill Valley in 1907, is a good example of the Craftsman phase of Mullgardt's work. Perched on a steep hill-side, it performs two visual functions: to the street above it appears in its homey, bungalow-nestled-into-nature image; from the street below, with its battered foundation walls, and the elaborately detailed, mas-sively cantilevered terrace/porch, it is quite monu-mental (despite its non-monumental materials). A prominent hillside landmark, it is in reality a modest house which makes maximum dramatic use of its commanding site. Entrance is through a narrow slice of space laid along the edge of the hillside and de-fined by low side walls and a pergola (the pergola, an important part of the design idea, was unfortunately omitted in execution). This leads to a reception room, and from the reception room into the main living space. Living room, dining room, and porch

MULLGARDT, *Evans house, Mill Valley, 1907* (Baer)

Evans house, early published drawing

are treated as subdivisions of this single space, interconnected by banks of glass doors which tend to dissolve any strong feelings of separation. The porch, with its emphatically stated modular structural system which integrates railings, planters, and supports, is not "outside" in the conventional sense: it is simply a portion of the major living space one degree less enclosed.

Mullgardt's career as an architect was star-crossed and erratic. Some of his most important designs were never built. Those which were built seem to exert an irresistible fascination upon bulldozers; many of the finest have disappeared. One of the greatest losses, and certainly the masterpiece of his residential work, was the Taylor house of 1908. To the battered walls and traditional roof line of the Mission Revival Mullgardt added the rough-cast stucco wall with which the Mission Revival recalled primitive adobe technology. It was an enormous house, which capped and dominated a visually prominent Berkeley hillside. The main rooms were grouped in a line along a gentle slope, separated only by arched openings which indicated, but did not separate, changes in social function. Although this series of subspaces shared a single ceiling plane, the floor level of each was stepped up the slope, a few steps above the space next to it, with the entrance at the very bottom. This must have been one of the most staggering pieces of spatial sculpture in the Bay Area oeuvre. Midway in this spatial cascade was a room-sized alcove to the west, with a large fireplace. On warm nights this alcove could be separated from the main space by sliding glass doors: the fire could thus be enjoyed visually, without the discomfort of added heat.

86

Evans house, interior (Baer)

But of all the Bay Area designers who worked in stucco, the one whose work is most consistently fascinating is the Berkeley architect John Hudson Thomas. Thomas' deliberate disruption of expected scale, his juxtaposition of seemingly unrelated formal elements, and his many-leveled references to the architecture of disparate times and places in the same design all relate his work, consciously or not, to the innovative buildings of Coxhead's and Polk's generation.

At the beginning of his career Thomas had designed, in partnership with George Plowman, a series of redwood bungalows which established his reputation. He continued to do wooden houses whenever clients wished him to, even when he was most deeply involved in exploiting the visual possibilities of the stucco wall. The Randolph house of 1913 is a handsome, apparently straightforward bungalow in the Craftsman mode. The first floor is sheathed in redwood shingles, the second in tongue-and-groove boarding with an exo-skeleton which symbolizes, rather than actually reveals, the building's structural system. The roof is a series of shallow gables with very generous eaves. All this is well within the Craftsman tradition. But there are traces, even in this quiet building, of the idiosyncracies which Thomas used with such forceful effect in his stucco buildings. At the north end of the building a small extension pushes out from the main body of the house until it is flush with the eave line. This extension is treated as a separate wing of the building with its own gable and eave. Half of its roof is, in fact, part of the main roof line; the other half is a separate plane directly below the main eave. This separate roof is superfluous in a strictly structural sense: it would have been simpler to run the extension to the main eave all the way across. But it is quite important in a visual sense: as a mannerist way of increasing the statement of roof and shelter. For a relatively unimportant structural event it creates considerable visual importance by using a minimum of means to imply a complexity and scale beyond the actuality of the building. On the interior too, there is an unexpected moment: a stair landing accommodated by the vestigial wing just discussed. With a gabled ceiling and a back wall which is almost entirely window, it is a visually expansive space with no clue as to its actual scale: in

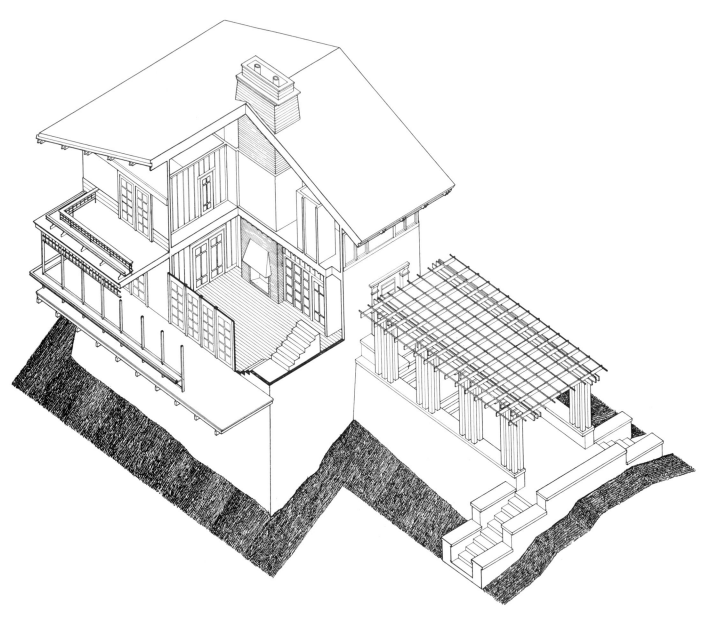

Evans house, axonometric

MULLGARDT, *Taylor house, Berkeley, 1908, original rendering*

THOMAS, *Randolph house, Berkeley, 1913 (Sally Woodbridge)*

THOMAS, *Locke house, Oakland, 1911* (Baer)

fact, the ceiling is so low that it is not possible to stand erect near the sides of the room. It is a grand ballroom designed for dolls. These two oddities of the Randolph house—a manipulation of expected form and one of expected scale—are the tools with which Thomas' endless and inventive variation created a series of powerful, startling, and sometimes unnerving buildings.

Probably the most startling, certainly one of the finest, and perhaps the richest of these buildings in the multiplicity of its sources and references is the 1911 Locke house. The massing of the Locke house, its tower, and its veranda, all seem legacies of the late Queen Anne. But there is nothing Victorian in its imagery. The massive arches, the buttresses, the deep

window reveals, and the rough-cast stucco are derived from the Mission Revival. Although in this house and others Thomas borrowed ideas from a staggering range of sources, they were never taken intact; they were transformed and integrated into very complex compositions. The interior organization of the Locke house, with its spaces expanded horizontally by alcoves and oblique vistas (sometimes through interior windows between rooms), shows many lessons learned from the Prairie School designers. From the Prairie School and from the Craftsman Movement in general, Thomas took the idea of total design: that window muntins, light fixtures, stair railings, and door panel arrangements should always be an extension of a controlling idea.

90

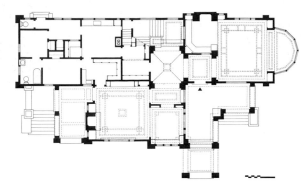

Locke house, plan

Bell (Wintermute) house, axonometric

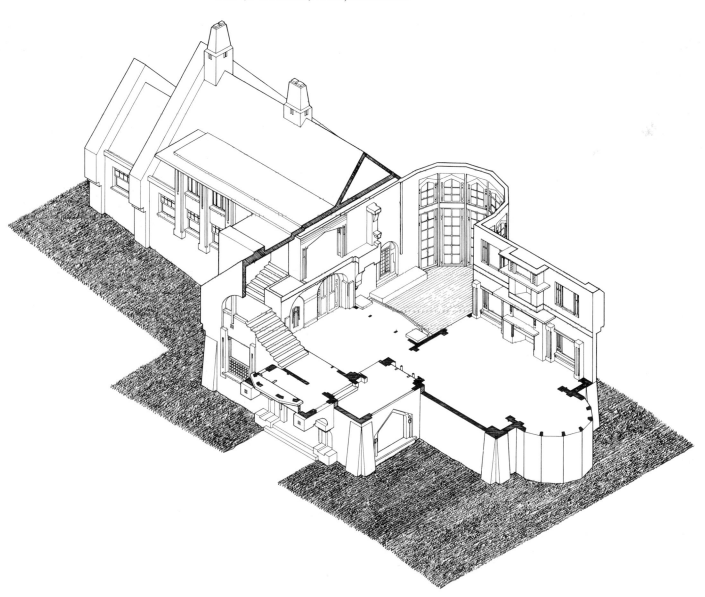

There is in Thomas' work generally a tension between control and chaos, between unifying devices and deliberately contradictory ones. That certain of his compositions do not fall apart visually defies some law of esthetic gravity. It is a principle of Thomas' design approach that each element should appear to have been designed independently. Windows in the same room, for instance, may be of different sizes, proportions, or even shapes; but a related muntin pattern will hold them in precarious harmony. In the Locke house certain formal devices (pylons, wide parapet gables, decorative motifs in tile) serve through repetition to unify masses which would not otherwise belong next to one another. Thomas also has an array of devices which serve the opposite function. In the Locke house the living room, halls, and dining room are a set of spaces which flow together into one single slightly subdivided space. But lest this lead to any visual confusion regarding separation of function, Thomas uses a different, quite emphatic ceiling treatment to differentiate between each subspace: the dining room ceiling is rather conventional; the hall sports a groin vault with a finely integrated Craftsman light fixture at the apex; the living room ceiling has deep coffers at the corners, an overlaid pattern of wooden stripping, and built-in light fixtures which are inverted pyramids of mica and hammered copper. The observer's path through the Locke house is a sequence of obviously differentiated but subtly related spaces; it is an experience of variety and surprise.

In 1914 Thomas designed a pair of houses for a hillside site in Berkeley; these flank a shared entrance court which makes maximum use of the only level area of the property which is not built upon. The client, E. R. Peters, writers of the period, and perhaps Thomas himself considered the house to be "in the Hopi style." (See illustration on p. 15.) Yet except for murals of Indian scenes and the decorative woodwork of the living room and dining room of the main house, there is little or no direct influence from primitive American buildings. The smaller of the houses indicates that Thomas was familiar with Irving Gill's Southern California exercises in pure cubic form; the larger house has forms, proportions, and decorative motifs which suggest the Austrian Secessionists. The spatial sequence of the stair, which includes a large

Locke house, interior (Baer)

Locke house, interior (Rob Super)

two-level landing, is one of Thomas' expansive circulation spaces; but contrary to his usual practice, it is not visible from the public areas of the house and so does not in the usual manner add to the visual expansion of the other portions of the house.

The largest residential commission Thomas was to receive was the 1913 Bell (Wintermute) house. Here it is the circulation path which establishes the spatial feeling of the building. The adventure starts outside; Thomas was always concerned about the way his buildings were approached, about the visitor's path, but in the Bell house this is controlled in an especially careful and dramatic fashion. Entrance to the first layer of enclosure is through an arch beneath a cantilevered, massively corbeled projection from which a bay window further projects. The path then leads through a loggia, up steps past a series of landings (turning a couple of times along the way), finally arriving at the front door. The entrance hall is the circulation hub of the design and is completely wrapped in a layer of space which the actual entrance must penetrate. The plan is an elaborate variant of the central hall layout. Living room and dining room flank the entrance hall. To the rear through glass doors and stationary panels is a two-story atrium/conservatory. On the living room side is an opening which leads up one step to a landing. This landing leads, in turn, to another, two steps higher, which cuts across the front side of the hall. The openings between the hall and this landing are quite proscenium-like, giving the landing much the feeling of a small stage. From this landing the stair continues up, turning at a landing to wrap around the third side of the entrance hall. Here, at the second-floor level, the circulation space rejoins the atrium through a series of glazed openings. In its overall form, with its grey stucco walls, parapetted gables, and stacked bays, the Bell house relates to the Tudor Revival buildings so popular at that period with the upper middle class. But there is also much of the Mission

Locke house, interior (Rob Super)

THOMAS, *Bell (Wintermute) house, Berkeley, 1913 (Baer)*

Revival; much Secessionist ornament; and many decorative devices derived from Roman sources. The dining room, with its gilded stucco surfaces, architectonic cabinetry, beaten copper fireplace, and filagree in wood and metal, is simultaneously Gothic, Oriental, and Prairie School. Of all the Bay Area designers of the teens, only Thomas, with his unique sense of synthesis and esthetic daring, could have used such potentially discordant elements to create such a powerful and coherent design.

By 1920 Thomas' design process had begun to undergo the same transformation as had those of his predecessors some fifteen or twenty years earlier; his eclecticism became more straightforward, the sources for single design much more limited. Synthesis was edged out in favor of picturesque reproduction. The visual elements which characterize this change were evident in earlier work, but as the teens ended Medieval imagery became the almost exclusive input to Thomas' design. With his abandonment of the attempt to synthesize a widely varied series of images and references, the first phase of the Bay Tradition came to a gradual close.

The past is reassessed by each generation of critics.

Bell (Wintermute) house, stair landing (Baer)

Bell (Wintermute) house, dining room (Baer)

In the 1950's, when there was an intense search for ancestors of the Modern Movement, Polk, Coxhead, Thomas, and others were simply unacceptable figures; but Maybeck, by judicious editing and selective blindness, could be transformed into an acceptable one. The reassessment of the 1970's involves a rejection of the heroic stance, a search for means which are expressive yet simple and economic. There is an attempt to define an attitude which encompasses both the serious and the playful, both the thoughtful and satirical. Confusion has been created by attempts to type the accomplishments of Polk, Coxhead, and Maybeck in "Simple Home" terms: in the verbal pleas of the Berkeley writer Charles Keeler and of Joseph Worcester for the simple, the unaffected and "unarchitected." The simplest buildings in California at the time, those which responded most directly to the demands of function, were the straightforwardly utilitarian wooden buildings of the immediate post-frontier period. But Worcester did not preach

◀ *Bell (Wintermute) house, conservatory (Baer)*   97

in one of the simple, gabled wooden boxes with a cross nailed to the roof which were the homes of many of San Francisco's churches: he utilized the most sophisticated designers the city had to offer. Keeler did not live in a miner's shack: he built a Maybeck house, a very fine one. The buildings of Coxhead, Polk, and Maybeck may be simple in a superficial sense: they are not covered with the turrets, towers, and fussy jigsaw ornament which sprouted all over most of San Francisco's turn-of-the-century buildings. Yet with their synthesis of historic fragments from a wide variety of times and places, with their manipulations of expected scale, their elaborately sculptural spatial concepts, their frequent experiments (both esthetic and structural), and their use of seemingly contradictory formal elements, they are not simple productions in any way. They are rich, complex, and sometimes enigmatic, and to deny this is to limit our experience, restrict our perceptions, and to reject work which has new significance for an age which is not without mannerist tendencies of its own.

2

Life in the Dollhouse

DAVID GEBHARD

During the past three to four decades we have tended to be so casual in the way we look at period architecture of this century that we have been oblivious to the striking differences which set off a period building of the teens from one built in the twenties, thirties or even more recently. If we pay a little attention to these buildings we will quickly become aware of how a system of historical imagery—say "American Colonial"—could be manipulated to produce very different effects. If we group together the variety of historical images used during these decades it will become immediately apparent that the borrowings which form these period styles are only incidentally based on the way they were used in the original historic prototype. We can only establish a meaningful picture of period style if we look at its totality and avoid becoming bogged down in discussing the prototype.

One of the periods which did establish a sharply defined personality of its own was the decade of the twenties, running from about 1919 to about 1932. This period experienced a wide range of historical borrowings from the American past (mainly, although not exclusively, Georgian and Federal) and from the European past (Mediterranean, English Medieval, English Georgian, and French Norman Provincial). Clients and architects did not employ historical references to suggest particular buildings

from the past, but gently used these forms and details to establish a mood. In this sense the use of historicism during the twenties was markedly different from that of the early nineteenth century, when the Greek or the Gothic was closely related to literature (the classics of Greek and Roman literature; the Gothic novel, etc.). The period buildings of the twenties were related to literature only by a vague similarity of mood.

All the period houses of the twenties shared a number of visual attributes, one of the most important being their fragile, almost cardboard quality. This thin fragility is apparent not only in the surface which defines volume, but in all of the details, and in the way the building is related to its site. Since these buildings were supposed to be modeled on historic images it was important that they appeared to "belong" and be natural to the site—and yet in a strange way, they never turned out to be. They are like the witch's cottage of gingerbread and cookies in "Hansel and Gretel" which has been magically but unrealistically set in a dark endless forest; the period houses of the twenties reassert their traditional relationship with their sites via historical illusion, not as a visual fact.

Externally or internally, these buildings create a peculiar set of opposites. They do not suggest the "real" past; rather they convey a 1920s version of the past. They evoke the feeling of personal handcraftsmanship which has been realized by the machine. As Gladding, McBean and Co. (the largest of the West Coast tile manufacturers) noted in one of their advertisements for "Medieval Shingle Tile" in the twenties: "Our new Medieval roof tile was designed to satisfy the sophisticated taste of those who find an inexhaustible delight in the roofs of ancient European country houses. Its coloring reproduces the stains of lichens and of storms. It smacks of storied antiquity. This *Medieval* is admirably suited to French, Norman, or English architecture. . . ."[1] And while life out-of-doors was becoming increasingly important, especially in the mild climate of California, these period houses were insistent that the inner spaces of the houses be private and secluded. Wall surfaces predominated over openings, thereby creating a feeling of tight enclosures; windows and french doors were almost always broken up with mullions or with leading which traditionally made the windows read as screens rather than as openings between exterior and interior space.

A final element which sets off the period houses of this decade from their predecessors and from those of the thirties has to do with the question of seriousness. These houses use the serious architectural style of the past in a non-serious fashion. They reveal neither a literary nor a visual intellectualism. As the Bay Area writer Eugene Neuhaus noted of W. R. Yelland's Tupper and Reed Music Store in Berkeley (1926), "it is playful, it appeals to the imagination in its happy surface variations of light and shade; its pleasurable details done with fine understanding of the material possibilities."[2]

To a marked degree this lack of seriousness was due to an open child-like quality. In the same article Neuhaus began by quoting his young son's reaction to the building: "Wouldn't downtown be interesting if all the stores were like that." He then went on to emphasize the knowing purity of the child's vision: "The boy," he wrote, "is too young to know about sacrosanct school traditions, the glamour of historic styles and all the other inhibitions of architecture, but he intuitively realized one thing—here was something stimulating, something interesting, something gratifying which gave him a vision of a different, of a happier environment."[3] Thus, for the twenties client and architect, the Golden Age of Greece, the purity

of the unspoiled savage, have been wholly replaced by the vision of the child.

Though the imaginative literary world of the child of the teens and the later twenties ranged from the detective adventures of the Hardy Boys to the scientific world of Tom Swift, the adult view of childhood hinged on the late-nineteenth-century fairy tale or romance. From this world the adult took a visual imagery which was almost exclusively Medieval—castles mounted on impenetrable crags, low-thatched cottages lining a village street, or small farmhouses situated in an untroubled forest. So the favored forms of the historic past which were projected into the adult world of real buildings tended to be packaged as English Tudor or French Norman (as they were referred to at the time).

Since a sense of childhood romance had already been a strong ingredient of the earlier buildings of the Bay Area Tradition from Coxhead through Maybeck, the clients and the architects of the Second Phase warmly and enthusiastically embraced these Medieval dollhouse forms. In the Bay Area, and especially in and around Berkeley and the University of California, these Medieval cottagey forms were readily taken up by the academicians and their camp followers. For after all, the university was a Medieval institution and, therefore, for a scholar to live in a small, steep-roofed cottage was as appropriate as for him or her to teach in a vine-covered Tudor building. Since the Medieval cottage was so closely associated with the sequestered life of the university, it was natural that it should be taken up by intellectuals or would-be intellectuals, by second-generation inheritors of modest wealth (with coupon in hand), and, to a degree, by other professionals such as lawyers and doctors whose image, like that of the academicians, looked back to a Medieval past. In looking over the clients of the architects of the Second Phase, we find that it seems to be the man rather than the woman who desired the Medieval dollhouse—perhaps indicating that the male remembrance of childhood (conditioned by tradition) tends to be less factual and "real" than that of the female.

What were the general characteristics of this dollhouse architecture? The setting of the building on the site, the landscaping of the site, and the interior spaces of the building communicate a contrived set of

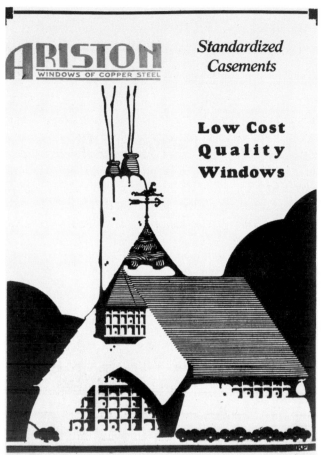

Back cover advertisement from Architect & Engineer, *October 1919*

YELLAND, *Tupper & Reed Music Store, Berkeley, 1926* (Baer)

chances (planned chances, if you will). The elements of the building and of the site provided the stimulus and stage set to act out the dreaming world of childhood romance. The ideal Hansel and Gretel cottage of the twenties announced that the man-made object cowered before nature, a nature which was rural and somewhat wild. There had to be a hint of hoary age, decay, and the witch-infested forest—not of the sublime as one finds in eighteenth-century architecture and landscape gardening but a remembrance of one's responses as a child to fairy tales. The form of the building—even if it was only one or two rooms—had to be as wildly irregular as possible, mysterious and impossible to "read" as a whole either externally or internally. Everything was to be scaled to the minuscule; with a sense that we as adults are like Alice in Wonderland, walking around in a world of which we are really not a part. The sense of mystery in these buildings was heightened by the complexity of passage, of movement from one space to the next, and in the way that light (both artificial and natural) was used.

Stucco, brick, wood, and stone—traditional "natural" materials—were employed both within and without. Generally these materials were kept small in scale and were used in a rough fashion to imply that they were rustic and rural, not urbane and polished. Favored details included small casement windows (with leaded mullions, if possible), simple board or paneled doors, rough plastered walls, "hidden" and/or irregular staircases, the appearance or fact of exposed structure, real or suggested changes in floor and ceiling levels, and above all a large brick or stone fireplace.

In the Bay Area there were three favored locales for the Medieval dollhouse—Berkeley and the East Bay hills, the Forest Hill area of San Francisco, and the coastal retreat of Carmel. Other examples were scattered hither and thither in northern California— as retreat cabins by Lake Tahoe, in the hills of southern Marin County, and even occasionally down the peninsula. As was the case elsewhere in the country, this architecture was a suburban architecture—not only in the sense of where it was located, but in its full-blown advertisement that it was anti-urban. Almost every architect in the Bay Area produced one or more variations of this theme, but the major expo-

nents were John Hudson Thomas, W. R. Yelland, Carr Jones, and the Carmel architect Hugh Comstock.[4] Among earlier practitioners of the First Phase, Bernard Maybeck, Henry Gutterson, and Walter H. Ratcliff also produced numerous cottages which fall fully within the Hansel and Gretel mode.[5] The shift from the Craftsman and Voyseyesque work of these older men (accomplished between 1900 and 1915) was gentle and easy. The use of segregated historic fragments and specifically Classical segments and the intense interest in expressing structure were replaced by what appeared to be a single overall historicism, where the total composition reads as an historical episode and where structure as a declared aesthetic entity was markedly played down. These cottages and other buildings were not blatantly "dishonest" in their use of material or of structure. Half timbering made no further claim than being a surface treatment. The occasional wavy lines and curled-around-at-the-eaves shingles read just as what they were, though they hinted at something they were not—namely Medieval thatching. Irregular stucco-surfaced walls never really departed from the two-by-four wood stud which lay behind them—no one was asked to take them for masonry—but like shingle roofs and applied half timbering they ask us to search in our memories for things past. One could go on and on about how other materials—brick, stone, wood sheathing—were called upon to make dual declarations: of their own reality as materials of the twenties, and of their employment to create allusions to the past.

Maybeck, who was in his fifties during the twenties, continued to follow the diverse paths which he had taken during the previous decades. His Kennedy house in Berkeley (1923) presented a Coxhead approach of posing separate historical remnants in and on a Maybeck Arts and Crafts form. A 1916 house in the Forest Hill section of San Francisco transforms the Maybeck forms and spaces into something very close to a fairy-tale cottage. And other designs, such as the Feudal manorial Anthony house (Los Angeles, 1927), used not fragments but an historical whole to suggest the Medieval (in this case Spanish Medieval) atmospheric mode of the place.

Thomas, along with his Berkeley contemporaries Gutterson and Ratcliff, settled down to two decades

MAYBECK, *Kennedy house, Berkeley, 1923 (Baer)*

MAYBECK, *house in Forest Hill, San Francisco, 1916 (Baer)*

of design in the dollhouse idiom. As in his work of the early 1900's and the teens, he sometimes succeeded and many times did not. But even when he did not pull it off, his admitted inconsistencies, incompleteness, and lack of resolve seem to end up as positive elements of a visual grammar. His own house of 1928 in Kensington—which is in fact a moderate-sized residence—was designed to be read in small increments, so that neither externally nor in the spaces within does it ever lose the small scale which is so essential for a fairy-tale atmosphere.

Gutterson, Ratcliff, and other Berkeley architects spotted their fairy-tale cottages all over the hills of East Bay. Many of them were really very small, like the little Raymond T. Farmer cottage in Berkeley (1918), which is essentially a one-room house with small auxiliary spaces provided for sleeping, cooking, and the bathroom. Others, even though larger, like Ratcliff's 1927 Naylor house, maintain their sense of an unreal stage-set fantasy by segmenting the building into distinct separate volumes and by carefully scaling everything down, including the walled gar-

THOMAS, *Dungan house, Berkeley, 1915 (Baer)*

Dungan house (Baer)

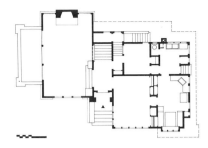

Dungan house, plan

Dungan house, interior (Baer)

THOMAS, *Thomas house, window, Kensington, 1928* (Baer)

GUTTERSON, *Farmer cottage, Berkeley, 1918* (Baer)

Farmer cottage, plan

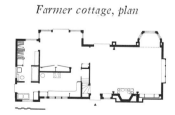

RATCLIFF, *Naylor house, Berkeley, 1927* (Baer)

RATCLIFF, *Naylor house* (Baer)

109

YELLAND, *Thornberg Village, Berkeley, 1928,*
exterior (Baer)

den and cobblestone stepping stones which lead to the house.

The most openly romantic of all of the East Bay architects was W. R. Yelland. After visiting the Auvergne district of France he wrote, "Everywhere there is a strange atmosphere of simplicity and contentment. I am inclined to feel that, partly anyway, the happy, informal way of building has affected their lives."[6] In his apartment complex, Thornberg Village (now called Normandy Village) in Berkeley of 1928, he took the conventional and rather dull H-shaped apartment plan and squeezed and pulled it apart so that we feel, in a "stage-setty" way, that we are in a Medieval village. And the illusion was carried all the way through—in the intimacy and mystery of the entrance to each apartment and then the irregularity of horizontal and vertical spaces which we encounter within each apartment. The delight of the fairy-tale Medieval is present in Yelland's Goss house in Piedmont (c. 1925), in his small hillside Garthwaite house in Castlewood Country Club (1927), and in his rural Marie-Antoinette French farmhouse for Harry E. Miller, Jr., at Atherton (1929).

110

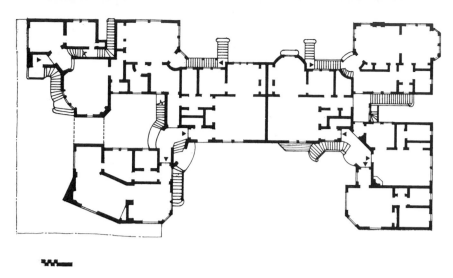

Thornberg Village, plan

Thornberg Village, exterior (Baer)

Thornberg Village, exterior (Baer)

YELLAND, *Goss house, Piedmont, 1925 (Sally Woodbridge)*

JONES, *house in Palo Alto, 1934, exterior* (Baer)

Equally taxing one's credibility are the scattering of low brick and stucco cottages—many actually very large in square footage—produced by the Berkeley designer Carr Jones and the "teensy-weensy" story-book architecture of Hugh R. Comstock of Carmel. Comstock's cottages and his Tuck Box Shop (Carmel, 1926) illustrate the built-in pitfall in the use of Hansel and Gretel imagery—if it is too self-consciously cute and coy, it will end up amusing us, but will no longer serve as a visual language to take us back to the reality of childhood.

The Bay Area Alice houses and other buildings of the twenties represent a peculiar and idiosyncratic episode within the Bay Area Tradition's Second Phase. Nothing quite similar occurred elsewhere at the time, nor has it occurred since. (Southern California's Hansel and Gretel architecture was quite different.) Within the current phase of the Bay Area Tradition, Charles Moore has injected historicism and a sense of the child's world. The new do-it-yourself work (the "Wood-Butchers" art) of the late sixties and the seventies also has its aura of childish fantasies—but neither the high art allusions of Moore nor the low art efforts at historical romance of the back-to-nature movement has been able successfully to carry on the dollhouse imagery of the twenties.

114

House in Palo Alto, entrance (Baer)

House in Palo Alto, living room (Baer)

House in Palo Alto, plan

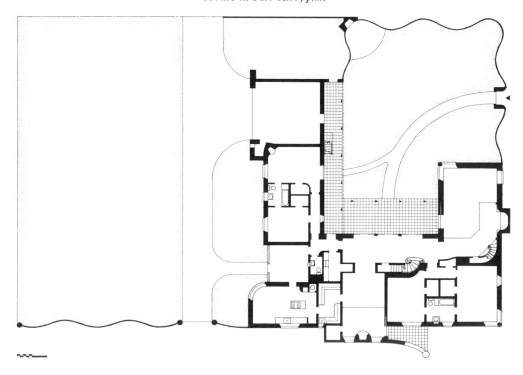

JONES, *house in Piedmont, c. 1930* (Baer)

House in Piedmont (Baer)

COMSTOCK, *The Tuck Box, Carmel, 1926* (*Baer*)

COMSTOCK, *cottage in Carmel, c. 1925* (Baer)

3

William Wilson Wurster
An Architect of Houses

RICHARD C. PETERS

Architecture is not a goal. Architecture is for life and pleasure and work and for people. The picture frame, and not the picture. www[1]

I like an unlabored thing, that looks as inevitable as something that comes out of a frying pan just right, like an omelet in France, for instance. www[3]

As a practicing architect, I can best describe my views on architecture as follows: when a hillside is given to me on which to place a house, I embrace it and do not long for a meadow; and conversely, when a site comes on a meadow, I embrace it and do not long for a hillside. www[2]

The "California way of living," that somewhat mythical and mystical ideal for which the state has become famous, deeply influenced its architecture. No one pursued this spirit more passionately than William W. Wurster. From 1927 to 1942 he designed over two hundred houses and became the recognized leader of a group of San Francisco Bay Area architects whose work, especially in domestic design, was important in the development of mid-twentieth-century American architecture.

Wurster perceived a special character in the geography and social framework of the region that stretched from San Francisco north, south, and inland for about a hundred miles. As a native son he felt called upon to give it physical expression. When he was asked to design or discuss architecture in other parts of the country he was always somewhat hesitant, stating that he only knew one region well enough to speak with authority. The regional values that called for attention were not dissimilar from the general concerns felt by architects everywhere. Special features of site and climate, added to the personal needs of the client, condition the design approach of all thoughtful architects. It was Wurster's personal interpretation of these factors and his deep concern that made the difference.

The San Francisco Bay Area has a variety of climate and landscape unknown in other parts of the country. Environmental conditions change within a few miles creating different indoor-outdoor relationships. In the hot, dry central valley the sun must be held at bay, whereas in foggy San Francisco it must be coaxed in. The areas in between require accommodation for both conditions. Throughout the region there is a lack of summer rain.

Rejecting the venerable and continuing approach in architecture of solving problems by balancing one style or idiom against another, selecting the best solutions from previously built and published work, Wurster reused and refined a set of architectural elements—the living porch, the glazed gallery, the screened verandah, and the garden-living room. These he derived from vernacular sources and adapted to contemporary situations with such skill and understanding that they continued and strengthened a regional architectural tradition. In fact, Wurster's contribution to local domestic architecture is so subtly integrated into the prevailing scene that it is often invisible to the passing eye.

His ideas were simply stated, often in a homey way that belied their sophistication:

Use the site, the money, the local materials, the client, the climate to decide what shall be. Make no arbitrary decisions to be against what has been or only for what is to come. See with eyes to the front, be appropriate in what you do, do not be barbaric in a conventional neighborhood, or unnecessarily prim in Bohemia.[4]

Or:

The most predominant single desire for most people is for personally controlled out-of-door space where the family can have a flower or vegetable garden at its door, where clothes can be dried in the sun, where the baby can be put in a play pen, where young children can make mud pies.[5]

He had a deep mistrust of style perfectly expressed by the following words:

A style has to do with periods and fashions and is something that is adopted by a number of not necessarily thinking people and pushed through to exhaustion. . . .[6]
In reality I like to think of the word [style] as meaning "of today" which means that it will be different tomorrow, in other words a constant term applying to changing modes and mediums.[7]

Given this attitude he could not accept Lewis Mumford's baptism of Bay Area work, much of which he was responsible for, as the "Bay Region Style." He preferred "atmosphere" or "tendencies" if need be,

but mostly he preferred to speak of the problems and solutions without labeling them in a formal way.

William Wilson Wurster was born in Stockton, California, in 1895. At home he was encouraged in drawing, in observation, and in reading, but he acknowledged that his was "more an intellectual than a drawing gift." During summer vacation periods from Stockton High School he worked for the well known local architect, E. B. Brown. In 1913 he enrolled in the University of California at Berkeley and graduated with a degree in architecture in 1919. He immediately went to work for John Reed, Jr., a San Francisco architect who did institutional work. While working on Galileo High School he came close to leaving the field, where, as it seemed to him at that point, people were put in niches with little possibility of experiment, communication, and exposure to the real world of building. His chance to change his "niche" came with an offer to become the architectural designer on the staff of the Filtration Division of the City of Sacramento. From 1920 to 1922 Wurster worked on the Sacramento Filtration Plant and moonlighted on four residences. These houses plus his previous experience were the basis for his state architectural registration in April 1922.

On May 21, 1922 he took his savings of $4000 and embarked on the standard architect's grand tour of Europe. After a year of traveling, studying, sketching, doing some measured drawings, and keeping a diary, he returned in 1923 to work in the well-known New York firm of Delano and Aldrich. He developed a life-long friendship with William Adams Delano and spent the summer of 1924 with the Delano family in Syosset on Long Island. He tutored their son, Richard, and experienced a style and scale of living markedly different from that of the Bay Area. In August of 1924 he returned to San Francisco to do the San Leandro Filtration Plant for a former employer in Sacramento, Charles Hyde. The job took two years, during which he opened a small practice doing houses in Berkeley.

Perhaps his most fortuitous meeting was with Mrs. Ralph Ellis, a friend of the Delanos, who had come from New York to live in Berkeley. He came to meet as well her friend Mrs. Warren Gregory, a Berkeley resident of many years. These two influential and gifted ladies launched him on his career.

WURSTER, *Gregory farmhouse, Santa Cruz, 1926-27 (Sturtevant)*

Through them he was drawn into the maze of relationships that characterize the landed gentry of any established region. As a native son and a professional whose work was the physical expression of the art of living, Wurster was well equipped to fill their needs. His success in this endeavor is well attested to by the fact that he did two and sometimes three houses for the same families in the course of his career.

The most important work of this early period and perhaps the signal work of his career was the Gregory farmhouse of 1926-27 near Santa Cruz, California. Originally commissioned by Warren Gregory from John Galen Howard's son Henry, the work was interrupted by Mr. Gregory's death. Perhaps the family had not been entirely happy with Howard's design. In any case, Wurster was invited to come down one weekend and offer his advice. He was deeply moved by the site, typical rolling coastal ranch country studded with live oaks, and wrote:

"The farm is a place of peace and rest, of the realities rather than the formalities of life, and so it seemed imperative to make the house simple and direct, free from any distorted or overstudied look."[8]

The simple sketch he made on that first visit, according to Gregory family legend, was built almost without alteration. The living quarters of the house form two sides of the courtyard plan, with a simple water tower marking the entrance and low walls forming the rest of the enclosure. As in the earlier Anglo-Spanish ranch houses, the interior of the house is accessible only by doors opening onto the continuous verandah along the court side or onto the terrace on the open side of the compound. The central living space is emphasized by raising that section of the roof. Redwood boards, left unfinished for the floors and painted white for the walls and ceiling carry the visual rhythm of the design.

For all its archetypal California ranch house look,

123

Gregory farmhouse, view from court (Sturtevant)

the Gregory house precisely satisfied its owner's needs. It aped no traditional forms. Rather, it embodied the region's essential spirit in a rare moment of creative genius. If any single house can symbolize the Bay Area Tradition in residential design, the Gregory farmhouse is that work.

The relatively small size of the Gregory commission was typical of most of Wurster's work in the pre–World War II period. Although a number of his clients were not severely restricted by the Depression, the times were generally conservative. In any case, a certain austerity was characteristic of the office's clientele; those who craved ostentation went elsewhere.

Wurster took great pride in perfecting the living quality of the house. He believed that building modestly was essential, but his was a vigorous modesty: "we should design up from the log cabin, instead of trying to compress the mansion," he said.[9] Organized in design teams, he and his staff worked out house design rules such as always placing horizontal window members so that they never interfered with the sight-line of anyone, whether seated or standing; a standard height for all electrical switches, and a means of coordinating the foundation elements of the house, known locally as the "Wurster footing." It avoided a level change from the outside to the inside, thereby welding the house more completely to the site. All wall siding was butt-jointed to square framing members at the corners instead of using the usual

Gregory farmhouse, living room (Sturtevant)

more costly mitered corners, and ways of constructing horizontal and vertical board siding were refined. Double-hung windows and re-sawn, flush-set redwood siding were other signatures of Wurster's work. An absence or simplification of door and window frames emphasized the "carpenter-style" approach.

This deliberate paring away of those very elements considered by most architects to be the life and breath of design did not earn Wurster the universal approbation of his peers. Those who disapproved labeled his work "shanty-style," implying a slip-shod imprecision that was far from true of his work.

Wurster's commonsense approach to design was equally important in the plan of the house, typically a diagram of the client's needs. The flexibility with which the office met those needs, no matter how eccentric, was truly remarkable. Many, many clients take great pleasure in recounting the lengthy planning period during which Wurster asked more questions than would ever have occurred to them to ask. The answers all contributed to the "big idea" of the frequently small house.

The dramatic expansion of Wurster's practice in the thirties began with a commission by the internationally famous golfer Marion Hollins to design her house and other residences as Pasatiempo Country Club and Estates. The site was in the foothills of the Santa Cruz Mountains. Wurster, along with Miss Hollins, also a friend of the Ellises, chose architect

125

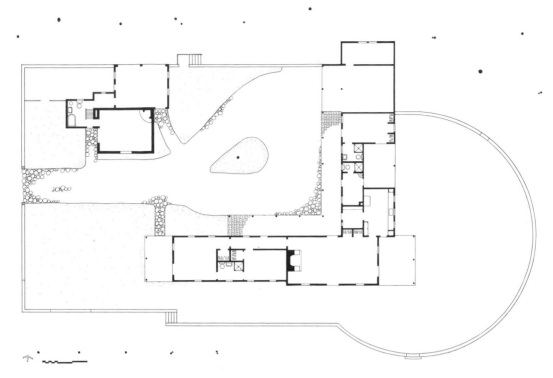

Gregory farmhouse, plan

Clarence Tantau and landscape architect Thomas Church to oversee its entire development. This gave Wurster the opportunity of working on numerous houses and it is in this Pasatiempo portfolio of 1931-32 that the aforementioned elements of his work emerge. The Marion Hollins residence of 1931 contains the "kitchen cave," which is perhaps his first inside-outside dining room space and the forerunner of what later becomes Wurster's "room with no name." The glazed gallery of the Kaplansky-Howes house is an indoor-outdoor link which is usable as a working space and not just a hall connecting adjoining spaces. The Butler house is a set of pavilions linked together with an open gallery space called the living porch, which allows the opportunity for simple country living in a quiet protected environment. The screened verandah of the MacKenzie house is another trademark of Wurster and recognizes the special requirements of out-of-door relaxation on the edge of the beautiful lawns of the golf course.

Wurster always gave special attention to those elements of a design that reflected special needs of the client. In the house of his close collaborator, Thomas Church, the drafting room, designed to maximize the use of natural daylight, is the major form determinant for the whole composition. Although deftly woven into the overall fabric of each house, the importance of these special places is prophetic for Wurster's work in the years ahead.

For the Voss house of 1931 Wurster had what he described as "an ideal client with an ideal site."[10] Built on a knoll in the Big Sur range, this house was designed to take advantage of dramatic vistas of the California coast; the two-story scheme with every room facing south is open to the view and to the out-of-doors. This house contains the essence of Wurster's design—the casualness of informal living combined with simple conventional wood frame construction, not unlike the vernacular barn construction which Wurster knew and admired. Closer examination reveals that the house is organized around the

WURSTER, *Hollins house, Pasatiempo, 1931* (*Sturtevant*)

Hollins house, "kitchen cave" (*Sturtevant*)

WURSTER, *Kaplansky-Howes house, Pasatiempo, 1931, gallery (Sturtevant)*

WURSTER, *Butler house, Pasatiempo, 1931-32, gallery* (*Sturtevant*)

Butler house, plan

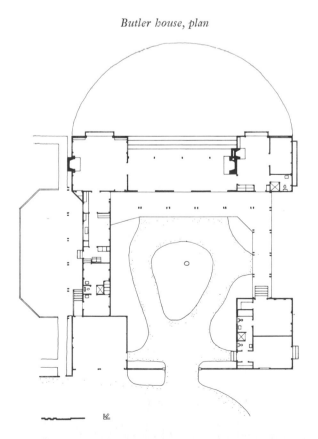

WURSTER, *Mackenzie house, Pasatiempo, 1931, screened verendah (Sturtevant)*

WURSTER, *Church house, Pasatiempo, 1931 (Sturtevant)*

Church house, interior of drafting room (Sturtevant)
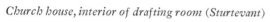

WURSTER, *Voss house, Big Sur, 1931* (*Sturtevant*)

Voss house (*Sturtevant*)

WURSTER, *Benner house, Berkeley, 1934,*
exterior of sun porch (Sturtevant)

Benner house, interior of sun porch (Sturtevant)

"big porch" on the upper level and the "kitchen cave" on the lower level, both capable of being closed and comfortable during harsh weather. These features, which allow the owners the opportunity of living with the land, recognize the uniqueness of life in a country place as a retreat from the complexities of urban life.

In contrast is a suburban stucco and frame home nestled in a small canyon in Berkeley. The Benner house, completed in 1934, was built for a large and active family. Here again are two special features. The "sun porch," which opens onto a simple lawn terrace and gardens by Thomas Church, is capable of many uses. Facing south, it could be a summer or winter room, a rainy-day room, a marvelous hideaway, or a place for active play. It is a room which has no real identification, and yet, because it is centrally located in relation to the entire house, it is a major feature in the design. The balcony is really a large porch connecting all the major living spaces to

133

WURSTER, *Clark house, Aptos, 1937* (*Sturtevant*)

a view deck and sleeping porch which look west to the Golden Gate. Of this house Wurster wrote: "We are in the throes of designing a house which shall take a fresh viewpoint—'call it modern if you will' but it is not to be a reactionary modern—in a word everything is done because of a positive wish—never to be different—and I hope it will give a pleasant, enlightened look—but not bizarre."[11]

In 1937 Wurster completed a beach house for the Clarks in Aptos near Santa Cruz. Here is the centrally organized kitchen cave on the beach level, flanked by wind-protected sitting places—outside living porches protected from the windy Pacific.

Two examples of the living porch are the 1937 Hammill house, oriented to a magnificent view of the Bay, and the Green residence of 1938 on the slopes of Mt. Diablo, open to the countryside and the rolling hills beyond.

Clark house, interior (Sturtevant)

WURSTER, *Hammill house, San Francisco, 1937 (Sturtevant)*

WURSTER, *Green house, Mt. Diablo, 1938* (*Sturtevant*)

The 1941 Turner house is located in the California Central Valley. The great covered porch provides cooling shade and allows enjoyment of outdoor living in the hot climate. The living room, wrapped by the gracious porch, becomes part of the garden through the open, airy quality of its interior space.

Wurster realized that the glazed gallery created flexibility in the internal organization of spaces, best illustrated in the Le Hane house, completed in 1937 (see illustration, p. 7). Never just a long hall, it is organized as a sun-drenched living place which allows the entire house to open to the enclosed garden.

The Pope house near Orinda (later bulldozed for a freeway) had an interior court of many uses which was more an open-air vestibule. It could be opened to the view of rolling hills or closed to serve as a central hallway. This duality was constant in much of Wurster's work. His use here of concrete block and corrugated metal siding was highly unusual in residential design.

WURSTER, *Turner house, 1941, living porch* (Sturtevant)

Turner house, living room (Sturtevant)

WURSTER, *Pope house, Orinda, 1940* (*Sturtevant*)

WURSTER, *Chickering house, Woodside, 1941* (*Sturtevant*)

Wurster spoke and wrote a great deal about the "room with no name." The 1941 Chickering house has such a space—a large, central loggia which is a link or connector between two rooms. (Strictly speaking, the house does not have what was called a bi-nuclear plan, a term popularized by Marcel Breuer.) The room is a multi-purpose space, either open or closed, freely relating with terraces and gardens, which connects functionally different areas. Formal, yet informal; elegant, yet casual, it is indicative of the effort necessary to understand the specificity of an individual room designed to meet diverse needs.

Chickering house, plan

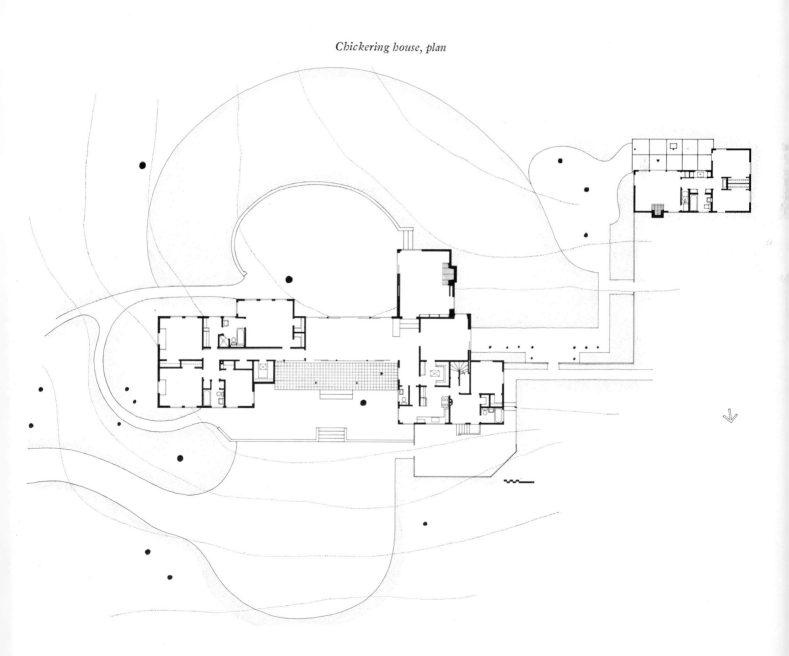

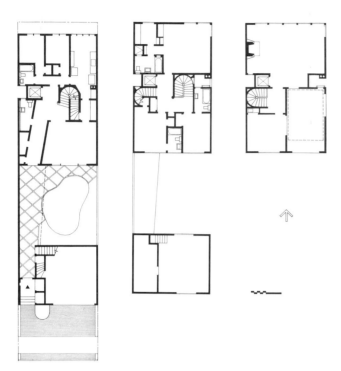

WURSTER, *Grover house, San Francisco, plan*

Wurster's townhouses for San Francisco reflect the distinctive microclimate and topography of the city. Sitting on a slim city lot, the Grover house of 1939 (see illustration above) reaches up to partake of magnificent views and at the same time turns its back on the wind by providing an intimate exterior Thomas Church garden accessible from the dining area on the lower level. A small deck on the upper level is related to the solarium and living room.

Sandwiched between two existing houses and built to the edge of the street, the Doble house is an

WURSTER, *Jensen house, Berkeley, 1937* (*Sturtevant*)

example of the "large-small" house in the city. The living spaces are placed both on the top level for the views and at the first level for access to out-of-door activity. The house also has a sun court on the south and entrance side, protected from the city's blustery western winds. In this and the Grover house the simple use of materials and details, coupled with the direct expression of an internal organization, clearly indicate the restraint of the Wurster idiom. They are appropriate examples of Wurster's belief that it is of "small matter in what you live; of great importance is

what you look at,"[12] be it views of the water and hills or small courts catching warm sunlight.

The following group of houses show different approaches to building in different settings in the Bay Area. The Jensen house, completed in 1937, is built in a secluded wooded grove on the side of the Berkeley hills. This little house with ship-cabin scale reflects Wurster's belief that no job was ever too small for his interest. On the terrace level the large "Wurster windows" look out from the living and dining areas to the view of San Francisco and also protect

Jensen house, living room (Sturtevant)

Jensen house, plan

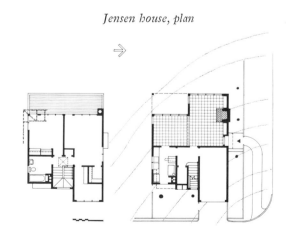

WURSTER, *Dondo house, Point Richmond, 1935 (Sturtevant)*

these spaces from the strong westerly wind. The bedrooms share the view and have a large sitting deck which is used as a sleeping porch on balmy evenings. The simplicity of the rather formal interior of the living room, with its plain white walls and tile floor, is designed to accommodate any kind of furnishing. "A good house should serve as a background for life which the people can augment."[13]

The Dondo house, 1935, located on the shore of the northern end of San Francisco Bay at Point Richmond, is a specific answer to the site and to the needs of the client. Built of "under down block," a precast concrete unit, the house is designed for minimum upkeep and maximum livability. The quality of such an economical material used straightforwardly is an appropriate instance of Wurster's insistence on freedom from care. The opportunity to live at the water's edge, to be a part of this unique setting, is found in

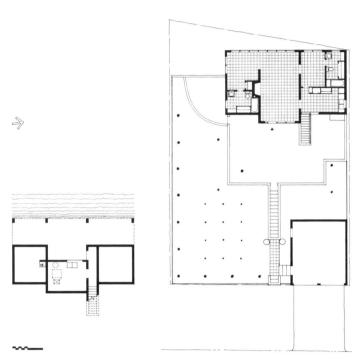

Dondo house, plan

Dondo house (Sturtevant)

WURSTER, *Corbus house, Palo Alto, 1941* (*Sturtevant*)

the logical and clear interior functions, including the "individual outdoor room" for the racing shell and water activities.

The Corbus house, 1941, was built in the then-rural countryside of the last developed peninsular suburban area near Palo Alto. This simple pavilion house, with what has been described as "Wurster's awkward scale," not only has a sense of spaciousness, though small, but also fulfills the ideal of a country place, though it sits on a standard suburban lot. It is a seemingly artless house, casual and carefree.

Thus, in the twenties and thirties when most of his peers were concerned with what to add to their basic designs to give them the proper tone, Wurster was intent on editing the extraneous and the pretentious to reveal the living patterns of his clients. Conse-

quently, his work commanded the attention of a generation then in school for whom appropriateness of materials and construction and flexibility of plan were paramount.

However personal, the work of the Wurster office of the period 1930-43 was not the result of a one-man design show, but of teams. In 1944 Wurster joined forces with his long-time employee and friend, Theodore Bernardi, and formed Wurster & Bernardi. He also felt he needed to broaden his understanding of urban problems, so he enrolled in graduate school at Harvard to study city planning. He had married Catherine Bauer, a well-known planner and author of *Modern Housing*, and they embarked on a venture in the East which lasted ten years. In 1944 he became Dean of Architecture at MIT.

In 1951 Wurster returned to his alma mater as Dean of Architecture at the University of California, Berkeley. World War II was over; architecture once again began to flourish. Wurster and Bernardi expanded the partnership with the addition of Donn Emmons, who had been in their office for some time.

Though the scope of their work increased dramatically, they steadfastly held to the belief that residential work was important and exciting. The houses of the firm were known worldwide and the diversity of design approach had enormous influence, not only in the Bay Area but throughout the United States. Based on timeless precepts Wurster had formulated and refined nearly thirty years before, these houses develop their own sense of appropriateness. Contained within them, however, are those personal design elements which were first seen in the earliest works in Pasatiempo. The Henderson house of 1954 (discussed in Chapter 4) shows the living porch in all its grandeur. The screened verandah of the Pope house (1958; also discussed in Chapter 4) recognizes the need for protection from bugs and rain in the hot Central Valley and at the same time is really another room without a name.

The most beautiful and sophisticated of the glazed galleries is in the Coleman townhouse of 1961-62. A crystal wall wrapped around an exquisite garden creates an elegant corridor of light which weaves the garden and the interior spaces together.

Another "garden house" in the city is the Salz residence. Here the characteristic San Francisco bay windows become demi-rooms capturing sunlight and providing a chance to walk out into the gardens.

A 1951 Lake Tahoe retreat, the Heller house, contains a magnificent room without a name. Bold, massive forms and materials combine with multiple-use spaces to develop the most striking example of this Wurster concept. Living, dining, working, and sleeping all take place in this setting, expanding what had initially begun in the kitchen cave or the individual room into a beautiful and robust "nameless" place for activities at the water's edge.

The retreat that Wurster built in 1962 for his family sums up the qualities this chapter portrays. It is at the ocean's edge, a special place for relaxation. The simplicity and directness of its spatial organization and the honest use of materials are as deftly handled

WURSTER, BERNARDI & EMMONS, *Henderson house, Burlingame, 1954, living porch (Sturtevant)*

WURSTER, BERNARDI & EMMONS, *Pope ranch house, Madera, 1958,*
living porch (Sturtevant)

WURSTER, BERNARDI & EMMONS, *Heller house, Lake Tahoe, 1951* (Sturtevant)

WURSTER, BERNARDI & EMMONS, *Coleman house, San Francisco, 1961-62,*
gallery (Sturtevant)

150

WURSTER, BERNARDI & EMMONS, *Salz house, San Francisco, 1954 (Sturtevant)*

Salz house, plan

WURSTER, *Wurster house, Stinson Beach, 1962* (Sturtevant)

here as in the Gregory ranch house of forty years before. Overlooking the sand and sea, the room with no name testifies to Wurster's belief that everyday use has symbolic meaning in the making of places.

If by regionalism in architecture we mean a commitment to the expression of the physical, cultural, and historical aspects of a geographical area, Wurster was a regionalist par excellence. When he left the Bay Area during World War II to go to Harvard and thence to MIT, it was as the pivotal intellectual leader in the field for a significant region of this country, a role then duplicated by no other architectural figure.

His influence, seemingly eclipsed by succeeding architectural fashions with different, more formal qualities, is all-pervasive and readily acknowledged by the generation of architects which his office schooled while contributing hundreds of buildings to the scene. Now that the built world has acquired a certain sameness from one coast to the other, Wurster's belief in and celebration of a particular way of life in a special place has crystallized, not as a style, but as a humanizing attitude of mind, a moment of truth.

Wurster house, "room with no name" (Sturtevant)

4

From the Large-Small House to the Large-Large House

SALLY WOODBRIDGE

Anyone who flew over the San Francisco Bay Area soon after the end of World War II saw large open spaces between the cities on the San Francisco Peninsula, vast prune orchards and truck gardens in the northern Santa Clara Valley, a few small sleepy towns amid the farms on the eastern side of the bay south of San Leandro, valleys and plains in eastern Contra Costa County still green with apricot orchards and walnut groves, and in the northern counties mile after mile of dairy lands, vineyards, and field crops surrounding historic towns and villages that had grown very slowly for decades.

MEL SCOTT[1]

Take-a-chance clients, mild, even climate, no insects or bugs, a long dry season and, above and over all, the immensity of the scene—all have their share in shaping the design. Is it small wonder to find the vitality of architecture with these as the starting points?

WILLIAM W. WURSTER[2]

If "human" is considered identical with redwood all over the place . . . I am against it. . . .

MARCEL BREUER

The scene described above by Mel Scott could not last. Of the more than half a million people who came to the Bay Area during the war years, a majority chose to stay. By the end of the decade the population increase was 947,014. One way or another, the rivers of people were bound to fill up the empty spaces.

If San Francisco became a city overnight during the Gold Rush, by 1950 it had become the head of a metropolitan region. In addition to new population centers created by the war effort, an influx of research-oriented industries plus growing diversification in the general industrial and commercial field reinforced smaller urban centers around the Bay. As a result Contra Costa, San Mateo, Santa Clara, and So-

lano counties competed in growth rate with San Francisco and Oakland. Housing accompanied industry.

During the war San Francisco engraved its haunting image deeply upon the minds of the G.I.'s who passed through the Golden Gate. Responding to the bewitching beauty of the place and its lingering frontier qualities, they vowed to return and did, in droves. Economic realities such as earning a living posed no great problem for most of the postwar pioneers. An era of prosperity was long overdue. California, at the end of the rainbow, was naturally going to get the pot of gold. Architects were as confident of the future as everyone else and with good reason; the housing shortage, already critical because of the reduced residential investment of the Depression, had reached monumental proportions by the end of the war. Through the Veterans Administration's mortgage policy every returning G.I. was assured of being able to participate in the great American dream of owning his own home.

California was attractive to architects for another reason. The generation of architects who established practices in the postwar period had been trained in the late twenties and thirties in schools still encircled by the long arm of the Beaux-Arts.[3] Although the prominent professional schools gave little inkling of them in this period, the works of Mies van der Rohe, Le Corbusier, Gropius and the Bauhaus, and Frank Lloyd Wright were well covered in the architectural press. But there were few geographic centers in the country where Modern design was accepted or practiced. The West Coast work of William W. Wurster, Gardner Dailey, Richard Neutra, and R. N. Schindler, also well published, exhibited an acceptance of the idiom and an experimental quality that gave California an early prominence as a center of the Modern Movement.

In the relatively narrow world of architects, artists, and critics the Movement was well established, but the general public felt uncomfortable in its presence. Rejection of the familiar visual vocabulary of traditional designs, usually variations of regional colonial themes, deprived Modern of a comforting symbolism; its stark simplicity reminded people more of institutions than homes. In addition a peculiar vocabulary was used to describe it. Instead of such words as *elegant, handsome, attractive,* or *comfortable,* which the public was accustomed to reading as signs of approbation, architects and critics used words like *clean, honest,* and *functional.* What they said sounded more like a platform for moral reform than a design for living.

When the public was asked to choose, as it was in a 1938 competition sponsored by *Life* magazine and *The Architectural Forum,* between the traditional and Modern designs of ten of the most prominent architects of the day, it almost unanimously favored the traditional. Published comments ranged from guarded statements about the appropriateness of the traditional "from an artistic standpoint" to the observation that "the traditional type seems to be more a part of the landscape in the Eastern states" to more personal responses such as "[Modern] looks uncomfortable from the outside" and "modern looks funny" —a comment by the children of one of the families.

If the man in the street viewed Modern architecture with distrust, his banker had an even more skeptical eye. Clients who were interested in Modern design found that the money-lending institutions were not. Both architects and clients complained of this recalcitrance to no avail; in the minds of the mortgage brokers a Modern house had no resale value.

A subtle combination of factors made California different. San Francisco, the oldest metropolis on the coast, was barely half the age of comparable urban areas in the East. Having received its major importation of foreign influence during the Victorian decades, its architectural heritage was less diverse. Its building practices were also more uniform. Because of a lack of good local building stone as well as the threat of earthquakes, there was no strong masonry tradition. The ubiquity of wood frame construction provided an unselfconscious but discernible continuity between the high-style Victorian buildings and the commercial vernacular.

Proximity to Europe maintained eastern receptivity to eclectic design. But in California, after the turn of the century, a growing chauvinism renewed interest in the state's architectural heritage, creating such revival styles as Mission, Monterey Colonial, and, after the San Diego Exposition of 1915, the Spanish Colonial. Not that the Bay Area did not have its share of eastern-oriented eclectic design, its mansions that resembled embassies for small countries. Still there was a clear line to the simple pioneer past if anyone cared to look for it.

Furthermore, a kind of frontier pride in leaving pieces of the past behind prevailed. Even those newcomers who wanted to bring the style of another part of the country or of another era with them were often persuaded by architects like William W. Wurster (whose skill in this was well known) that it would not suit their new life in this special climate and landscape.

Finally, the new environment offered possibilities for a life style that was particularly well suited to the tenets of Modern architecture. It was climatically possible to have the interpenetration of interior and exterior space so dear to Modern doctrine, and the requisite large glass areas usually framed incomparable views.

The San Francisco architect who perceived all of this most clearly was William Wilson Wurster. In his first published house, the Gregory farmhouse of 1926-27, he took the body of Modern architecture and gave it a regional soul. This unadorned structure of vertical redwood boards painted white recalled the traditional California ranch house with its courtyard composition and outside circulation system of covered walkways. It was well published and well remembered by the generation of students then in architecture schools around the country. Reflecting upon its design in an interview in 1963, Wurster said, "That house illustrated that if you want to do small work like a carpenter, do it with good sense, so it

doesn't look architected at all." Although he subsequently designed houses in the prevailing eclectic styles of Monterey Colonial and Regency, Wurster's work had a studied artlessness that contrasted strongly with the formality and use of traditional cliches that were typical of the current architectural scene.

Another San Francisco architect, equally famous at the time, who also opened his office in 1926, was Gardner Dailey. Although there was a general similarity between Wurster's and Dailey's work, there were also marked differences. Unlike Wurster, Dailey was not a native son, although he was educated at Stanford and Heald Engineering College in San Francisco; nor was he so committed to capturing the regional spirit in his work. His use of the indigenous did not interfere with his interest in the exotic. Fi-

WURSTER, *Gregory farmhouse, Santa Cruz, 1926-27* (Sturtevant)

DAILEY, *house in Woodside, 1940 (Baer)*

nally, he had a feeling for elegance that Wurster firmly rejected. Those who worked for Dailey in the thirties speak admiringly of his skill in composing circulation schemes and furniture arrangements for the living areas of his houses that accomplished the passage from entrance or stairs to living or dining rooms with the maximum effect of graciousness. If Wurster's houses were carefully designed from the inside out so that they often "hardly looked architected at all," Dailey took great care with ordering fenestration and refining moldings and other architectural detail.

This urbane and charming man also designed superbly in the rural, regional spirit. In 1940, he transformed the California barn into a simple house with only 800 square feet of space. Small as it is, the living room is doubled in scale by raising the ceiling to the height of the roof and dissolving the walls with large areas of glass. Perfectly sited in a dip in the rolling landscape, the design expresses California's enduring romance with the rural scene.

In another rural-suburban retreat of the same year in Marin County (then more remote from San Francisco than it is today), Dailey proved that he was equally at home with the Japanese influence, a prevailing current in West Coast architecture since before the turn of the century. The one-story, Y-shaped, post-and-beam structure, divided into three segments covered with interlocking, double-pitched hip roofs, recalls both Japanese residential and Cali-

DAILEY, *house in Ross, 1940 (Sturtevant)*

fornia rural compounds. The entrance, approached diagonally by a flight of brick stairs, shares its importance with a monumental brick chimney. Beyond the oak-paneled door, designed to look like a shoji or screen, the visitor finds himself in an entry hall. Turning right, he descends a few steps into the high-ceilinged living room whose end wall—two-thirds window—focuses his attention on a perfectly framed view of Mt. Tamalpais rising Fuji-like from the valley below. Behind him and up a few steps is a dining or garden room which may be closed off, like the entry, by sliding screens. This room in turn opens to a brick-paved courtyard closed on the opposite side by a landscaped hill. The choice of materials—golden woods for the interior wall panels, floors, and sliding

screens, dark-stained redwood for the exterior, and slate for the roof—creates a rich and balanced scheme of colors and textures. A walk around the house reveals a sequential pattern of decks and roof planes that reinforces the Japanese image of a series of pavilions strung along the edge of a hill.

In contrast to the suburban villa, the urban townhouse, restricted by narrow, rectangular lots, adhered closely to the box as the compositional unit. In the hands of Wurster, Dailey, and their successful contemporaries—John Ekin Dinwiddie, Hervey P. Clark, Mario Corbett, and Francis Joseph McCarthy—this box was stark and simple. Only such structural elements as the beam ends, visible under the projecting roofs and often painted white like the window frames

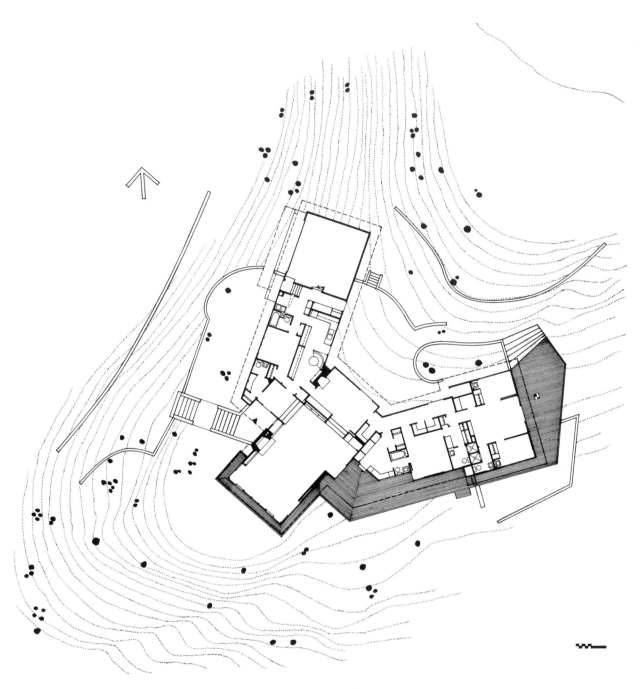

House in Ross, plan

and sunshades over them, broke the austere silhouette.

Almost alone among the townhouses designed for San Francisco in the prewar era, the Roos house of 1938 by John Ekin Dinwiddie directly reflects eastern brand, International Style design. Essentially a horizontal box with its living floor slightly extruded, the house is composed of carefully articulated planar elements. The south elevation wall, notched by a window at the corner, features a large, centrally placed bay window, slightly canted to catch the view and set in a bold, white frame. The extension of its white base line, tied to the ground by narrow white poles, defines the entry. A curved, free-standing chimney at the rear of the house completes a composition controlled by the Cubist aesthetic that had dominated the Modern Movement in the preceding decades. This formalistic, pictorial approach was of no interest to Wurster or Dailey, whose townhouses of two and three years later represent the informal, understated character of current Bay Area Modern.

There were two characteristic plans for the townhouse: a tall rectangular box set flush with the street with enclosed garage on the ground level and a small garden at the back; or two boxy structures, the smaller on the street and the garage and the larger box to the rear of the lot, with living and sleeping quarters direct to the view (at that time there usually was one, of either the Bay or the city). This left a small courtyard between the two volumes for an intimate, outdoor landscaped room that was one of the hallmarks of Modern in the Bay Area.

DINWIDDIE, *Roos house, San Francisco, 1938* (Baer)

Roos house (Baer)

Although mild temperatures permitted a lush green garden all year round, summer fog and a strong, cool summer wind from the ocean required that outdoor areas be protected for use. Weather being more a day-to-day than a seasonal matter, the garden was most useful as a kind of showroom, as important to look at as to be in. The man who explored most intensely the design possibilities offered by this special combination of circumstances was Thomas Church.

A native Californian, educated at the University of California, Berkeley, with a graduate degree in landscape architecture from Harvard, Church opened his office in 1929. During the thirties, as landscape architect for Wurster, Dailey, and others, he designed numerous residential gardens. To the design of the small garden in particular he brought an architectonic sense that, while not entirely new to the field, was so well articulated and publicized that he emerged in the postwar period as the father of contemporary landscape architecture in this country. Church banished the concept of the front and back yard. Instead he zoned the garden for use like a room, often controlling the circulation through the placement of raised planters, paths, and built-in sitting areas. Typical of his small-garden design was the asymmetric composition with a path or paved area curving around a planted one, achieving the effect, optically, of enlarging the space. Partitions, like those in the house, screened areas from view and enhanced the flow of space; textured walls and pavements further diverted the eye. These were principally gardens for living.

As the decade of the thirties turned, the atmosphere of innovation and excitement in fields of design, soon to be interrupted by the war, charged the Bay Area with enough magnetism to draw outstanding talent in the postwar years. Not only in design but also in planning there was confidence in the power of ideas to work changes in the world. With this went a feeling of kinship and mutual concern which prompted practitioners to consult with each other and exchange ideas. This interchange was particularly lively in the field of new materials, which had become important during the Depression. Locally, Michael Goodman had pioneered in the development of exterior plywood in the mid-twenties. Later it became almost synonymous with contemporary design, but initially it had a kind of stylishness

WURSTER, *Harley-Stevens house, San Francisco, 1940* (Baer)

Harley-Stevens house, plans

Harley-Stevens house, rear view (Baer)

WURSTER, *Grover house, San Francisco, 1939 (Sturtevant)*

that was almost perverse. Wurster, with his predilection for the cheap and unpretentious, is reported to have said, during a design conference for a house, "Well, sheet rock is cheaper than Douglas fir plywood, but Douglas fir plywood looks cheaper so let's use it."

The war also focused attention on another theme popular during the Depression—prefabrication. Wartime construction, which was to absorb the energies of many an architect, opened up the possibility of imposing a meaningful order on both the design and the economics of building. Even as the United States entered the war, the postwar house was already on the drawing boards. In the September 1942 issue of *The Architectural Forum*, Gardner Dailey and Joseph Esherick wrote of their "House D-2, Magic Carpet Series":

The pre-fabricators have pointed the way to mass-produced shelter and the day when the consumer will benefit just as he benefitted from mass-production when automobiles ceased being made by hand.

. . . Occupants of the house of 194X will not be asked

DAILEY, *flats on Telegraph Hill, San Francisco, 1941* (*Baer*)

to live in anything monotonous and dull. They will have a wide choice of arrangements to suit their needs, tastes and environments. Should space requirements change after the years they will not be forced to move because the house is too small or too large. They can simply add to or reduce the number of segments as required. Demountability will afford the opportunity to move the house as often as necessary. Being light it can be carried on a small truck.[4]

As they served the war effort in a variety of ways, architects polished this image in their minds until it seemed inevitable.

Actually there were grounds for this idealized projection, but it was social change that made the difference. The postwar family had acquired mobility as a permanent trait. Not only did this family move frequently; it also began to plan for the different stages

166

CHURCH, *small garden in San Francisco* (Baer)

167

LANGHORST AND LANGHORST, *house in Lafayette, 1947-49,*
Thomas Church, landscape architect (Sally Woodbridge)

House in Lafayette, garden side (Baer)

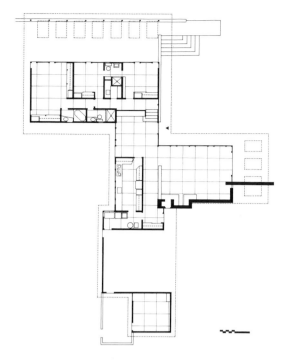

House in Lafayette, plan

of life. As the traditional family, with more than two generations living under the same roof, vanished, the nuclear family with one set of parents and their children became the ideal type. Finally alerted to the possibilities of flexibility, this family wanted a house that could expand and shrink when it did.

Although the American family was at last in tune with two of the basic concepts of Modern design—open planning and flexible use—their assimilation by the building industry had as much to do with economics as with ideology. Reducing the number of interior partitions and making possible a more efficient organization of mechanical equipment and plumbing reduced construction costs. "Freeing the plan" also stretched the small budget of the postwar family.

As for the magic carpet of pre-fabrication, as Dailey himself observed, his and others' postwar prefabricated dream houses never left the drafting boards. On-site construction proved still to be the equal of the factory. Besides, the term "pre-fab" had a pejorative connotation in spite of architects' efforts to talk it away.

According to a United States Bureau of Labor Statistics notice published in the summer of 1949, the typical house in the San Francisco–Oakland metropolitan area was a one-story detached structure of

wood frame construction with wood or stucco exterior, five rooms, and approximately 1000 square feet of floor space. It had one bathroom, a one-car garage, and a fireplace in the living room.

The custom-designed postwar house typically had 1000-1500 square feet of space. In the catalogue of an exhibition titled "Domestic Architecture of the San Francisco Bay Region," which took place in 1949 at the San Francisco Museum of Art, Gardner Dailey described it:

In comparing this exhibition to one which we might have seen here two decades ago, we note the disappearance of the large house, and in its place the appearance of what may be termed, "The Large-Small House." The Large-Small House has one very large room, and the balance of the house has been compressed wherever possible to eliminate waste space, long halls, and stairs. The elimination of space has been accomplished by reducing the service section to a one-maid or no-maid unit. The basement has disappeared. The garage, as such, is usually but a roof. Almost all of the houses shown use what has become popularly known as the dual-purpose room. By this we mean the Playroom-Garden Room, the Study-Guest Room, the Living-Dining Room, the Dining-Kitchen Room; the pantry has become only a vestige, and it is only man's basic instinct to worship fire which still keeps the fireplace intact in the Living Room.

The suburban house designed in 1947-49 by Fred and Lois Langhorst and landscaped by Thomas Church is an excellent example of the large-small house. It is placed at the edge of the kind of beautiful knoll that was a favored and typical building site of the time. Because of the bounty of natural beauty provided by the landscape and the organization of the plan to take advantage of it, the relatively small spaces are not confining.

In 1945 and 1946, on the eve of the postwar era of unprecedented prosperity, architects opened or reopened offices confident that a great building era was just around the corner. It took a while to retool the war machine for peacetime construction, but soon a steady flow of houses, mostly in the modest $10,000 category, began to support what continued to be one of the largest areas for private residential practice.

Though nearly a decade had passed and public taste had adjusted to a more tolerant view of Modern design, its proper definition was still unresolved for the relatively small segment of the public and of the profession which was concerned with ideology.

The "carpenter" style brand of the International Style developed in the Bay Area by Wurster, Dailey, and Mario Corbett was generally viewed with distain by their eastern counterparts. Frank Lloyd Wright called Wurster a "shanty-builder"; to others he was known as "Redwood Bill." Being neither radically modern nor traditional, this home-grown style fell between the slats and, in the black-and-white world of the architectural press of the forties, presented a troubling perversity except to critics like Lewis Mumford. In his *New Yorker* column "The Sky Line" of October 11, 1947, Mumford wrote:

People like Bernard Maybeck and William Wilson Wurster took good care that their houses did not resemble factories or museums. . . . I look for the continued spread, to every part of our country, of that native and humane form of modernism which one might call the Bay Region style, a free yet unobtrusive expression of the terrain, the climate and the way of life on the Coast.

It is difficult at this date to recapture the urgency of the issue these remarks raised. Suffice it to say that it prompted a symposium for architects at the Museum of Modern Art in New York on the evening of February 11, 1948, that produced an impassioned airing of the design ideology of the day. Among the heated statements was this one by Marcel Breuer:

I don't feel too much impulse to set "human" (in the best sense of the word) against "formal." If human is considered identical with redwood all over the place, or if it is considered identical with imperfection and imprecision, I am against it; also if it is considered identical with camoflaging architecture with planting, with nature, with romantic subsidies.[5]

Meanwhile, back on the Coast, the controversy produced a salutary reaction in the form of an exhibition at the San Francisco Museum of Art in September and October of 1949. Writing in the catalogue, Mumford—the only non-resident who contributed—said:

This exhibition repairs a serious omission in the existing histories of American architecture: it establishes the existence of a vigorous tradition of modern building, which took root in California some half a century ago. Apart from the building of Irving Gill and the Brothers Greene, some of the best examples of this work were produced in the Bay Region area; and the early work shows qualities of boldness, directness, and human sensitivity, combined with a certain quiet restraint, that seem

imbedded in the very character of the region. The Bay Region architects have given form to their very informality. . . . a few years ago I characterized the buildings that have been assembled for this exhibition as examples of the "Bay Region Style," and contrasted it with the restricted and arid formulas of the so-called "International Style." . . . What I was calling attention to, in the work of the Bay Region school, was the fact that, though it was thoroughly modern, it was not tied to the tags and cliches of the so-called International Style: that it made no fetish of the flat roof and did not deliberately avoid projections and overhangs: that it made no effort to symbolize the machine, through a narrow choice of materials and forms: that it had a place for personalities as different as Maybeck and Dailey and Wurster and Kump. What seemed to me admirable in the style was that it was a steady, organic growth producing natural forms as natural and appropriate by both client and architect.

In general the term "style" was decried by the authors of the catalogue. Elizabeth Kendall Thompson, Western Editor of the *Architectural Record*, wrote in the catalogue:

There are many styles of architecture here as there are in any city or region, and there is no predominate one which can be termed "Bay Area Style." But there is a group of houses, relatively small in number, built during the last fifty or so years, which because of an individualistic insistence on principle rather than on style has withstood the rigors of time and fashion and which, to trained and untrained eye alike, remain good architecture.

This common approach to design was clearly apparent in the works chosen for the exhibit. The boxy and planar compositions of the Americanized International Style with horizontal bands of windows and/or glass walls predominated. The common denominator was the use of redwood, usually left unpainted, in a post and beam construction. One of the best examples of the Bay Area version of the International Style is the unpretentious but crisply detailed redwood box that Ernest Born designed for himself in 1950-51.

Some of the work, such as that of Henry Hill, who had been a student in Gropius' and Breuer's first design studio at Harvard, showed a strong relation to the East Coast scene; the work of Fred and Lois Langhorst leaned toward Frank Lloyd Wright. But the majority of the buildings exhibited by such prominent firms as Francis Joseph McCarthy, Clark &

BORN, *Born house, San Francisco, 1950-51* (Baer)

Beuttler, Campbell & Wong, Anshen & Allen, Confer & Ostwald, Mario Corbett, John Ekin Dinwiddie, Joseph Esherick, Gardner Dailey, and Wurster, Bernardi & Emmons, gave the impression of a consciously operating tradition in good health.[6]

The man whose work was closest to the mainstream of the Modern Movement in the U.S. was John Funk, a native of Southern California with a graduate degree in architecture from the University of California in Berkeley. His first house for his sister-in-law in Modesto became a landmark of the Modern Movement by gracing the cover of the Museum of Modern Art's first *Built in U.S.A.* book, published in 1944. In the late forties Funk designed a

series of houses in the Bay Area which, though neither large nor complicated, were classic expressions of the state of the art. Although built of wood, they would have fit comfortably into the scene of either Southern California or the East Coast. There was no imprecision about them; any quality of informality lay in the way they related to their sites and to the out-of-doors. Funk's 1948 house for himself in Lafayette well illustrates a major contribution of the Bay Area to the Modern Movement, what Marcel Breuer referred to backhandedly as "camoflaging architecture with planting, with nature, with romantic subsidies." Working closely with landscape architects like Robert Roysten and Lawrence Halprin,

FUNK, *Funk house, Lafayette, 1948;*
Robert Roysten, landscape architect (Sally Woodbridge)

Funk completely integrated his floor plans with the landscape designs. His crisply detailed buildings achieved an extension of the living area either by notching the long, rectangular plans with lushly landscaped courts and patios or by dividing the living and sleeping zones into two blocks set perpendicular to each other and connected by a glazed entrance hall, as in a Marin County house of 1948. It was Breuer who originated the phrase "bi-nuclear plan," but here the off-set block of the studio-workshop and garage with its wide trellis contributes another important element to the landscape composition. By stepping back and forth the plan creates areas for planting, which, in Halprin's scheme, blends into the native flora of the site at its edges. The use of trellises over the courts and entrance walkways and even, at times, attached to the raised floor line of the house was, according to Funk, a means of forcing the client to "camoflage." The strong horizontal line of the roof plane unifies what is otherwise perceived as a discontinuous structure.

This idea of masking parts of the house with planting was also prevalent in South California, particularly in the work of Richard Neutra. However, it rapidly became generally accepted in the Bay Area which, under Thomas Church's tutelage, was the dynamic center of the profession. Church called the concept of grading the manmade landscape into the

FUNK, *Woerner house, Marin County, 1948,*
Lawrence Halprin, landscape architect (Baer)

Woerner house, house and garden (Baer)

surrounding site "airplane circle design." A circle, designated the design area, was drawn on the site. Within it were described the living zones of the house and garden, which were then graded into the surrounding area, making total design of the site the first step. An accepted program today, this approach was revolutionary at the time, when landscaping was an after-the-fact matter of spending a certain amount of the budget on plants to punctuate the site or frame the house, like parsley around the roast.

One of Church's most famous works of the postwar period was a garden for a ranch near Sonoma that was designed around a swimming pool which preceded the building of the house. Under the hands of Church and his staff, which then included George Rockrise, who designed the pool house, and Lawrence Halprin, a softly rolling hill rising above the plain at the edge of the Bay was gently scooped out near the top. The site was inlaid with a free-form pool echoing the salt-flat pools below, decks which permitted existing oak trees to poke through, paved areas, and planted mounds around the pool. The effect was such that the viewer at ground level or in the pool felt magically suspended at the world's edge.

This garden of 1947-48 was widely published, giving Church an international reputation. His practice was enlarged to the extent that he began to travel around the country consulting with architects for whom he provided an initial concept or scheme which was drawn up in the architect's office. Church's own office remained small, as he wished it, with the staff spending much of their time on job sites. Church is often described as looking like a real gardener in khakis and an old felt hat with pruning

Woerner house, detail of landscaping (Baer)

CHURCH, *Donnell garden and pool, Sonoma County, 1947-48* (Baer)

shears hanging from his belt. Whether or not his appearance was calculated, it had a marvelous effect on clients in all categories from homeowners to the boards of directors of corporations and institutions. From Church's office came a group of landscape architects, among them Robert Roysten, Douglas Baylis, and Lawrence Halprin, who profoundly influenced the profession. When Halprin opened his office in 1949, his first commission was a garden for his wife's parents in Woodside; Wurster, Bernardi & Emmons were architects for the house. The site plan shows the two wings of the house, one containing bedrooms and the other service areas, set at a wide angle and hinged in the middle by the entryway. On the entry side the largely blank walls give the effect of a wall defining the public area. On the other side large areas of glass open the house to the garden.

Here Halprin preserved an open meadow as meadow rather than mowed lawn, which both contributed to the modified rusticity of the house design and kept down maintenance, a major client requirement. In the spring the meadow is green, studded with yel-

175

WURSTER, BERNARDI, & EMMONS, *house in Woodside, 1949,*
Lawrence Halprin, landscape architect (Baer)

low daffodils; in the summer it is golden brown. Garden areas bordering the house interweave paving, rammed earth paths, and planted areas around the spreading oaks, making a total composition that is a deft fusion of the manmade and the natural.

One of the persistent images of San Francisco Bay Area architecture was of the natural house taking its place unpretentiously in the environment. The bewitching embrace of this environment, or as Wurster put it, "the immensity of the scene," militated against the house as a highly polished object set against a backdrop. Dramatic wooded or barren hillside sites were left relatively untouched while the house perched on, clung to, or nestled into their

sides, sometimes with only a peephole through to the view.

The man who was the master of this natural house or, as others would have it, this shack or shanty, was Mario Corbett. According to Henrik Bull and Charles Moore, who were later to contribute to the Bay Area Tradition, the picturesque qualities of these redwoodsy boxes, with stovepipe vents wired to the roofs and decks like trays hanging over the void, inspired in them a deep longing to come west. Corbett's work epitomized the spirit of impromptu design. No two houses were really alike: some were round, some rectangular, and some, like his own, segments of a circle.

House in Woodside, house and garden (Baer)

House in Woodside, house and garden (Baer)

House in Woodside, living room (Baer)

House in Woodside, house from meadow (Baer)

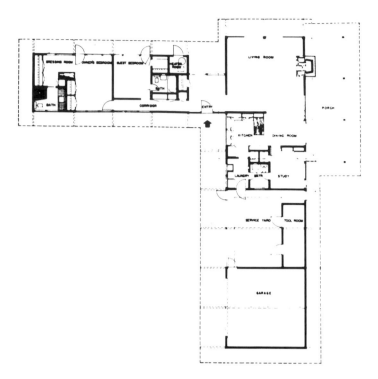

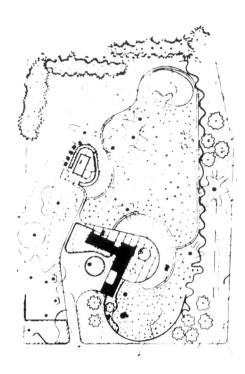

House in Woodside, plan

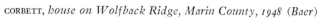

CORBETT, *house on Wolfback Ridge, Marin County, 1948* (Baer)

House on Wolfback Ridge (Baer)

House on Wolfback Ridge, plan

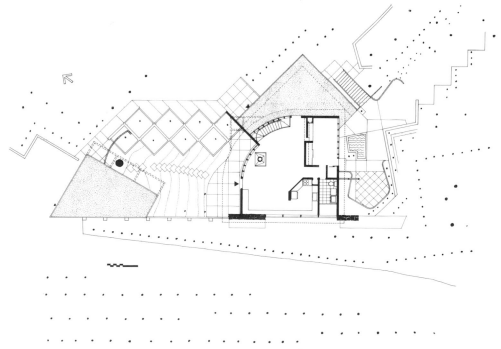

CAMPBELL & WONG, *house on San Francisco Peninsula,*
fireplace wall (Baer)

So many young designers—Alec Yuill-Thornton, Daniel Warner, Charles Moore, Albert Lanier, Henrik Bull, James Leafe, Ellis Kaplan—who later established practices worked for Corbett at one time or another that his office was, like Wurster's and Dailey's, a kind of graduate school of design.[7] Its freewheeling atmosphere was unequaled; most of those who worked there thought it invaluable. Inexperienced designers found their ideas taken seriously and often built. Though varied, Corbett's production had much in common with the prevailing carpenter-style school, with site orientation a major concern. The house achieved a sense of place that was consistent and remarkable.

Through the forties and early fifties most custom-designed houses, like the best known of Corbett's, were competitive in price with the mass market. Land and construction costs were within the range of the middle-income clientele whose demand for homes was high enough to maintain a remarkable number of small firms in residential practice. The important ingredient in this situation was not the average size of the commission, but the volume of work.

Worley Wong of Campbell & Wong recalls that although architects occasionally dreamed of large-scale work, it was the steady stream of small houses that provided the opportunity for experiment. Such standard components of the contemporary house as the symbolically important fireplace wall, the cabinet or storage walls, the systems of proportions for glass areas and room sizes—all were worked out in the process of repetition. As is true in other periods of consistent demand and relative unanimity of design ideology, the houses being produced in the Bay Area by the early fifties were a well-honed product with little display of innovation for its own sake.

Another architect who also used residential design to test new ideas was Joseph Esherick. A native of Philadelphia and graduate of the University of Pennsylvania in 1937, Esherick was greatly influenced by early association with his uncle, Wharton Esherick, the well-known sculptor-builder in wood. This Craftsman influence, plus an enthusiasm for Le Corbusier, logically put Esherick out of step with the firm Beaux-Arts tradition of Penn's School of Architecture, where his deep curiosity about the structural workings of things did not earn him a high place on the academic scale. After graduation and a brief period of work for George Howe, the memory of a summer vacation in San Francisco persuaded him to try the area again, not for its architectural promise, which he felt was equaled in Philadelphia, but for its social freedom and tolerance. After some time in Europe, in 1938 he made his way to San Francisco, where he found part-time work in the office of Walter Steilberg, structural engineer and former head draftsman for Julia Morgan. Through Steilberg he was introduced to the work of this earlier generation of architects of the shingled and woodsy Bay Area Tradition. He met Maybeck, studied his work, and also greatly admired the spatial composition of Willis Polk's Russian Hill house, where he visited Wurster in his small apartment. The strength of the tradition seemed quite clear to him, although, as he observed, it was less layered with a variety of images than that of the East. During an early friendship with John Yeon, a brilliant designer from Portland, Oregon, he was taken on a tour of barns and rural vernacular architecture that made a lasting impression on him.

His work with Gardner Dailey on such early milestones of the Modern Movement as the Owens house of 1939 in Sausalito and the Coyote Point Training School of 1942-43 shows an emphasis on modular expression in wood frame construction. A strong belief in the consistent use of a module to clarify design at times put Esherick at odds with Dailey, who favored changing modules to achieve spatial variety. Much of Esherick's interest in the possibilities of prefabrication for standardizing the construction industry in the postwar world lay in his belief that the public would be better served by buildings whose consistent use of a module would clarify the plan for the occupants.

Esherick's first houses from the office he opened in 1945 reflected his apprenticeship with Dailey in their verticality and use of high airy spaces punctuated by tall, relatively narrow windows. An ordering device which he used in his first San Francisco townhouse, as well as later buildings, was the restatement of the modular frame of the house on the exterior by means of a free-standing grid of two-by-twos. This quest for clarity, although it was not intended to formalize the structure, differentiated Esherick's work from

DAILEY, *Owens house, Sausalito, 1939, original rendering*

Owens house, plan

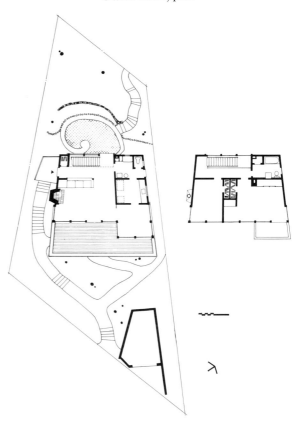

that of Wurster, Bernardi & Emmons. A comparison of Esherick's second townhouse of 1951 with one of the same year by W. B. & E. illustrates the difference. Although both houses have splendid views of the Bay, the latter is a thorough response to the site; its most important statement is the dramatic orientation of the living areas to the view. The de-emphasis of the entrance and the closing of the basement story create an appropriate nautical image; the house is often called the "ferryboat" house. By contrast the Esherick house deals equally and formally with the Bay view and the position of the house on a corner

184

lot. The L-shaped plan creates a private garden and processional entranceway culminating in a two-story, glazed entrance and stair hall. The vertical emphasis of the focal space is carried throughout the living areas. The stark simplicity of the form is lightened by a generous use of glass—welcome in foggy San Francisco—on the south and east elevations.

Both houses have a woodsy simplicity compared to John Funk's townhouse of 1948 or Henry Hill's of 1952-53. The emphasis on intersecting vertical and horizontal forms in the former and the streamline, ribbon form of the latter reflect the International Style of Gropius and Breuer to a degree unusual in the area.[8]

In several houses built between 1946 and 1951, Esherick stated the two themes which were to occupy him in the coming decades: one he called "packing a box"; the other he might have called "packing a triangle." Both exhibit a love of spatial intricacy in more than one plane.

ESHERICK, *San Francisco townhouse, 1951* (Baer)

San Francisco townhouse, entrance court (Baer)

San Francisco townhouse, entrance (Baer)

San Francisco townhouse, plan

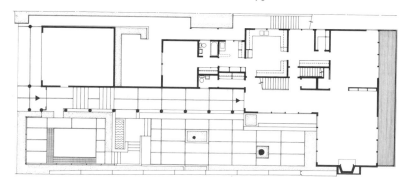

San Francisco townhouse, entrance hall (Baer)

WURSTER, BERNARDI & EMMONS, *San Francisco townhouse, 1951* (*Baer*)

San Francisco townhouse, view from distance (Baer)

San Francisco townhouse, plan

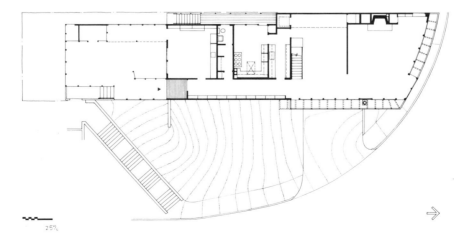

FUNK, *San Francisco townhouse, 1948* (Baer)

HILL, *San Francisco townhouse, 1952-53 (Sturtevant)*

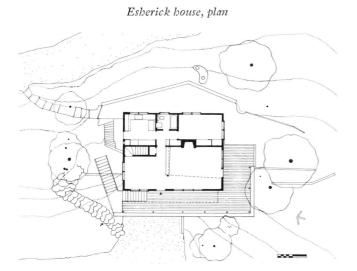

Esherick house, plan

In a 1946 house for himself in Ross, Esherick first dealt with the problem of packing the box. The game was to fit the living requirements into a hierarchy of spaces, with the living area given the greatest volume through height rather than floor area. The house is a straightforward box on the exterior; the interior is carved out to make the appropriate one- and two-story spaces. Their interpenetration is emphasized by an interior sheathing of hemlock whose fine, even grain makes a satin-smooth wood skin. Here also for the first time Esherick used the device of a large window wall set flush with the corner of the room to wash the adjoining wall with light. By his own account he felt a need during this period for large opposing glass areas to open up the interior and permit the outside to flow through.

ESHERICK, *Esherick house, Ross, 1946, living room (Sturtevant)*

ESHERICK AND ESHERICK, *Esherick house, Kentfield, 1950,*
Lawrence Halprin, landscape architect (Baer)

Esherick house, Kentfield, garden side (Baer)

Esherick house, Kentfield, interior of living room (Baer)

In the second house he designed for himself, with Rebecca Woods Esherick, in 1950, full homage was paid to the California barn. The gable is set across the long axis, as Esherick had often observed in real barns, to open up the largest area to the sun and air. The long sweep of the gable gives ample space to fit the service and sleeping quarters to either side while opening up the main living area to the full height of the structure to create a feeling of spaciousness with a relatively small floor area. Landscaped by Lawrence Halprin, the house is perfectly sited to take advantage of a magnificent live oak on the garden side. From the street side it offers a closed facade punctuated simply by an opening in the middle with a balcony over an understated entrance.

These bows to the rural past were an architectural

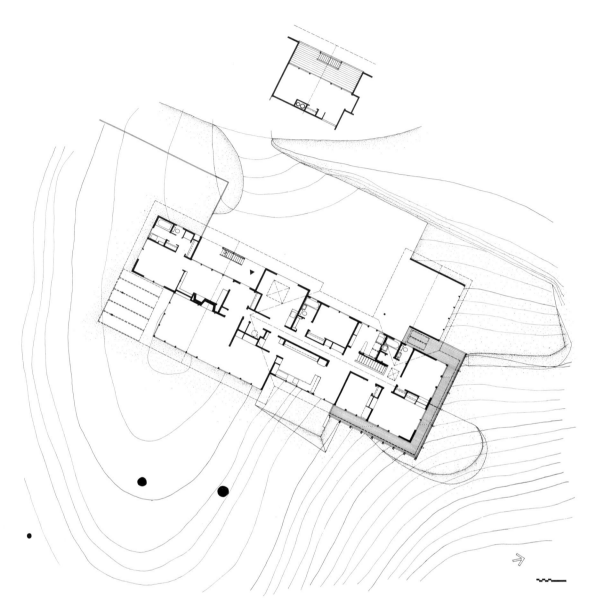

Esherick house, Kentfield, plan

trademark of the period. Both of Wurster's partners built houses for themselves—Emmons in 1948 and Bernardi in 1950—that captured images from the rural scene. The use of barn framing to articulate the essentially single space of Emmons' house, with its bedroom loft approached by ladder, and the wooden truss supporting the monitors on Bernardi's house were both drawn from vernacular rural usage. In fact, this sanctification of the ordinary, originally Wurster's contribution, was still the most character- istic trait of local architecture at the turn of the decade, although it was soon to mutate under the influence of the economy of plenty. In the mid- fifties the character of the Bay Area Tradition changed from modest understatement to masked opulence. Although architects continued to use the simple, informal life as a frame of reference, it was somewhat stretched out of shape by clients whose budgets and demands were not so limited. Though no longer inappropriate to the times, affluence was still a difficult concept for the Bay Area Tradition, with its Craftsman legacy of the natural house, fur- ther freighted with thirties and forties images of the anonymous and the ordinary. Once more it is inter-

EMMONS, *Emmons house, Mill Valley, 1948* (*Sturtevant*)

Emmons house, interior (Sturtevant)

esting to compare the work of Esherick and of Wurster, Bernardi & Emmons with respect to their responses to the changing times. In a W. B. & E. house of 1954 in Burlingame there is no vestige of the woodsy, utilitarian house of the thirties and forties. Instead, a stuccoed country villa handsomely painted in ochre and white with a dark frame is formally organized around a central court. The axial symmetry of the composition is carried through by Thomas Church into an equally formal garden with reflecting pool.

BERNARDI, *Bernardi house, Sausalito, 1950, section*

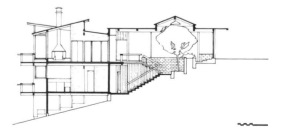

198

WURSTER, BERNARDI & EMMONS, *house in Burlingame, 1954,*
Thomas Church, landscape architect (Baer)

House in Burlingame, atrium (Baer)

House in Burlingame, garden side (Baer)

House in Burlingame, garden (Baer)

In a 1957 house by Esherick in the same area of Marin County as his original 1950 "barn," the same form and spatial arrangement are used, but the difference in scale, in addition to the breaking of the volume with an extended service wing that forms one side of the entrance court, creates more the impression of a lavish, shingle-style villa in the line of McKim, Mead and White than of the California barn.

In 1958, in Madera, Wurster's firm designed an omega to the alpha of the Gregory farmhouse. With its conscious use of vernacular materials—adobe and corrugated metal roofing—and its pointed reference to such monuments of California's Colonial past as General Mariano Vallejo's great adobe ranch headquarters near Petaluma, the building represents Wurster's mature vision of what a real regional architecture could be: a carefully referenced restatement of the past with form and materials still appropriate to the present.

Growing budgets had an effect on the living patterns and the house plans of the American middle and upper-middle classes. The large-small house described by Dailey became the large-large house. Since families with growing children could now afford to separate the activities of the one large room,

ESHERICK, *house in Kentwoodlands, 1957, Richard Heims, landscape architect (Baer)*

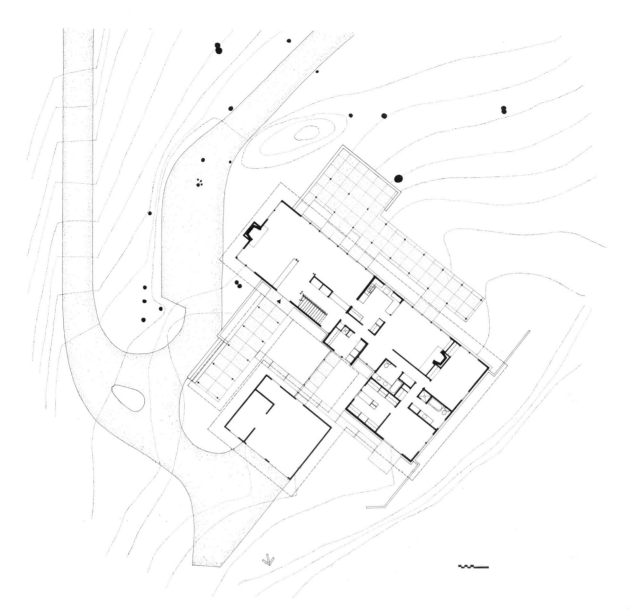

House in Kentwoodlands, plan

the ideology of the nuclear family living its undifferentiated life was relaxed—it was obvious from the variety of snide remarks passed about the "open plan" that most of it had not worked for family harmony anyway. Now the special requirements of the members were emphasized: the children needed playrooms, the parents needed workshops, sewing rooms, and dressing rooms, plus dens and other private spaces. Even the more minimal tract house had a fam-

ily room, laundry room, and often a workspace added to the usual living area. As interior spaces proliferated, so did exterior ones with decks or play areas for children and adults.

A suburban villa of 1951-53 by Henry Hill is an excellent example of the large-large house. Client requirements included a private space for each member of the family and a family room for everyday living in addition to the formal living room. In answer to

WURSTER, BERNARDI & EMMONS, *ranch house, Madera, 1958* (Rob Super)

HILL, *house in Orinda, 1951-53* (Baer)

the increased spatial needs, which had to be accommodated on an oblong site, 218 feet long by 100 feet at its widest point, Hill designed a one-story structure which skirts the outer edges of the site, leaving an interior court. Level changes dictated by the slope permit the two main wings to be separately oriented; fortunately the main living wing overlooks a golf course. The house is so well integrated with the site by Eckbo, Roysten & Williams' landscaping that it is hardly apparent that most of the land is occupied by building. The spatial progression from the parking area up the steps to the main entrance off a small terrace continues up to the court. On the opposite side a stepped ramp leads up to the bedroom wing. Stone walls tie the house to its site and, in many cases, the

outside to the inside by intersecting the exterior envelope. Instead of altering the horizontal plane of the roof, Hill permitted the rising floor level to change the character of the living spaces—the formal living room has the highest ceiling, the dining area next, and finally the family room gains a sense of intimacy as a low-ceilinged space. Exterior materials are treated differently at different levels: the horizontal redwood, siding of the lower level is stained grey-gold, while the upper levels are vertical board-and-batten stained grey-green. On the interior natural woods vary as the walls change their course. The complex and painterly articulation of the design is most characteristic of Hill's work.

In general the box, notched to the center of its

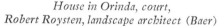

House in Orinda, court,
Robert Roysten, landscape architect (Baer)

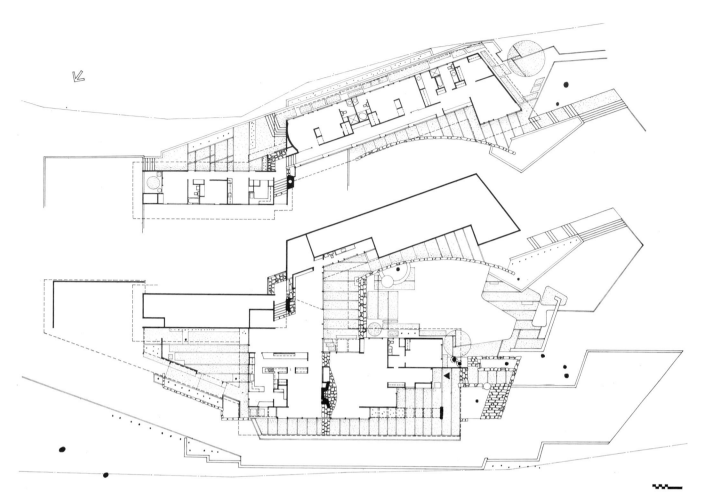

House in Orinda, plan

long axis as in Funk's earlier houses, was either strung out further or exploded, with its component parts moved around like checkers on a board. One of Funk's last houses, a villa of 1955 on a peninsula hilltop, is a fully developed expression of the large-large house extended, apparently infinitely, into the landscape. Funk achieved this spatial extension not by angling or curving the plan but by alternating open and closed spaces so that the whole is never visible from one viewpoint. The landscaping by Eckbo, Roysten & Williams shares in the achievement.

Another example of this serial house is one of the same year by Roger Lee. Lee was one of the most versatile practitioners in the small-house field and a leading contributor to the Bay Area Tradition. This Berkeley house of cottage scale sensitively sited over a creek in a small wooded glen illustrates the kind of image which Lee and his fellow designers Campbell & Wong projected so successfully as the "Bay Region house" of the postwar period. His later Mill Valley house, composed of a series of boxes strung along a creek, was one of the few for which he had a lavish budget. It states a persistent image: the woody, lightweight, post-and-beam house glimpsed piecemeal in the landscape, here studded with redwood trees. From carport to entrance, reached by a covered walkway, and on through the interior, the experience of the space is linear and processional, rather than hierarchical.

Vestiges of the early Mexican-American ranch

FUNK, *house in Los Altos Hills, 1955,*
Robert Roysten, landscape architect (Baer)

House in Los Altos Hills, garden side (Baer)

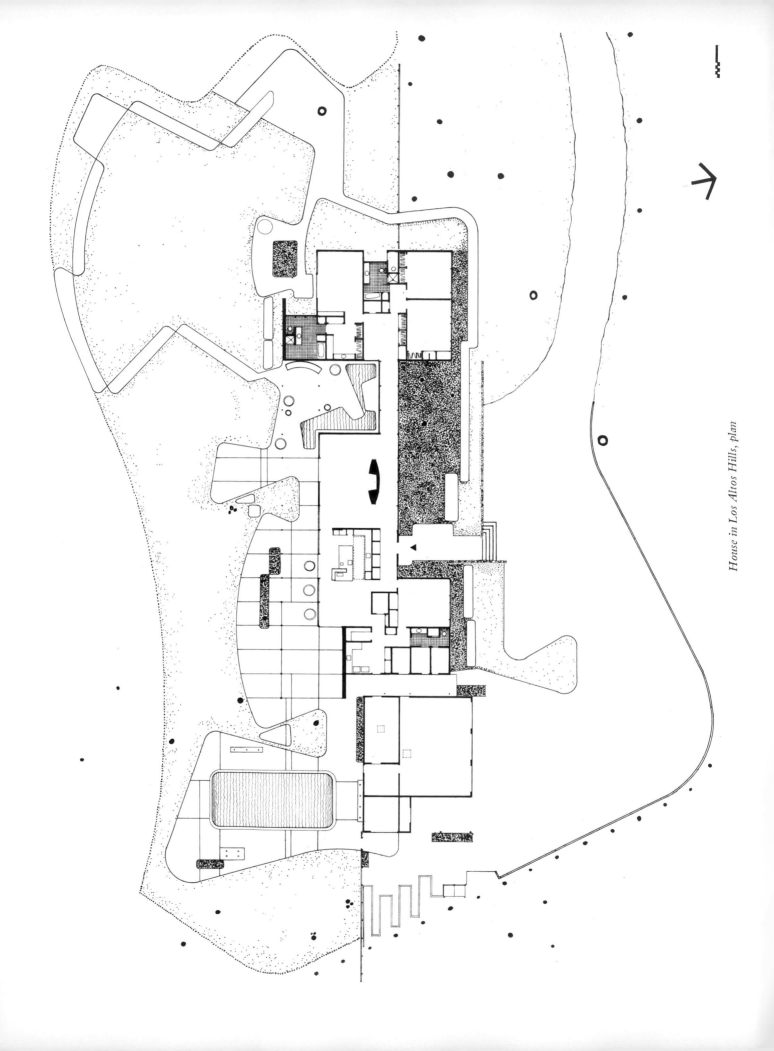

House in Los Altos Hills, plan

LEE, *house in Berkeley, 1955* (Baer)

LEE, *house in Mill Valley, 1956* (Baer)

House in Mill Valley, creek side (Baer)

CAMPBELL & WONG, *house in Saratoga, 1962,*
exterior of living room wing (Baer)

house were combined with those of Japanese country villas and palaces, as in a 1962 house by Campbell & Wong. The light, rigid frame of post-and-beam construction was ideal for making repeated spaces of horizontal rectangular proportions whose sides could be infilled with glass or wood, if exterior, or screens if desired instead of solid walls on the interior. The plan of the house and its immediate landscape is organized on a free rectangular grid which interrelates the indoor and outdoor spaces.

Another logical plan for this villa type used a central courtyard as a solution to problems of privacy which, although they might not exist on many suburban sites, were a factor in waterside areas like the

Belvedere Lagoon, a famous development begun in the postwar decade. By dredging and infilling part of the Bay near the Belvedere Peninsula, many narrow waterfront lots were created. By and large the houses designed for them presented blank, walled surfaces to the street or public side and opened dramatically, as does a 1958 house by Campbell & Wong, to the water and to an inner court. The prime importance of the automobile is straightforwardly acknowledged —another difference between East and West Coast— while the pedestrian entrance is discreetly placed at the end of a processional walk along the side of the garage.

The work of George Rockrise, who began his ca-

House in Saratoga, interior of living room wing (Baer)

House in Saratoga, plan

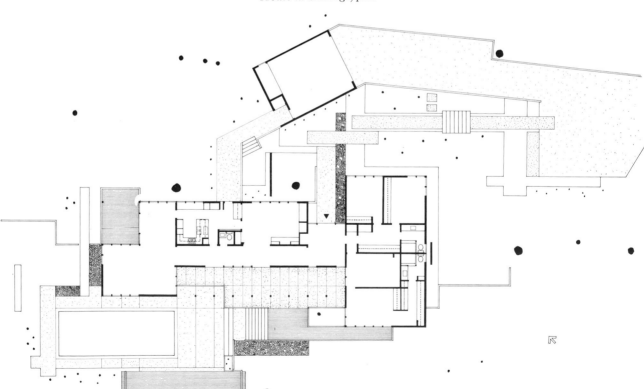

CAMPBELL & WONG, *house on the Belvedere Lagoon, 1958,*
view from water (Baer)

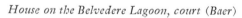

House on the Belvedere Lagoon, court (Baer)

reer on the West Coast by designing pool houses for Thomas Church, contributed to the flowering of this "Japanesque" villa. In his peninsula house of 1957, landscaped by Eckbo, Roysten & Williams, the wish of the client to have an unobtrusive design and to save every tree influenced the low-slung, horizontal profile of the house which, with living areas arranged around a central court, merges discreetly with the landscape.

The architect who used Japanese architectural forms most literally was Charles Warren Callister, for whom its major appeal was structural expression and intricate wood joinery. He shared this interest with Jack Hillmer, his University of Texas classmate, with whom he came to San Francisco to set up in practice. Both Hillmer and Callister became acquainted with San Francisco during the war. In the auspicious year of 1946, after canvassing Bay Area architects on the lookout for practice, they got rent-

free space in a downtown building in return for remodeling it. After three months they had not only altered the space but built all the furniture they needed. Fortunately the work was greatly admired by the owner of the building, who then commissioned a house. As the architects recall, the irony of the commission was that their client did not ultimately want a contemporary house. He had lived in one and had not liked it, but as he was unable to build his traditional dream house at that time, he wanted a temporary structure that would be torn down when the new one was built. Another side requirement was that, to reduce costs, the house be built of salvaged wood from a stable on the property. Given this unpropitious beginning, Hillmer and Callister designed one of the most famous and influential of Bay Area houses. Essentially the house is a great, hovering, irregular roof formed along three radiating lines that pass through a single point. The slightly

House on the Belvedere Lagoon, plan

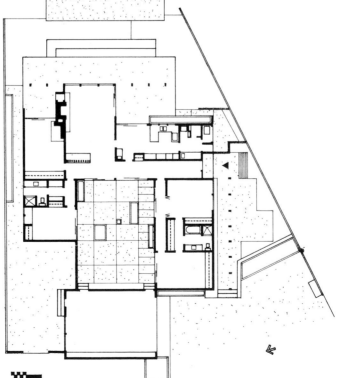

ROCKRISE, *house in Atherton, 1957,*
Eckbo, Roysten & Williams, landscape architects

HILLMER & CALLISTER, *house in Kentwoodlands,*
1946-47,
plan (drawing by Hillmer)

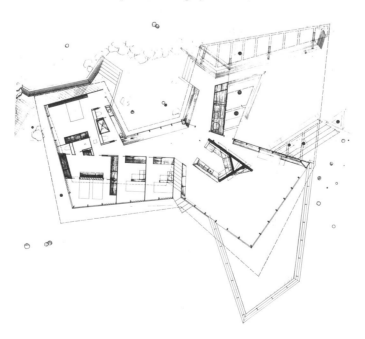

House in Kentwoodlands, view from above (Minor White)

House in Kentwoodlands, detail of wall treatment (Minor White)

tilted planes of this roof converge on a single point which becomes a downspout for rain. At the terminus of one of these lines, a pointed roof over the living area is echoed by a prowlike deck below. From above the roof, punctured by different-sized holes which accommodate trees, appears as a subtly formed plane magically suspended in air. Supports between it and the ground plane are minimized. The floor-to-ceiling glass of the living room has only a thin bracing, so that the horizontal flow of space is barely interrupted. Although the structure is poised on a concrete foundation tied by reinforcing to the floor (which in the bedroom wing was the first post-tensioned slab in the area), the flaring form stepped out slightly at the junc-

ture of each board, emphasizes the use of "the board" as the basic decorative unit. Boards slanted in a series to make vertical ventilating louvers for the bedrooms reinforce this statement, which is continued in the vertically set tongue-and-groove two-by-twelves of beautifully weathered salvaged redwood that form the walls. These variations on a theme give the house a unity of expression both forceful and natural.

After this joint venture Hillmer and Callister, pursuing separate practices, continued to produce houses which, recalling both Wright and the Japanese, emphasized structural geometry and highly articulated wood joinery—quite the opposite from the mainstream carpenter style originated by Wurster.

CALLISTER, *house in Berkeley, 1948* (Baer)

CALLISTER, *house in Berkeley, 1958 (Baer)*

Three houses designed respectively in 1948, 1952, and 1958, show Callister's affinity for traditional Japanese design. A strong modular emphasis combined with careful scaling of the repeated members, from the heavy posts and beams of the frame to the lighter, stick-like elements of the balconies, stairs, windows, and screens, gives rhythmic definition to the simple static forms. These forms develop an increasing complexity on the interior to complement the exotic roof forms of the late fifties. Callister expressed a poetic

regard for the Bay Area in the June 1950 issue of *Western Architect and Engineer* which featured his work:

Rather than reform the architecture of San Francisco, I would wish to find the inspiration which is in the traditions of the area. I will use the new techniques within the traditional sense as I am now using prevailing techniques. My concern is not with recreating the old, but rather with creating our own unique eclecticism.

Hillmer's work was less concerned with evoking

220

the landscape through the forms of the buildings than with structural integrity and expression. The most intricately integrated work of the postwar period is a house on the Belvedere Peninsula designed by him in 1950. Hillmer virtually lived on the site during the two-year period of design and construction, observing the sun and wind patterns and supervising construction. Three intersecting, diamond-shaped structural members, which strongly recall Wright, anchor the house to the hillside on one side while suspending it dramatically over the beach on the other. The living areas float in a long, horizontal plane with a notch cut out to express the separation of living and sleeping spaces. The first tatami (straw mats) to enter the

House in Berkeley, living room (Baer)

United States after the Korean War were sent by a friend to Jack Hillmer. He used them in the bedroom, which had a Japanese bed stored in a cabinet when not in use. Although this was the only strictly Japanese moment in the house, the three-by-six-foot measurement of the tatami set the module for the rest of the design as it did in the traditional Japanese house. Hillmer's meticulous care in eliminating all extraneous detail gives the house an austere and elegant simplicity. A most remarkable expression of this is the fireplace, a single slab of rough-cut gray granite about twelve feet long by six and a half feet high with the hearth to one side, which forms one end of the living room wall. Its monumental scale plus the fact that its exterior face is visible from the glazed gallery connecting the living and sleeping sections makes it more a living element of the landscape than a manmade artifact. As a work of uncompromising high art of the general time and place, this house has no peers.

House in Berkeley, bedroom (Baer)

HILLMER, *house in Belvedere, 1950 (Baer)*

House in Belvedere, plan (drawing by Hillmer)

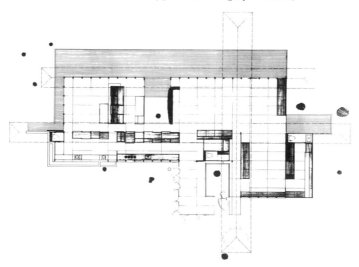

House in Belvedere, living room (Baer)

House in Belvedere, view of deck (Baer)

House in Belvedere, view from beach (Baer)

ROCKRISE, *house in Belvedere, 1957,*
Lawrence Halprin, landscape architect (Baer)

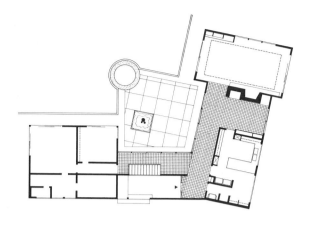

House in Belvedere, plan

The work of Hillmer and Callister also reflected the growing interest in the exotic and the picturesque. Symptomatic of the passing of the classic International Style influence, the flat roof went out of fashion in the Bay Area in the late 1950's as it did in the rest of the country. An increase in verticality and complication of the roof form signified a changing attitude in design. Qualities of the picturesque that appear, for instance, in Callister's roof forms are also evident in the composition of a house by George Rockrise of 1957 on the Belvedere Peninsula. Another example of the rewarding teamwork between architect and landscape architect, the site plan reserved the only flat area, the top of a knoll, for a garden court where Lawrence Halprin placed a mature oak tree. The living areas are ranged along the steep outer edge of the site and, in the case of the living room, projected out over the water. The structure restates in dramatic, manmade terms the natural forms of the coast.

More critical than changing formal attitudes was the changing structure of the economy. By 1960 the Bay Area had been radically redesigned, not by architects and planners so much as by housing developers, bankers, highway engineers, industrial designers, shopping center entrepreneurs, and others involved in land transactions. The building boom had not only greatly enlarged the residential practice of Bay Area architects, it also aided the rationalization of the merchant builder's side of the construction industry. It was increasingly difficult for the architect to compete in the middle-income market. The combination of the beginning inflationary spiral in construction costs and a scarcity of reasonable building sites began literally to cut the ground from under the custom-designed suburban villa and townhouse. As architects looked to other types of practice to take the place of dwindling demand in the residential field, the long postwar development from the large-small to the large-large house drew to a close.

The architectural legacy of this period was not an original concept of form nor a design vocabulary. Rather it was a planning concept, a way of giving expression to that almost mythical ideal, the California way of living.

5

Mass Producing
Bay Area Architecture

ROGER MONTGOMERY

Alongside their preoccupation with high art for elite clients, San Francisco Bay Area architects exhibit a continuing concern for popularizing current architectural ideas. The Newsoms published copybooks so that every Californian could have a miniature gingerbread house. Maybeck's friend and patron Charles Keeler wrote a book to popularize the natural house. The dollhouse designers and Spanish Colonial Revivalists of the twenties gave the builder Doelger his model for the Sunset district in San Francisco and for Daly City. Heavy conversations among underemployed architects and landscape designers in the thirties focused attention on the New Deal and wartime housing. After the war a concerned minority among developers and designers tried mass-producing the residential architecture of the 1950's. Finally in the late fifties, major changes in the housing economy helped produce a popular-market version of current elite architectural ideas. From this came a ubiquitous condominium vernacular for export to the nation.

Recent events in the continuing effort to mass-produce and popularize serious residential architecture form the theme of this chapter. It begins in the 1930's and extends over forty years to the present, where it ends with a momentary return to New Deal social motives. Before embarking on this account, the analytical bias of this chapter needs explanation.

Architectural ideas, in this view, flow along channels embedded at characteristic places in the social system. In residential architecture, for instance, the artist-architect typically designs for upper-middle-class clients. This work forms the locus of invention. From there innovation flows more or less directly to upper-class and mass-middle-class markets. In this process these groups are responding to the upper-middle-class dominance of the media and other communication channels. Working-class and poor people remain strikingly untouched by high art innovations. Architectural invention reaches those at the bottom of the social stratification system only when upper-middle-class professionals design for them without their participation. Public housing projects provide notorious examples: notorious because of the almost automatic conflict between what we call "user needs" and the artist-architect's design values.[1] Architectural innovation appears in housing projects directed at the working- and lower-class masses because the professionals who design the projects work in the context of their own upper-middle-class values. Most project management is upper middle class and naturally enough selects architects from its own familiar level in the stratification system. And these designers work in a context set not by poor people's needs but by their own professional and social class peers. Architectural innovation tends to be imposed on the occupants of social housing, not to be an expression of their values.

A second prefatory point concerns localism and the geographic boundaries that limit ideas. No matter how strong the local component, imported architectural ideas figure very importantly. In the period between the 1930's and now, a set of ideas, largely European in origin, often labeled the Modern Movement or the International Style, had enormous influence on architecture everywhere, the Bay Area included. Among these ideas were two concepts that led to the idea of social housing or social architecture: physical determinism and equalitarianism. The first of these notions held that good environments made good people. It focused on rebuilding nineteenth-century industrial slums and replacing squatter settlements in the countryside. The other idea came from an equalitarian, social democratic ideology focused on the masses. It led architects to seek a mass clientele among the workers instead of the wealthy elites that traditionally employed their services. Public housing became a more respectable kind of work than villas for the rich. These motives hang on still, albeit not so single-mindedly. For some designers, social housing remains even today the work of choice. Symmetrically, this chapter opens and closes with architects trying their hands at a special type of social housing, namely housing for migrant agricultural workers.

Only late in the 1930's, in the effort to shelter these migrants, did New Deal initiatives really penetrate to the Bay Area and trigger there the modest beginnings of social architecture. This contrasts with the eastern part of the country and with Europe, where from the beginning the Modern Movement in architecture had strong social overtones and mass housing formed a principal focus for leaders in the movement. Yet, when social architecture *did* reach San Francisco under Depression-spawned welfare programs, it found a responsive climate among the architects and landscape architects and the small emerging group of urban planners. Quickly these people produced work that gained international recognition. Then, almost immediately, the war caught up everyone in a vast effort to transform the Bay Area into a world class arsenal and navy base. The enormous population flow needed to sustain this led to a great spurt of social

housing project design, much of it directed by well-known Bay Area architects. Hundreds of thousands were housed almost overnight.

As quickly, social housing began to falter. By the middle of the war, the draft, patriotic volunteering, construction work in the Pacific Theater of Operations, and special service assignments had largely dispersed the architectural and environmental design community. Talk about the postwar world kept some interest alive. The war ended, and a great building boom began. Federal policy shifted away from supporting social architecture. The environmental designers found themselves up to their ears in other work: custom housing, schools, commercial and institutional buildings. Aside from some small groups of liberal true believers interested in a utopian communal life, and a brave few agitating for regional planning, social motives in design seemed quiescent, if not dead. Only in Richmond, a Bay Area backwater transformed by the war, did the movement live.

Another postwar Bay Area occurrence, though, held even greater promise for popularizing local, high art architectural ideas and making them available to a mass clientele. The remarkable Joseph Eichler successfully mass-produced the 1950's Bay Area–style house. Scores of his subdivisions, large and small, scattered throughout the area testify to the validity and adaptability of these motives.

Following the years when Richmond and Eichler tried their distinctly different approaches, another kind of movement to socialize Bay Area design took a far stronger hold. After an apprenticeship in the ateliers of the Bay Area, a group of architects evolved a new mass housing style splendidly timed to coincide with the near-disappearance of the single custom house market and the rise of a market for condominiums and other multiple housing. For a decade now, versions of the Sea Ranch Condominium designed by Charles Moore and his partners have dominated the design of group housing. It has swept across the country and become a national condominium vernacular.

While this was happening, a curious event took place outside the local architectural mainstream. A newcomer to the Area regenerated a bit of the New Deal by turning once again to housing migrant workers. His reconstructed old camps, many now blessed by mature trees set out according to the original designs of the 1930's, provide a splended conclusion to this chapter of the social housing story in the San Francisco Bay Area.

NEW DEAL, FSA, AND THE BIRTH OF SOCIAL HOUSING IN THE WEST

The first of the Depression-era housing programs to penetrate into Northern California came during the early Roosevelt years in the utopian efforts of the Rural Resettlement Administration. This most pure of New Deal agencies sought to establish self-sufficient, land-based production cooperatives somewhat on the lines of the early Zionist *kibbutzim*. In 1935 a western regional office of this agency located in Berkeley with responsibility for design and development in the West. There, Burton Cairns headed a small team of engineers assisted by a few architects and a lonely landscape architect or two. In the few years he had to live before dying in a work-related automobile accident, Cairns played the pivotal role in forging a commitment to social architecture and mass housing among Bay Area practitioners. Landscape architect Francis Violich, who worked in RRA in the beginning, remembers him as "the most inspiring person I've ever worked with in my life. . . . He [understood] the social problem in . . . design. . . . He saw the importance of social problems from the functional design point of view, and from a pure esthetic design point of view."[2]

Some efforts to start production cooperatives, in Arizona especially, began in the first two years. But major social housing work started only after Roosevelt's second inaugural in 1937. At that time, reorganizations of New Deal programs coincided with accelerated migrations of dust-bowl refugees to the promised land of California. RRA merged into the new Farm Security Administration of the U.S. Department of Agriculture. The regional office moved to San Francisco. There Cairns took charge of a much-expanded staff. The group included at least two designers who would play a major role in social housing over the decades to come, architect Vernon DeMars and landscape architect Garrett Eckbo.

Like Cairns himself, both of these men trained at the University of California, Berkeley. Eckbo came from a proletarian background but managed to attend Cal, where he discovered landscape architecture. He did graduate work at Harvard. There he participated in overturning the academic tradition in favor of a Modern Movement approach, a pivotal event in the history of American landscape design. He returned to the Bay Area and FSA with a vigorous sense of social purpose.

DeMars, who was to become the region's best-known social housing designer, a "people's architect," in Harry Ransom's phrase, started with no developed social conscience. He explained that he joined FSA

only because it paid five dollars a week more than working for Clarence Mayhew. I went in with absolutely no social preconditions at all. And as a matter of fact, I didn't have a germ of sympathy with that kind of thing— I didn't even know about it. I'd never been motivated in school in this direction at all. Then I was interested a little bit, and I found it interesting to design a collapsible, portable privy. This was really an interesting problem. You knew it was needed by somebody, and it was really rather rewarding. Then I began to feel—and maybe this is where my social consciousness arose—I had been working for Clarence Mayhew, doing eclectic English half-timber stuff in Piedmont, and I was just bored to tears by it. I worked all alone doing that, and it didn't seem very important. Even without any pre-conditioning, I suddenly felt that this really could be important. And then one day they took us down to see the *Plow That Broke the Plains*, in the United Artists theater, and I went out singing. . . .[3]

Today the spirit of hope infused by the New Deal in its managers and planners and designers seems exotic, almost unbelievable. The experience of working in these agencies clearly transformed their lives. The connection between architecture and justice, good environment and good health, the integral relationship between physical community and social-moral community—these ideas seemed self-evident and tremendously exciting. What power lay in the designers' hands!

Violich recalls:

we turned to . . . the notion of architecture and development, which is based heavily on principles of social welfare, namely health and psychological well-being . . . more sunlight through large panes of glass and therefore . . . different shaped windows, a certain amount of space between buildings . . . and orientation of buildings played *very* heavily. In the Farm Security Administration I did more fiddling around with buildings to meet solar orientation diagrams than I ever did in school.

We were motivated to try to improve people that we got to see, even to know personally, in the migratory labor camps. So that those factors of social well-being, like schooling and health [were] a very important motivation. Another was the very real feeling for the Bay, and for the state of California's own climate, ecology, and the form of the land. . . .

We were concerned with bringing to the people in those sites a certain kind of dignity to their everyday life that wasn't possible in the squatter camps. That's why we had the theaters, we had the plazas. I was always the one that was trying to get someplace where people would congregate, and have them properly planted with trimmed sycamores and that sort of thing. A certain kind of dignity which we thought we could offer them at the same time we were being very sensitive to what their basic needs were.[4]

Such was the spirit in 1938 when work began in earnest on the settlements for migrant workers. It was a spirit very much of its time, and it was one aided by special circumstances at the San Francisco office. Helping house migrant workers, for instance, provided a rationale that seemed more broadly acceptable to the public than trying to establish farming communes, which remained the program's purpose in other FSA district offices. The San Francisco Regional Office became a widely recognized leader in architecture and in New Deal social reform.

On a very different level, a decision of the University of California to employ Catherine Bauer as a lecturer in 1938-39 had nearly equal impact. It furnished the Bay Area another catalytic personality who played a major role in social housing from then on. Miss Bauer brought to Berkeley a rich background for so young a woman. Protege of the New York circle of Lewis Mumford, she wrote the immensely influential 1934 book *Modern Housing* and, largely by virtue of the book, became part-author of the landmark 1937 U.S. Housing Act that started public housing. Her enthusiasm, confident knowledge, and the fact that she fit in so well socially made her almost immediately a powerful influence in the FSA circle of designers. Though her influence in direct architectural design was not great, in the broader sense she had an enormous effect in developing the norms for community design and building a sense of camaraderie in doing critical, socially consequential work.

Later she would marry William W. Wurster, and after the war become a regular member of the university faculty. From 1938 to her death in 1964, she played a major role in local housing and planning matters.

At first the settlements FSA designers built were little more than camps containing minimum sanitary facilities and regimented rows of tent platforms. As time went by and some of the emergency needs were met, more permanent dwellings were erected. By 1939 and 1940, several more or less stock designs were evolved culminating in the Yuba City prototype used at other sites as well. This design for a two-story row house marked a high-water point in the penetration of International Style into Bay Area practice. DeMars admits that the work of the Swedish housing cooperatives, designs firmly in the International Style vanguard, had a general influence on his FSA work; and that Le Corbusier's hypothetical design of 1934 for a farmstead directly influenced the Yuba City designs.[5] Perhaps this acknowledged debt to European Modern architecture explains the swiftness with which the FSA work appeared in the international architecture press, recognition greatly aided by selection of these designs for the Museum of Modern Art *Built in USA* show of 1944.[6] Low-cost Le Corbusier in California made a terribly potent idea.

At the community design scale, these migrant settlements produced two ideas that also met with a good deal of international interest. In site design, they demonstrated clear connections with International Style prototypes. The most common motive, used at Yuba City and elsewhere, was the straight CIAM-type[7] *zeilenbau*: parallel lines of row houses each facing in precisely the same way, determined by careful solar orientation studies. Another more startling but less rational pattern appeared in a number of camps. In these, dwellings, particularly platformed tents, were arranged in a geometrically perfect hexagon. Yuba City exhibited this motive too. Was this literally the kibbutzim? It certainly echoed the forms of early radially symmetrical Zionist camps.

After installing basic shelter and plumbing, the FSA designers turned to developing communal facilities. The Woodville settlement near Fresno represented the high point of this movement. There a school, day-care center, clinic, community center,

FARM SECURITY ADMINISTRATION, *migrant farmworkers' housing near Visalia based on Yuba City prototype, 1939*

FARM SECURITY ADMINISTRATION, model of Firebaugh

FARM SECURITY ADMINISTRATION, *aerial view of migrant farmworkers'*
housing near Yuba City, 1939 (Lee)

even a coop store served the inhabitants. All exhibit
a consistent style, rather artless, made directly from
wood siding, stock millwork, low mono-pitch roofs,
and the like. It was a vocabulary drawn in part from
the same international roots as the housing. But—and
this seems crucial in hindsight—it also had clear affinities with the Bay Area Tradition, especially with
Wurster's work. His easy acceptance of the esthetic
results of unsophisticated-looking carpentry was
clearly shared by the FSA team.

Taken together, the integrated design of site,
house, and common facilities developed for an obvious and pressing social purpose provided in the
FSA communities a splendid beginning for the social
housing movement in the Bay Area. Yet the designs
did not represent the popular assimilation of ad-

vanced architectural ideas. And they certainly did
not show much assimilation of local, regional ideas.
Instead, they embodied the understanding and enthusiasm of an architectural in-group well schooled
in recent International themes. They designed *for*
people caught in poverty, people unable to command economic attention in the housing market-
place. Despite the noble motives instilled by Cairns
and Bauer, social architecture and the effort to bring
well-designed housing to the masses remained the
concern of a very small, turned-on elite. The house
forms used in FSA work related directly to Le Corbusier and William W. Wurster. They had yet to
awaken any real popular sensibility. Social architecture had set down roots among the Bay Area practitioners, but its forms remained importations.

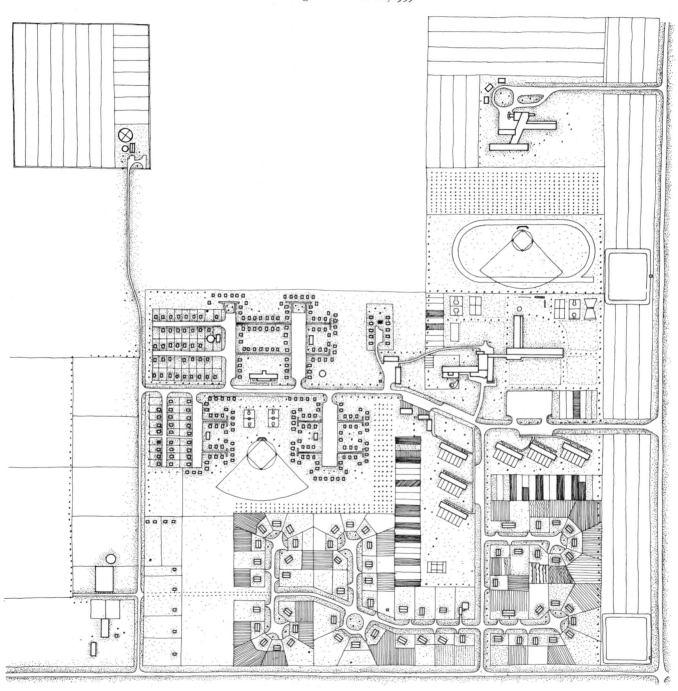

THE WAR HOUSING EXPLOSION

Simultaneously with the final burst of FSA construction for migrant agricultural workers, a new emergency loomed and a new group of migrants needed housing. By 1940, the war in Europe had begun, the U.S. became a main supplier to Britain, and conflict with Japan seemed imminent. The San Francisco Bay Area was transformed in two or three years into an "Arsenal of Democracy."

Nowhere was this transformation more disruptive of old patterns, and powerful in terms of new patterns, than in Richmond, California. This East Bay town had begun at the turn of the century as a small working-class satellite around a railroad yard and oil refinery. By virtue of both a deep-water harbor and plenty of nearby mudflats suitable for shipways, in 1941 it became the ship-a-day complex of Kaiser maritime facilities. Employment increased tenfold. By 1943 Richmond provided jobs for enough people to support a city of half a million, counting service workers, spouses, and children. Not more than a quarter of these people actually lived in Richmond; even so, the population rose in three or four years from 24,000 to over 100,000. Overnight a crowded shack town settled on the mudflats around the shipyards.

Private and public agencies constructed more than 30,000 new dwelling units in Richmond. These

Woodville community building

Atchison Village, Richmond, 1941-42 (Sally Woodbridge)

ranged from slapdash dormitories to all manner of shacks, from conversions of existing buildings to large projects of new houses and apartments. Some few were carefully done, as at Atchison Village, a group of temporary multiple houses that remain in service today. Most were not. Mel Scott, historian of urban development in the Bay Area, calls Richmond a "war casualty." Certainly the prewar city was destroyed by the enormous war effort. And the new city never has quite erased the war's scars, despite a determined social housing effort that is treated in a later section of this chapter.

Richmond, despite the magnitude of its wartime housing program, was not favored with works of major architects or with projects that had a wide influence on later events. Pure production motives dominated. In some other parts of the country distinguished architects did work on war housing. In San Pedro, a port and shipbuilding center in Southern California, Richard Neutra built his landmark community, Channel Heights. In the Bay Area there were architect-designed projects in Vallejo and in Marin County just outside of Sausalito. And in this work some regional influence became visible.

Vallejo, site of the major naval installation at Mare Island, was, next to Richmond, the most impacted district in the Bay Area arsenal. Its population doubled, and the shipyard work force increased several times that. Large projects developed in Vallejo provide some of the most characteristic examples of wartime housing. Among these, Federal Terrace remains the only extant example. It was built of permanent materials to public housing standards. Good maintenance has preserved it as an attractive enclave somewhat like Atchison Village. The others, now long gone, were less positive.

At Chabot Terrace, a few miles outside of Vallejo on the north, and Carquinez Heights, south of town, more than 5000 dwellings were erected practically overnight. Some of the Bay Area's most distinguished designers, including William W. Wurster and Ernest Kump, took part in these developments. Their design in hindsight seems almost a caricature of the barracks idea. Hundreds of little identical shelters, lined up mechanically, marched up hill and down dale, without schools, community facilities, without even sewers.

Taken individually, the barracks-like little houses looked right out of the artless Wurster tradition of residential design. They were soundly laid out internally. The triumph, though, in this Vallejo work was the extraordinary rationalization of the construction process itself. Two assembly lines, one based on wallboard technology, the other on plywood, were set up. In production terms, the result must have been among the first real successes in factory-built housing. Perhaps the most interesting incident in the Bay Area with respect to war housing construction appeared as an offshoot of the Vallejo projects and their concern with production processes. Wurster and his team convinced the federal authorities to release a small amount of material and money for experimental work. Largely under the guidance of Fred and Lois Langhorst, who were employed in Wurster's firm, twenty-five dwellings were designed and built as demonstrations of constructional alternatives to the standardized factory-built barracks. At the time this experiment had no direct influence on the course of war housing. But these twenty-five units received more attention in the architectural press than all the other thousands of houses in Vallejo and the Bay Area. The experiment offered a glimmer of what might be done to mass-produce a more humane and varied popularization of the Bay Area custom house.

In contrast to the obsessed monotony of the Vallejo projects, Marin City looked like an ideal community. It served the Bechtel Marinship yards in Sausalito. Developed by a design team directed by Carl Gromme and including such talented associates as Francis Lloyd, Hervey Parke Clark, Thomas Church, and Lawrence Halprin, this project gave a very clear sense of the complete settlement idea implied in the last of the FSA work.

Marin City was built on a dramatic bowl-shaped site. It provided a complete residential community for 6000 people. Larger group dwellings and the common facilities were disposed across the flat bottom of the bowl. Neat little redwood houses, their barrackslike quality relieved by adroit hillside design, ringed the central area. The public buildings, more generous than the FSA prototypes, achieved the same integrated architectural expression. Marin City must have stimulated many to dream of a postwar world in which such communities, albeit more permanently constructed and more commodiously disposed, could be made available to all.

During the war, Marin City received lots of favorable attention. Mel Scott quotes Congressman George W. Bates of Massachusetts on an inspection tour of wartime naval bases. "We have visited hundreds of war housing projects in the United States and we have seen none that so ideally meets the requirements of a community of war workers as does Marin City. [It has] all the essentials that go into the makeup of a well rounded . . . project. Marin City furnishes sound housing at low cost and it builds up an active community life."[8]

As a kind of postscript on the war housing experience, Marin City remains today, partly rebuilt as a reminder of this dream. The actual wartime structures are long gone. Public housing and other subsidized housing have replaced some of the earlier accommodations. Much of this work is very successful social housing designed by such luminaries as Vernon DeMars, John Carl Warnecke, and the Frank Lloyd Wright–trained Aaron Green. The community buildings and stores have disappeared, but there remains on this handsome site a hint of the early hopes for large-scale community design. It was a starting point toward the individuation of dwellings within planned unit clustering that would finally succeed in popularizing and mass-producing Bay Area design.

POSTWAR DREAMS

By 1943, the war housing boom had petered out. Most of the social housing design group had left San

WURSTER, *Chabot Terrace, Vallejo, 1942*

Chabot Terrace

Chabot Terrace, experimental houses

GROMME, LLOYD, CLARK, CHURCH, AND HALPRIN, *Marin City, war housing and community buildings, 1942*

War housing and community buildings

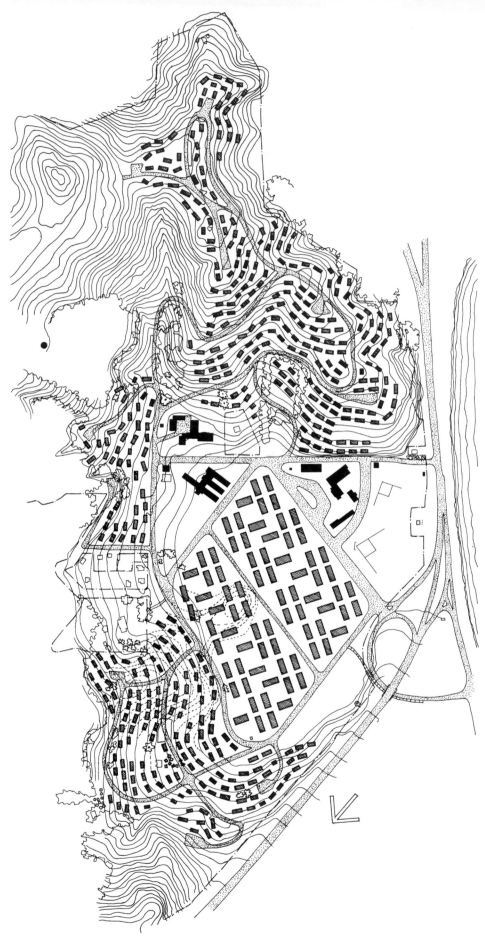

Marin City site plan

Marin City c. 1975, buildings by Green and Warnecke (Roger Montgomery)

Francisco to go to war. The few who hung on had little to do but dream about the kind of postwar world they should build. Typically, they dreamed of making neighborhoods for everyone, themselves included, that followed the idealized principles of the best New Deal and war project design. During the closing years of the conflict, they expressed these dreams in a number of published hypothetical projects.

Characteristic of this postwar dreaming was the proposal by Francis Lloyd, H. P. Clark, R. N. Campbell, and David Bohannson to reconstruct the Candlestick war housing project in San Francisco. They proposed replacing the two-family temporary units with single-family one-story ranch houses neatly lined up on the concrete floor slabs of the tempos in such a way that even the plumbing hookups could be retained. A splendid combination of economy—in

this case through maximized re-use of the permanent installations—and concern with New Deal ideals of communitarian site organization dominated these dreams of a postwar world. It was a world dedicated to economy, equalitarianism (with limits), the Modern Movement (a generation late), and the authentic good feelings of a decade of masterful work in social housing.

Among the most interesting of these efforts at idealized postwar environments were those that the architects developed for themselves. All across the country, as the Second World War ended, architects helped bring into existence small communities that integrated more or less successfully Modern design, responsible and conservative land management, the spirit of communitarianism and cooperation, and an enlightened upper-middle-class life style. In the West, these ideals produced communities like Mutual

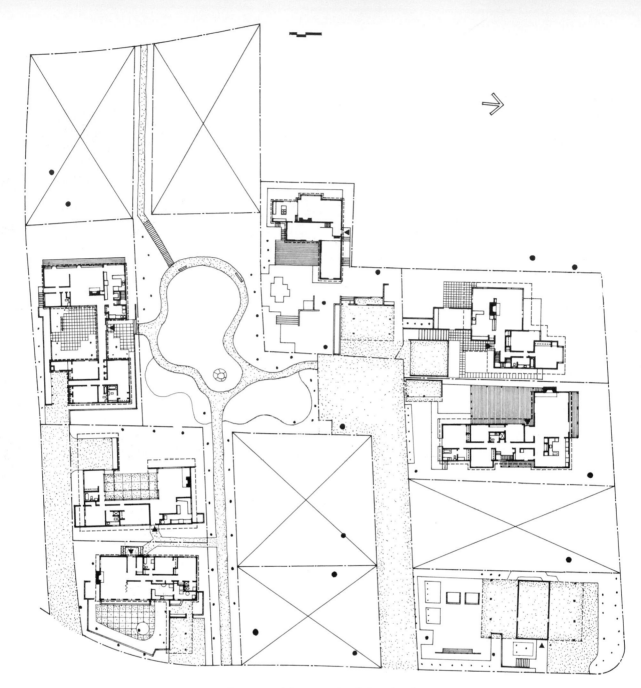

HALPRIN, *Greenwood Common, Berkeley, site plan, c. 1950*

Homes in Los Angeles. Best known and most complete among Bay Area examples is Ladera on the San Francisco Peninsula. Here John Funk, who did considerable war housing work in addition to his wide custom-house practice, Joseph Stein, who had a reputation as a particularly political type among designers in the mid-forties, and the widely experienced social housing landscape architect Garrett Eckbo planned an ideal residential community. A significant fragment of this community actually got built before the postwar housing boom, inflation, lending institution hostility, and a decline in utopian optimism conspired to halt development. Interestingly, Joseph Eichler, the great mass-producer of pure 1950's style Bay Area design, would partly finish the project a decade later. Ladera remains one of the few palpable indica-

244

Greenwood Common, general view (Baer)

tions of the special spirit that informed mass housing as the Second World War closed.

Much less idealistic, more pragmatic, somewhat later, and more conventionally architectural rather than social, another project of the postwar era, Greenwood Common, merits special mention. About 1950 William W. Wurster inherited the opportunity to buy the Gregory property in Berkeley, a small es-tate owned by his and John Galen Howards's patron, Mrs. Warren Gregory. Wurster subdivided the land in a very special way. Instead of covering the area with lots, he made a ring of relatively small sites around a central, communally held park. The result-ing cluster plan became a milestone in group housing design, in a sense the first of the planned unit devel-opments (PUDS) that by the 1970's would dominate

HARDISON & DEMARS, *Easter Hill Village, Richmond, 1954,*
Lawrence Halprin, landscape architect

Bay Area mass housing. In this elite enclave, with its zoo of Bay Area houses by top designers, two motives appeared that would reappear again and again until they emerged in final form fifteen years later in Charles Moore's Sea Ranch Condominium. The themes of Greenwood Common, planned unit design of dwelling groups married with an exaggerated effort to individuate each actual dwelling, led to the ubiquitous condominium vernacular of the late sixties and early seventies.

THE SPECIAL CASE OF RICHMOND

Among all the Bay Area communities, as observed previously, the war transformed none more than Richmond. When it ended many people left town to go home. Richmond found itself a big, somewhat

empty, and very jerry-built town. This triggered a vigorous community development effort, one unique in the Bay Area for its innovative directions. For instance, some wartime housing was preserved and remains today, lovingly maintained. Atchison Village stands as a testimony to the relativity of housing standards.

During the late forties attention focused on cleaning up the shack towns and planning for redevelopment. As the fifties began, so did the actual reconstruction. First came a small-scale public housing effort. Don Hardison, a Richmond architect, teamed up with Vernon DeMars, who had just returned from tours in the Navy, with FHA in Washington, and teaching at MIT. They in turn brought in landscape designer Lawrence Halprin. Together the three produced a landmark in public housing design: the Eas-

246

ter Hill Village Project. Few public housing projects in the history of the program have had the architectural impact of this cluster of 300 dwelling units perched on a small hill once quarried to fill the mud flats below. For the first time in a Bay Area public project, the twin themes of planned unit development and strong individuation appeared here intentionally combined.

Halprin's inspired decision to leave the boulder-strewn land boulder-strewn, and the cluster site design the group used to integrate buildings and open spaces into a larger planned unit disposed along the contours, broke sharply with the FSA-style geometric rationalism. Here the Bay Area architects put behind them International Style formal motives and chose an *ad hoc* directness. They responded to the

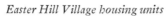

Easter Hill Village housing units

personality of the site and their interpretation of social preferences of the residents, rather than insolation, rationalized access systems, and construction economy.

The dwelling design also pioneered new approaches. Hardison and DeMars sought to build individual houses, not apartments. These individual units, though grouped into buildings of various sizes, read like individual dwellings. The architects used setbacks and offsets, paint schemes and roof colors, porches and fences to individuate them. Vernon De-Mars explains that during the years since his FSA experience,

I had been stewing on all these things . . . I just had concluded that a row house was not six families living communally in a piece of sausage that hadn't been sliced yet. They didn't share anything, except their party walls. . . . As an architectural expression, it was not a bar. If you had an apartment house with a single entry, and had internal halls, then the expression was a unit. Row houses, even if they're built at once or whatever, are discreet family things. I had the feeling that our Chandler project [FSA project in Arizona] with its adobe walls, had been on the right track, as expressing this separateness . . . I even feel that our later Corbu thing in Yuba City was less good. . . .[9]

At Easter Hill different sizes and types of houses appeared in a single building, an unheard of irrationality in FSA or war housing work. The architects went to great lengths to produce a separate front stoop for each family. DeMars explains that the houses were paired, one plan a mirror image of its neighbor, to economize on a single plumbing stack, but that

to break apart this mirror image, we simply took the absolutely unthinkable move of taking the front door and moving it across the room from where it was in the standard plan. We thought that what we gained externally would make up for the fact that the door was in the wrong place in the living room. After it was built, we found more people liking it better in that location than in the other. . . .[10]

To return to the special world of Richmond, Easter Hill Village successfully kicked off a remarkable, publicly stimulated cycle of group house building. Over the next fifteen years, a series of projects further refined these themes, especially the individuation idea. In the appropriately named Pilot Project,

Hardison and DeMars developed a design vocabulary that would hold up through the succeeding years; after the designers had gone on to other things and merchant builders took over design responsibility. The intentionally miscellaneous-looking experimental dwellings of the Pilot Project group were conceived of as prototypes for use in the enormous urban renewal needed to reinhabit the war housing sites. Today thousands of permanent, suburban-looking houses cover these acres, the direct descendants of the Pilot Project prototypes. They represent a very special and impressive accomplishment in the mass production of Bay Area residential design. Nowhere else was this architecture popularized in a way and for a market so nearly like that envisioned in the enthusiastic New Deal days. Richmond, and DeMars and his colleagues, present one of the few American monuments to social housing ideas.

EICHLER

Forty miles south of San Francisco in the Santa Clara Valley, another fascinating episode in the popularization of Bay Area design occurred. It started in the late 1940's, when Joseph Eichler decided to become a homebuilder. He claimed a mission to bring good architecture to middle America. The improbable, but often repeated, story tells how the experience of living during the war in the Frank Lloyd Wright house on Reservoir Road in Hillsborough, south of San Francisco, transformed butter-and-egg salesman Eichler into a homebuilder and patron of the arts. "I never ceased to marvel about that house, always making new discoveries," he explained. "It was during that time that I became interested in houses. . . . I had never been interested in houses and such before. . . . This is when I came to the conclusion that after the war I was going to enter the homebuilding business."[11]

After some short involvement in prefabrication, by 1947 or 1948 Eichler had bought his first land, twenty acres near Sunnyvale, and had begun to build the first primitive version of his own personal kind of tract house. At first his houses were semi-stock: Eichler remembers that he bought parts from his former prefab operation. He worked with a now-forgotten designer. Very quickly, however, he

HARDISON & DEMARS, *Plaza Project, Richmond, 1957, later development
from the* Pilot Project, *Richmond (Sally Woodbridge)*

HARDISON & DEMARS, *Potrero Project, Richmond, 1963 (Sally Woodbridge)*

turned to well-known Bay Area architects. By 1950 he was working with the San Francisco firm of Anshen & Allen, an association that would continue for years.

Eichler had worked with Robert Anshen earlier, when, between giving up his lease on the Wright house and beginning business as a homebuilder, he had sought to build a house for himself. Though they never got to building that custom house, they discovered a mutual interest in mass building. Thus began the remarkable passage in architect-designed, mass-market housing that would end only in 1974 with Eichler's death at a still very active seventy-three. The houses began as flat and shed roof "ranch houses" that looked startlingly like some of Wur-

ster's most modest custom houses from the 1930's. Within a few years, Eichler, Anshen & Allen, and the Los Angeles firm of Jones & Emmons had designed and built hundreds of houses in a number of subdivisions. Later Claude Oakland, who had worked for Anshen & Allen, set up his own firm and became the third member of Eichler's stable of architects. Though designs of the firms were recognizably distinct, together they created an Eichler style that characterized his projects for twenty years. All of the elements came from the typical Bay Area custom house of the 1950's, with the exception of some special quirks the Southern California people added—drooped eaves, for instance, were a Quincy Jones trademark. By 1954, Eichler had started Greenmeadow, one of a

Eichler home, Sunnyvale, 1948 (Sally Woodbridge)

number of tracts he built in Palo Alto—he was still working in that city at his death. The houses here typified the style: low, glassy, post-and-beam, an unmistakable Bay Area look, though stripped of decorative detail and fancy finishes. Floors were concrete slabs at ground level. Large garages integral with the house dominated the facades. Entrances through atrium courtyards were a particular trademark of Eichler and his architects, one that harked back to many Wurster designs and to the complicatedly fretted junction between outdoors and inside in John Funk's work. The atrium idea became an export to homebuilders in many places around the country.

Until the general slowdown of single-family house building in the middle 1960's, and his own financial crisis of that period, Joseph Eichler increased the scope of his operations to encompass the entire Bay Area. He moved beyond Santa Clara County to build in San Mateo, San Francisco, Marin, Contra Costa, and Alameda counties. He built houses in urban renewal projects in San Francisco, in the new town of Foster City, and in a number of swankier outlying suburbs like Walnut Creek. As time went by, his typical house got bigger, considerably more expensive ($16,000 in 1954; $35,000 in the mid-sixties; $75,000 in 1972), and generally more luxurious. The style remained largely unchanged.

A late example, such as the Lucas Valley houses in Marin County, suggests that as the custom-house market dwindled in the late fifties and early sixties,

ANSHEN & ALLEN, *Eichler home, Terra Linda, 1955*

ANSHEN & ALLEN, *Eichler homes, Walnut Grove, c. 1960*

Eichler took up some of the slack. The great custom-house architects of the day went on to other things as the incredible increase in prices dried up their custom-house work. In part, perhaps, Eichler's enterprise filled the gap. Ironically, what had started out and continued for a decade as a remarkable popularization of a high art architecture ended its twenty-five year campaign serving not a mass market but an elite one, sociologically the same market that had created the style in the first place.

THE RISE OF CONDOMINIUM VERNACULAR

The waning of Eichler's heroic efforts to mass-produce Bay Area architecture happened simultaneously with major secular changes in the American and West Coast housing economies. In but a few years, these changes led to a new thrust of popularization, more successful quantitatively than any previous efforts at marrying high art architecture and mass housing. By the end of the sixties, low-rise mul-

tiple and group housing had taken over as the modal type of new production housing. In the mass market, fully as much as in the elite, custom-house market, the single detached house seemed a dodo, brought nearly to extinction by significant changes in family composition, by sprawl and distance problems, by land costs, by rising construction costs, by shifts in consumer preferences, and by new government housing programs including an enormously productive subsidy program.

Most metro areas had begun to run out of close-in, well-located land on which large-lot single-family tract housing could be built. The few remaining sites were too expensive. Otherwise reasonably well-located or inexpensive sites were too steep for efficient construction operations. In the Bay Area, such relatively distant places as the Livermore Valley in eastern Alameda County and the southern part of San Jose were developing swiftly. In even these far-off places condominiums were built because detached houses used too much land.

Other dimensions of the housing cost equation had similar, cumulating effects. Changes in preference and family composition began to be felt. Fewer conventional, nuclear families sought conventional family housing. The presence of more unattached young adults, single-parent households, people whose children had grown, and elderly people ("empty-nesters" and "senior citizens," in housing jargon) set up a demand for small dwellings without extensive yards and gardens. Such dwellings could be compacted into multiple and group housing. The Latin American and Southern European notion of condominium ownership was quickly adapted to preserve in these group dwellings the psychological and income tax advantages of single-family ownership.

Government policy, changed by the new social outlook of the Kennedy-Johnson years, had by 1968 finally hit on a subsidy formula that worked in terms of mass production. Payment of a part of the interest charges directly to the lending institutions meant that a large pool of investment capital became available to people who otherwise were priced out of the market. The number of new people brought into the market was staggering—at least in comparison with previous subsidy programs like public housing. In the years 1969-73, 800,000 subsidized units were built as against a total of 600,000 dwellings in the thirty-five-year history of public housing. Most of these new units were perforce multiple or group housing.

Another factor, less powerful but of central interest to architects, figured in these changes. Starting during the heyday of the mass tract building of single detached houses, designers had set up a continuous stream of propaganda in favor of high-density, close-together, low-rise group housing. A whole series of buzz words associated with this movement make the idea clear. Housing should be "clustered," not "sprawled." It should take the form of "town houses," "court houses," "zero-lot-line houses," "patio houses," and the like. Housing should be grouped in "planned unit developments" that respected natural site features and made "communities" of the groups.

These changes were in no sense unique to the San Francisco Bay Area. They were felt in every metropolitan housing market and even in smaller cities. Some typical architectural characteristics accompanied these changes. Differences in the mode of practice were most important. Designers, architects, and landscape architects now worked in a way that tended to integrate the site design and the architecture in a single overall concept. This stood in sharp contrast to the institutional arrangements for single detached houses, whether tract or custom. In those, the site was designed by an engineer, surveyor, or land planner; and a house designer, be he or she architect or lumberyard draftsman, did the dwelling design. Typically, no communication occurred between the two. The land planner sought to lay out the maximum number of lots permitted under zoning law. The house designer tried to make "feature-filled" models for the sales staff. Community design values fell by the wayside.

In group housing, powerful economic, constructional planning, and legal forces encouraged integrated design. This in turn led to the first really widespread design of all aspects of housing in relatively large projects and the general acceptance of the planned unit development process. Architects became relatively more important in the development process, and some significant changes in consumer preferences seem to have made their essentially high art designs more palatable in the mass market. Relatively few buyers of single detached houses could accept the Eichler-style houses, whereas a much larger segment willingly bought equivalently high-style group houses. Among both renters and condominium buyers there seemed little reluctance to live in seriously artistic architectural surroundings. These changes in preference reinforced the newly dominant position of architects in mass-market housing.

In terms of the forms and ideas that appeared in the new group housing, Bay Area designers played a very significant part. They provided images that captured a major national market, spreading their regional ideas throughout the country. The Sea Ranch Condominiums, a 1965 design by Charles Moore and his partners, so perfectly packaged these ideas that offspring of Sea Ranch can be found now from New England to Florida, all across the Midwest, and everywhere in the West. This project, obviously one of the seminal events in Bay Area architecture, epitomizes the twin motives of planned unit clustering and distinct individuation of each actual dwelling

M/L/T/W, *Sea Ranch Condominium, 1965 (Baer)*

unit. Moore quotes a friend who characterized the Sea Ranch Condominiums from a distance as "like a large wooden rock." Moore calls it "a community" of ten dwellings "with tower, courts, bays, and solaria, ranged around two common courtyards . . . ," splendidly integrated with the powerful landscape into a single evocative unit. Yet against this runs an equally powerful individuation. Moore argues in explaining this project "that the fundamental principle of architecture is territorial." He made each "great room" a dwelling different. Each shows itself powerfully distinct within its basic vocabulary of materials, forms, and spatial layers within layers.[12]

Other major Bay Area architects played important roles in evolving the condominium vernacular. Wurster, Bernardi & Emmons did large planned-unit projects. At Woodlake in San Mateo, built in the same year as Moore's condominium, they achieved, with Lawrence Halprin, a splendid standard of site amenity coupled with a rather artless building. This was typical of a number of Wurster, Bernardi & Emmons' projects of this scale in the Bay Area and beyond.

Charles Warren Callister turned even more dramatically to group housing projects. He and his firm built a number of them in the Bay Area, such as the early part of Hiller Highlands in the Berkeley Hills above Tunnel Road. Perhaps his most characteristic project is Heritage Woods in Avon, Connecticut. In this work Callister offered a national version of the Bay Area Tradition. So successful was it that its architectural details become images as ubiquitous as the Sea Ranch cluster-form. It seems to have struck a nearly perfect note within the conflicting pulls of economy, constructional ease, and a demand for warm, woodsy forms constructed in a craftsman-like vernacular.

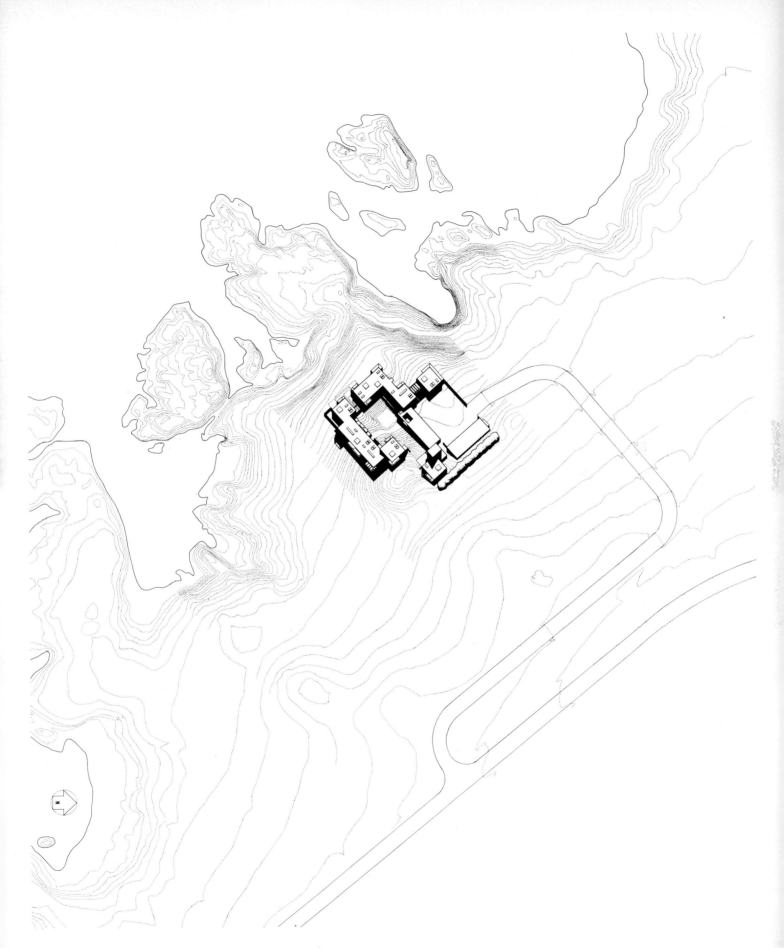

Sea Ranch Condominium, site plan (office of M/L/T/W)

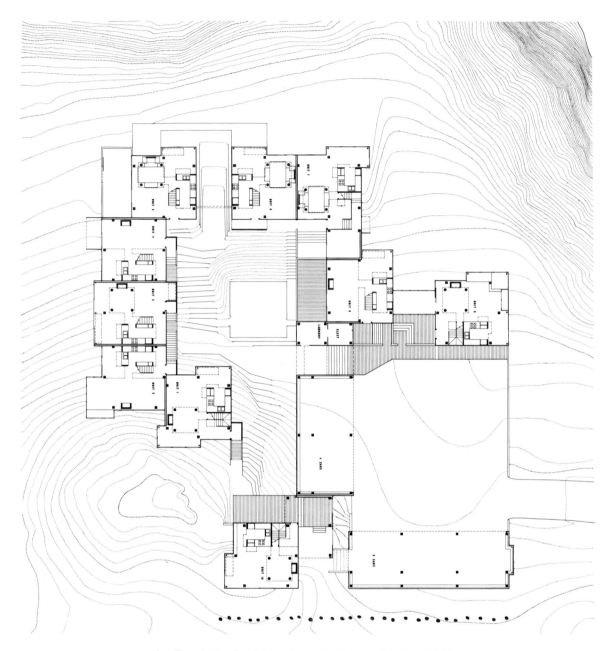

Sea Ranch Condominium, floor plan (office of M/L/T/W)

WURSTER, BERNARDI & EMMONS, *Woodlake, San Mateo, 1965, Lawrence Halprin,*
landscape architect (Sturtevant)

CALLISTER & PAYNE, *Hiller Highlands, Berkeley, 1967-72, Roysten,*
Hanamoto & Beck, landscape architects (Philip Molten)

MARQUIS & STOLLER, *St. Francis Square, San Francisco, 1962* (*Karl H. Riek*)

Another group housing design, perhaps equal in overall influence to Moore's Sea Ranch Condominium though not so memorable an image, appeared four years earlier in a San Francisco urban renewal area. There Marquis and Stoller, who had done a number of custom houses, designed for the longshoremen's union a project named St. Francis Square. Ranged around open courts that formed highly usable communal open areas, the houses successfully picked up the rhythm of traditional San Francisco vernacu-

lar row houses. As an early user of the Great Society's federal subsidy program, this development had a particularly important impact later on in the post-1968 subsidized housing boom. And as an early exemplar of the planned unit development process it played a critical role in the rise of the condominium style.

Some of the Bay Area's best known small-to-medium firms specialized in developing and spreading this branch of the Bay Area tradition during the late sixties and early seventies. Firms like Sandy & Babcock and Fisher-Friedman have achieved something not accomplished before during the many stages of local architectural development. Their group housing work, solidly derived from the central ideas developed during the last phase of the Bay Area Tradition, appears everywhere in the area today. Thousands, perhaps scores of thousands, of dwellings attest to the fact that they have finally mass-produced the local style. Sandy, Friedman, and other designers in this group work now in all parts of the country. And in all parts of the country their followers, and the followers of the more central figures like Moore and Callister, have forged, largely from the high-art Bay Area Tradition, a new vernacular scaled to the spe-

cial needs of the seventies housing market. They have constructed a condominium style, done not in a truly vernacular way like the wood-butcher single detached houses, but by architectural professionals.

RESURRECTING NEW DEAL MOTIVES

For a few moments beginning in the mid-1960's a wonderful architectural postscript occurred in the history of Bay Area social housing. The federal government under Lyndon Johnson tried to resurrect pieces of the New Deal in the form of the Great Society's War on Poverty. Once again the housing plight of migrant agricultural workers became a matter of concern to some Bay Area architects. But the

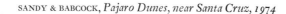

SANDY & BABCOCK, *Pajaro Dunes, near Santa Cruz, 1974*

FISHER-FRIEDMAN, *Islandia, Alameda, 1966-69* (*Joshua Freiwald*)

HIRSHEN & VAN DER RYN, *migrant farmworkers' housing, plyform tent, Indio, 1965 (Joshua Freiwald)*

similarity to the work of thirty years earlier ended there. This time no design and construction bureaucracies were founded. Whereas in the 1930's a part of FSA's function was to provide public jobs for designers, in the 1960's the Office of Economic Opportunity directly hired private professional firms for the services it needed. This time the effort began as such a low-profile undertaking, and the mainstream architectural establishment was so busily at work elsewhere, that it fell to a young newcomer to California to start building migrant facilities. Sanford Hirshen, less than a year in the state, with his then-partner Sim van der Ryn, began this work in 1965.

Hirshen brought with him a well-formed Internationalist perspective on social architecture and design. He had been trained in the East, worked there and in Europe, and had come under the influence of the great third-generation International Style teacher Louis Kahn, the same teacher who had so influenced

Moore. Hirshen brought to this work a new functionalist environmentalism and a sophisticated approach to the rationalization of construction. On the one hand, his thinking had been influenced by the radical critic and sociologist C. Wright Mills; on the other, his ideas about building had been formed in the context of Buckminster Fuller's mystical yet rational constructivism. This time the people who designed communities for migrant workers came from a cosmopolitan and sophisticated global base, not from a regional one.

In terms of production, Hirshen, who practices in a small, highly decentralized partnership, out-produced the FSA directorate. Between 1965 and 1975, he built or rebuilt and expanded some nineteen communities containing rudimentary dwellings for nearly 1600 households, as well as communal facilities. The first of these, such as the one at Indio in Riverside County and three early San Joaquin County camps,

261

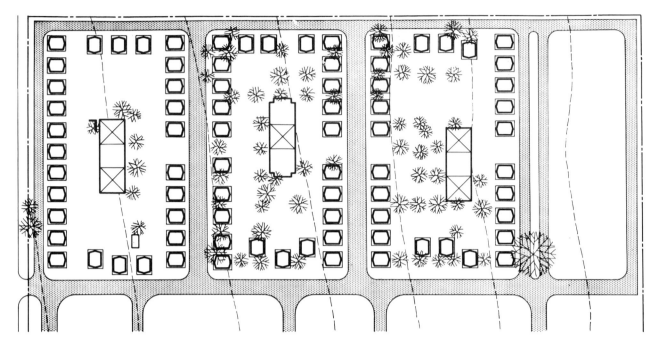

Indio site plan

HIRSHEN & VAN DER RYN, *migrant farmworkers' housing, Watsonville,
1967 (Joshua Freiwald)*

used folded-paper technology to produce pole-free tent-like structures. Later camps used modular prefabrication to produce quite house-like standardized dwellings. The constructional affinities between these later units and the mass-market condominium style seems clear enough. It may explain something about the economies in this mode of building that influence both public and private developers.

The early Hirshen site plans for migrant camps returned to the military camp formalism exhibited by the earlier FSA designs. Is there something about such tasks that makes designers think only in regimented terms? Later designs, such as the one at Watsonville, show more affinity with the planned-unit idea. The rigid symmetry of the camp has been broken somewhat by attention to the landform and the social patterns of its inhabitants.

The wonderful symmetry Hirshen's work gives to the story of mass-producing Bay Area residential design has many intriguing dimensions. Perhaps the most significant concerns the radical change in social context of practice between the 1930's and the 1970's. Asked about the ideas that powered the FSA work forty years ago, Violich observed,

One of the reasons our group succeeded was because we knew each other for a long period of time, we were knitted together in the social sense, we therefore had a system of communication. . . . We knew that we shared common interests . . . loved the Bay. We loved the smell of salt. We loved the seagulls. We loved the beach. We loved hiking in Marin County. . . . When it came to doing something professionally, . . . we were very open and at ease with each other, and we were all from here.[13]

Hirshen, asked the same question, observes that his reference group consists of an architect in St. Louis, a psychologist in L.A., and some designers and planners in the East.

This suggests how difficult it is now to maintain any semblance of regional tradition. In Melvin Webber's words, we live in a "non-place world" in architecture as much as in any field. Charles Moore belongs to the world more than the Bay Area, and so does Hirshen. A careful look at the process of popularizing architectural ideas shows that local traditions have their roots in local social networks. As social networks lose their spatial bounds, it seems that architecture loses its geographically limited character.

Or does it? The idea of regionalism exists first in

Watsonville, diagram of unit

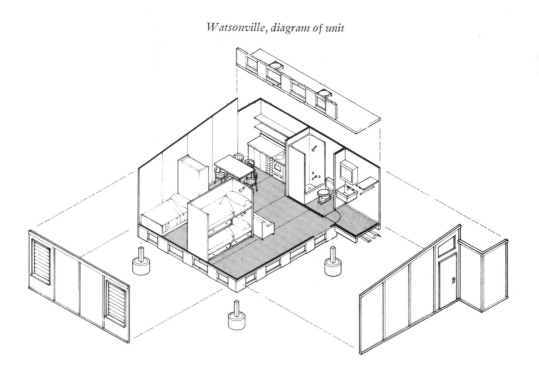

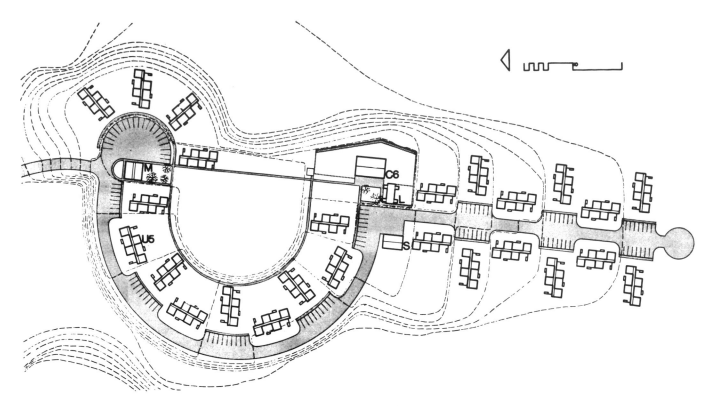

Watsonville site plan

our minds. Local groups can construct a local tradition and continuously renew it. If the recent history of mass-producing Bay Area architecture has any meaning, it is that any area could be a center of innovation in terms of a North American style, if not world style. Ironically, as the Bay Area emphasized its architectural uniqueness, it became a component in a universal architecture. To the extent it succeeds in reviving Newsom's copy books, Maybeck's details, Wurster's plans, and Moore and Hirshen's motives, the San Francisco Bay Area gives these architectural ideas more to the world at large than to itself.

6

The End of Arcadia

CHARLES MOORE

The fifteen years since 1960 form a separate chapter, the third and perhaps final act in the drama of a special Bay Area architecture. If it is an obituary, it is a strangely uncertain one: did the Bay Area Tradition ever, in fact, exist? Is it gone? Or perhaps alive and well but somewhere else? It is, at any rate, incontrovertible that there was a series of impulses which produced a number of modest but memorable houses, according to a set of principles generally shared, and now that impulse has gone. The splendid sites which transformed generations of modest houses into a kind of arcadian paradise have mostly been used up, and the rest are being jealously guarded by groups which have come to equate the public weal with public picnicking.

The future of domestic architecture around San Francisco Bay seems manifestly to lie in a whole new realm, shared with many other places—in fitting new buildings, not into arcadian sites, but into existing urban and suburban settings and even into existing buildings, uniting past and present, making ourselves a part of a continuous popular history. It is worth wondering where the sylvan past went, why the natural style that we continue to admire doesn't persist. There is, certainly, not just one reason why it went away, but a set of interconnected ones. If we take the norm from which the Bay Area has departed as the Wurster houses of the thirties and forties, one

evident change since World War II is an inflation of expectation: people thirty years ago were delighted to have a house that had a thousand square feet in it, two bedrooms, one bath, and very simple equipment. In San Francisco in 1947, when the standard builder's house contained a thousand square feet, architects felt very lucky if someone came in and asked them to do a 1200-square-foot house. That meant a $15,000 budget instead of, say, the $13,500 that might have gone with the builder's product. All the numbers, of course, have gone up from there; up also with them is what people not only expect but demand by way of space and equipment. An even more important inflation, in addition to the generally rising cost of construction, is, of course, the increasing expense and rarity of beautiful pieces of land. They used to be all over; now they represent an altogether finite resource, much of it used up.

There has been, in the thirty years since World War II, a growing disparity between the cost of builders' houses and of individually designed houses, for a number of reasons. One of these is the proliferation of regulating agencies intent on protecting people from everything from earthquakes to each other. They used to be happy with scratches on the back of an envelope; now they require endless structural calculations from an expensive structural designer, ruminations about the soil from people who find it profitable to dedicate themselves to that role, and most recently a set of regulations almost unenforceable in their complexity dealing with insulation, the size of windows, and other elements which can be rigidified in panicked response to the energy crisis. All this has forced an increase in the fees architects must charge.

In the thirties William W. Wurster, with a great many simple houses to do, could make money on a 6 per cent fee for a $10,000 house. By the late forties there was pressure to raise the fee from 9 per cent to 10; now architects discover that even on a 15 per cent fee for considerably more expensive houses they lose their shirts. That, of course, has contributed, for somebody who wants an individual house, to the difficulty of finding an architect at all. Generally architects willing to do houses are either young designers (who will do anything), academics like myself, who count on making up the deficit from their teacher's pay, and architects either of ample means or very simple tastes.

With all those difficulties accelerating from 1945 on, we find ourselves staring retrospectively at houses of a genre which started out earnest and humble but, by the end of the fifties, had gone out in a blaze of luxury, expanded, puffed out, grander and grander, fatter and fatter, and less and less easy to see the shape of. The underlying impulse for the careful individual dwelling had started from the "large-small house" that Gardner Dailey, William W. Wurster, and others talked about after the war, a place where the simple life could be led in generously simple buildings drenched in a lush landscape. By the beginning of the sixties, with shrinking budgets and rising expectations, instead of the "large-small house" architects found themselves, on purpose, begetting the "small-great house." It is small-great houses which are central to any survey of the scene from 1960 to the present. In the early sixties it seemed that the leading architects were trying hard to pare off the fat of the overfed house, to lay bare the formal ideas that had been obscured by the fat, and to find again in the diagram a source from which to wrest some order. The houses which illustrate this struggle here are chosen from hundreds of possible examples, in order to distinguish three particular architectural routes that seem especially useful to identify.[1] The first route starts from and seeks a return to the California barn and the Bay Area house of an earlier period. The earlier process of "packing the box" is again essayed, but within the simple shoebox are developed much more articulated details, more interesting finishes, and generally more complexity. This repacking took many forms: works of Marquis & Stoller, Henrik Bull, and William W. Wurster himself will illustrate some of them.

A second route, also out of the California barn and owing a great deal to the Philadelphia architect Louis Kahn, will be illustrated mostly by the work of myself and my partners. Again, it starts out trying to regain an earlier simplicity, but it works itself up into a frenzy of baroque spaces within the rather gentle limits of the shanty. A third route (again out of Bay Area houses, barns, and Kahn) is best seen in the work of Joseph Esherick and his partners in Esherick, Homsey, Dodge & Davis, as well as Peters Clayberg & Caulfield and Dmitri Vedensky, who have ties with the Esherick office. Their efforts lead toward proficiency in making form with light and its passage, rather than by concentrating, as my partners and I had done, on establishing surprising dimensions in space. The differences, within this local compass, seem surprisingly like the differences between Renaissance and Baroque art as Heinrich Wöfflin described them.

The sophisticated richness of the work of Esherick and his friends, spartan in its intellectual rigor but almost baroque in the sensuous play of light over surfaces, prompts an observation about sources and their appropriation: in the decades after World War II, the most malevolent adjective available for architects' use was "eclectic" (though note Warren Callister's early use of it in Chapter 4). Frank Lloyd Wright had pioneered in the pejorative use of the adjective, so that by the forties architects sat at their drawing boards confident that their every line was a clean one, unsullied by previous use. By the fifties, the more observant members of the profession had grown uneasy about this stricture, but were uneasy as well about seeming to admit that their work bore some connection to the existing world.

In the sixties, and especially in the early seventies, an increasing degree of candor allows us to admit that we have actually looked at existing places before we sat down at the drawing board to do the work at hand. We nurse much less anxiety than we used to about our capacity to take over whole chunks of an earlier work without its destroying us. The previous attitude emerges in a tale about Frank Lloyd Wright, who in a conversation with James Fitzgibbon was maligning painters, who he said were eclectic and irrelevant. Fitzgibbon queried: "But Mr. Wright, I have noticed that you have a great affinity for some painters; haven't you, for instance, been influenced by Gustav Klimt?" Wright replied: "I have been *refreshed* by Gustav Klimt."

At this much later date, by my citation of Louis I. Kahn's 1955 bath house for the Trenton, New Jersey, Jewish community center as the immediate progenitor of houses in the Bay Area in the 1960's, I don't mean to do the influenced works a disservice. The Trenton bath house is an especially potent influence on later Bay Area houses because it is such a clear instance of an urgent attempt, in a modest building, to get back to a clear connection with the underlying diagram. The diagram comes out of the desire to distinguish served from servant space; it is ordered by a plaid (i.e. unevenly spaced) grid of big and little which forms spaces inside hollow columns that are large for holding up the pyramidal hats that cover the dressing areas, but are able to hold plumbing and to serve as visual baffles to screen the segregated spaces. This form, meant to provide a strong architectural framework for making decisions, could be continued as the formal base for a much larger and more complex structure adjoining.

A scheme of 1962 by M/L/T/W for the Jenkins house, which was meant to lie in vineyards near St. Helena, responds to the same desire to develop a formal, geometric base which will firmly guide the architects' decisions. In a shanty version of the Kahn clarity, four roofs lean against each other to surround a square high space that is open to the sky. The dimensions of each shed are regulated by the system, so the plan couldn't be changed without abandoning the whole set of relationships.

The one house in the Bay Area which keynotes the efforts of the years since 1960 is, I believe, George Homsey's Rubin house in Albany, which signals an introduction to a whole new world. A splendidly pared down and precise world of space and light

(especially of light), this house managed to be a clear diagram of itself, altogether modest, yet at the same time rich in its development of spaces. The casual, almost shanty idiom of the Bay Area is mated with a precision of shape and an almost baroque drama of space and light. Following in what I'll call the mainstream of the last fifteen years of the Bay Area effort, Marquis & Stoller's Green-Johnston house of 1960 is an attempt to pare down, clarify, make neat and precise and airy the Bay Area idiom, taking advantage of the beautiful landscape, setting a simple house in it, doing in fact what the small houses of the forties had done, but with considerably more precision and more sophistication, as befitted the rather later date. The house is for two single people, so it is in most ways two houses adjoining; this may contribute to the delicacy of the scale and detail, which made the pieces appear as thin as was plausible and paid careful attention to surfaces like the wood deck, as well as to the connections that the region has always delighted in between indoors and out and to the extension of living areas to the outside—even though the cool coastal climate reduces to very few the chances to sit down in the outdoors. The house subscribes to the traditional Bay Area (and Modern) architectural division of walls into panels either of glass or of solid, so that windows are not holes poked into walls, but figure rather as part of the fabric of the house at the scale of the whole house.

A few years later, in 1965, the Marquis & Stoller Pence house was published across the world. It is a group of pavilions like those in Kahn's Trenton bath house, but arranged in a more leisurely and expansive way, set on an overpowering site so as to get excitement out of the relation between the buildings and the site and (with influences from Japan) an easiness in their relation to each other. They connect in an irregular line, much less formal than Kahn's plaid of served and servant space. The plan shows that the pavilions are simply divided into the rooms one would expect in a not-very-large dwelling; it is the siting which gives this little house its magnificence.

Inside in two of the pavilions the closeness between the inside and the out is apparent, as is the structural clarity of these pavilions, though that clarity is obtained at some price, to avoid using tie rods which would have gotten in the way of the space that was

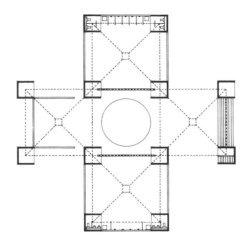

KAHN *bath house, Trenton, New Jersey, 1960, plan*

M/L/T/W, *Jenkins house (unbuilt), axonometric*

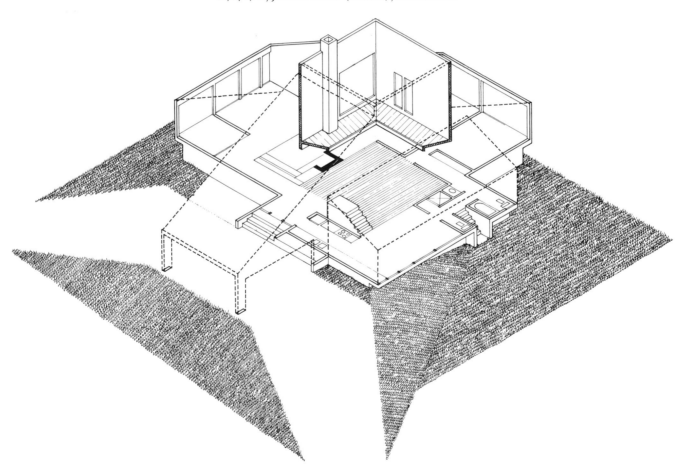

HOMSEY, *Rubin house, Albany, 1960 (Baer)*

Rubin house, plan and section

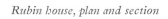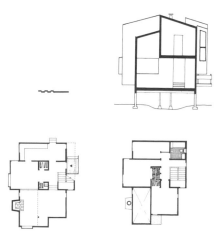

MARQUIS & STOLLER, *Green-Johnston House, Sausalito, 1960,*
model from above

Green-Johnston house, plan

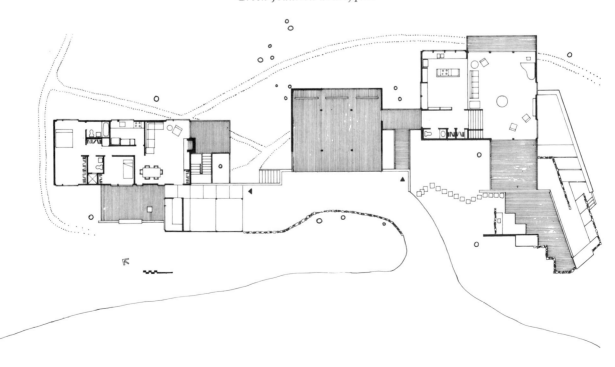

Green-Johnston house, deck (Ezra Stoller)

MARQUIS & STOLLER, *Pence house, Mill Valley, 1965 (Karl H. Riek)*

Pence house, interior of living room pavilion (Karl H. Riek)

BULL, *Sims house, San Francisco Peninsula, 1961* (G. E. Mitchell)

seeking to be clear. Close attention to the surfaces of these rooms is a special characteristic of this work of the mid-sixties.

Henrik Bull, too, is an architect in what I am calling the mainstream of the sixties, with highly elaborated buildings pushed back into simple shapes. In the Sims house of 1961, the plans which had been spreading and sprawling through the fifties in most Bay Area houses are pulled back into a neat box with lots of care expended on the making, articulating, and elaborating of detail in ways that are more and more overtly reminiscent of many places around the Pacific, especially Japan. The clarity of the plan is es-

pecially noteworthy, as is the clarity of the frame of the house on the lush and beautiful land, sitting quite clean in it but not separate from it, very much a part of the site.

The architect allows a single interruption of the simple gable shape. Close relationships again are insisted upon between indoors and out through walls made largely of glass, and details inside are strongly reminiscent of Frank Lloyd Wright and redolent of other times and places. This is not mistakable for a Bay Area house of the forties; it is much too knowing in its eclecticism and in the relatively high style of its design, with some glamorous jumps of scale to the

Sims house, plan

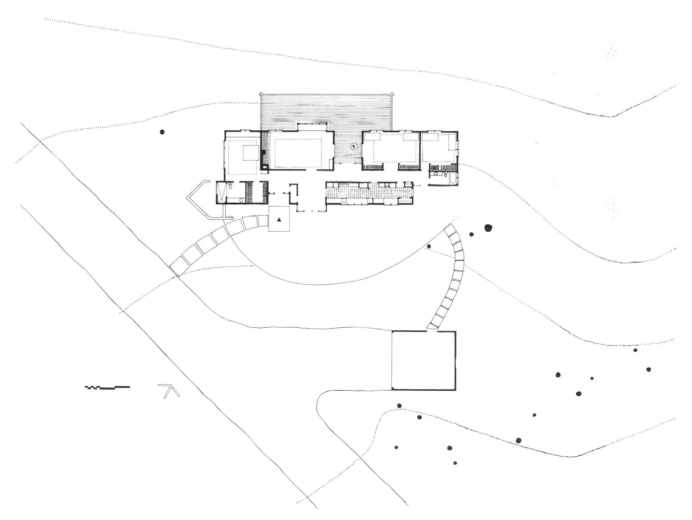

BULL, *house in San Rafael, 1966 (Baron Wollman)*

big hood over the fireplace or the high windows in the gable end of the main room, which are far more self-consciously dramatic than they would have been fifteen years before.

There is, as there probably would not have been a decade earlier, pleasure in the juxtaposition of elaborate old furniture and the fairly simple new structure, relaxing into the expectation of more objects inside, more furniture with more interesting recall piece by piece than the earlier period had allowed. Behind the furniture lie beautifully finished surfaces exposed in light. A characteristic of sophisticated Bay Area houses of the sixties quite different from their predecessors is a use of details to emphasize the self-consciously continuous space, edging up and across the house as well as just along corridors and rooms. On the outside, there is by now a much more active and complex detailing of, for instance, the beam ends, which carry our recollections past the simpler dictates of the thirties and forties to what Bernard Maybeck and other architects of the teens might have done. The surfaces don't just stop but

House in San Rafael, covered entrance way (Baron Wollman)

fray out at the end, modulating the plane and breaking up the light. Joseph Esherick points out that the advantage of this modulation parallels the human advantage of having eyelashes and eyebrows instead of pieces of steel glued onto the top surface of our eyeballs.

By 1966 a house in San Rafael, also by Henrik Bull, is more than ever a shoebox with all its rooms lined up in a row. The same organization of spaces, albeit with much more complex shapes, had been used by Frank Lloyd Wright in his Usonian houses of the decades before. Here the tensions between Wright's orders to break out of the box and the simpler local tendency to pack the box become evident. The box is there (and packed), but visually broken wide open by a skylight that goes down the middle of the gable. Beside the house a set of exotic, very Japanese pieces of roof hooked under one another form links down the hill from the garage to the house itself. There are exactly these shapes in various Japanese imperial palaces, and a close relationship could be noted to what Frank Lloyd Wright built at Fallingwater to link

House in San Rafael, interior (Baron Wollman)

House in San Rafael, section

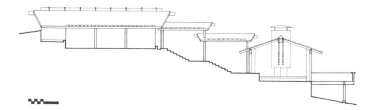

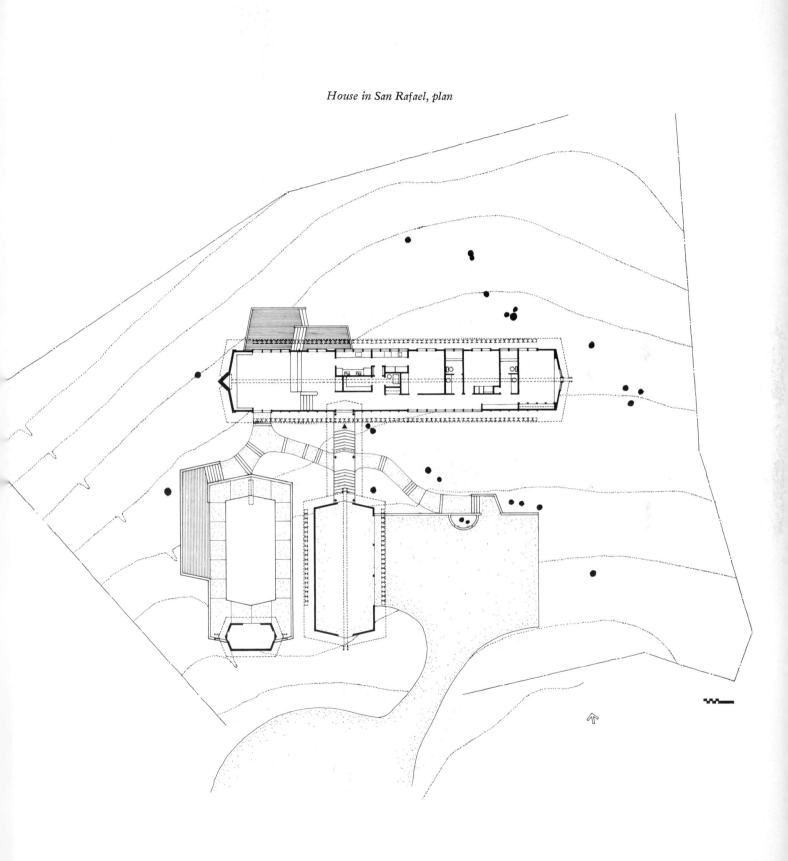

House in San Rafael, plan

the guest house with the main house, though the idiom is much more reminiscent of the Japanese sources than of Wright. The inversions and the tolerance of tensions in this work of Henrik Bull and the others included here open it to the label "mannerism," a nomenclature not, I think, particularly appropriate, since it suggests a super-sophisticated and generally purposeless playing around, in the manner of Giulio Romano. The surprises in this house of Bull's are, instead, hard at work in the service of the solution of problems. The gabled shoebox itself, for instance, is sliced open at the ridge, so that a glass strip up the end of the house and across the top and down the other side pulls the house apart in search of escape from claustrophobic enclosure, in a gesture which seems to be one of the prime psychic characteristics of these last years of Bay Area architecture. The details around the glass slot engage in a very sophisticated harking back to precedents from Frank Lloyd Wright and from the first decade of this century, and to the Japanese progenitors of those precedents, but where both Wright and the Japanese were modulating deep shadows, Bull's version is in the service of light.

The second parallel route through the third phase of the Bay Area Tradition is, for me, most easily describable in the work of myself and my partners in Moore Lyndon Turnball Whitaker. Three of us counted ourselves Californians. Three others of us had studied with Louis Kahn, and were excited by his diagrammatic clarification space as it had been developed in his Trenton bath house and after. And we were very much affected by California barns, and the responsive way they were put together. We had, among us, two basic versions of the Kahn diagram, both put together like a California barn: the first, a central served space with servant spaces hung on like saddlebags (though they really looked more like sheds), is illustrated in the Bonham cabin of 1961 and the Talbert house of 1962. The second is based on a central space with four posts, and manipulates servant spaces between that center and the edge of the house. Two quite different versions of that format occur in the Jobson house of 1961 and my own house in Orinda in 1962.

The Bonham cabin in the Santa Cruz Mountains cost not much over $7000 when it was built in 1962. Located in a dark redwood grove, it is built around

M/L/T/W, *Bonham house, Big Sur, 1961, axonometric*

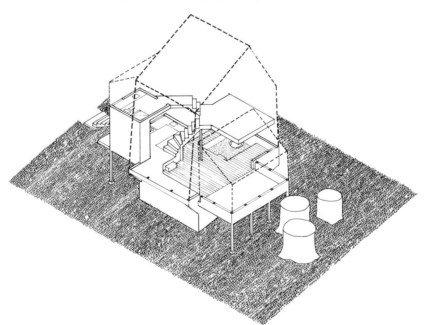

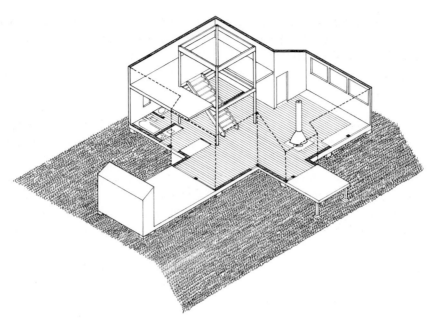

M/L/T/W, *Jobson house, Big Sur, 1961, axonometric*

a fourteen-foot square central space, really a miniature tower lined in white, with lean-to "saddlebag" spaces containing a bathroom and kitchen, a fireplace area, and a screened porch. We didn't at all mind, at that price, if it looked cheap. We were all delighted with Catherine Bauer Wurster's appraisal of her husband's practice, which by then had included some very expensive houses: "No matter how much it costs," she had said, "it will never show," and since our own buildings boasted the authenticity of tiny budgets, we exulted in the overt cheapness of asphalt roll roofing (dolled up with two-by-two battens), plywood siding, a flimsy chimney, and industrial sash, which was then the least expensive window available. But we were anxious for grandeur, too, in what was meant to be a very small great house, and looked for it in the great height of the main space, and the extraordinarily large window. The floor area of the house is so small that there is hardly any room for furniture; the substitute is seat-height changes of level, which allow you to sit anywhere with your feet on the next level below, so as to minimize the distance to the upper bedroom deck, permitting a short flight of stairs (which was all there was room for) to bridge the gap.

In 1962 the Talbert house, on a very steep site in the Oakland hills, gave a chance to extend the Bonham cabin diagram vertically. Here again is a central space with shed-roofed "saddlebags" hung on it, but this time the central space is higher and has large balconies alternately on the north and south sides of the tower which allow space inside to snake continuously down. On the top (entry) level is a bedroom, with a panoramic bathroom in a saddlebag. Stairs (also outside the central space) lead down to a dining balcony, with the kitchen in an adjacent saddlebag. Farther down still is a glassy bay, then at the bottom of the central space, seating around a fireplace.

Our other idea was initially represented in the Jobson house in Big Sur, a cabin only slightly larger than Miss Bonham's. We had read in Sir John Summerson's *Heavenly Mansions* about the importance of aediculas, four-postered pavilions where Egyptian pharaohs had ritually had their vigor renewed and statues of medieval saints had been enshrined. Summerson said that modern architecture did not include such an element, a situation we thought should be remedied. Primitive huts, we had also been told, were often formed around four posts, generally with a hearth in the middle, the edges of the hut then con-

Bonham house, exterior from chimney side (Baer)

Bonham house, interior showing big window (Baer)

M/L/T/W, *Talbert house, Oakland, 1962 (Baer)*

M/L/T/W, *Jobson house, Big Sur, 1961 (Baer)*

Jobson house, dining room (Baer)

figured to meet specific requirements of the inhabitants. In the Jobson cabin, we sought to base a scheme on an aedicular center (though here used for a stair to a mezzanine instead of for a fireplace), with a skylit top and a roof sloping off regularly on all four sides from the four posts ("like a redwood tent," according to a celebrated tent maker). The width of the space, therefore, is a determinant of its height, so that when the space is narrowest the high eave allows for a sleeping mezzanine; when it is slightly wider, in the dining area, it forms a high space, which allows vertical windows to frame the spiky redwoods outside; over the wider living room seating area the eave is lower, the space cozier, the windows pushed more horizontal, which accords with a gentle view up the valley. A special low window allows a view into a creek outside. All this, as in the Louis Kahn plaid, creates a very strict spatial framework within which many of the architect's decisions are fixed beforehand.

A second house based on an even more extensive set of geometries was built for me in 1961 in Orinda.

Jobson house, living room (Baer)

MOORE, *Moore house, Orinda, 1961* (Baer)

Moore house, interior with shower (Baer)

It includes two aediculas of different sizes, formed by large wooden columns placed to hold up a symmetrical roof over a square plan, though the symmetry of the openings lies about a diagonal axis, so that patterns are overlaid. There is yet another pattern here, of layers of implied insideness (from the shelves to the shower in one of the aediculas), to enhance the diagrammatic quality of the dwelling without losing the apparent easiness that goes with the location of this little square house on a round meadow in a grove of oaks. Here every decision, from the purchase of the large columns before there was even a design for the house, to leaving off any corner supports which would have solidified the square plan, was taken to press for a kind of toy grandeur, as would befit a (very) small great house.

Three other houses of M/L/T/W show a variety of changes rung on these two themes. The Jenkins house of 1962 (already illustrated on p. 268) is a version of the saddlebag scheme which puts the rooms themselves into shed-saddlebags and stacks

Moore house, interior with barn doors open (Baer)

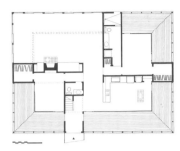

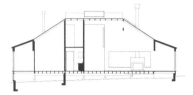

MOORE & TURNBULL, *Budge house, Healdsburg, 1966, plan*   *Budge house, section*

Budge house, bedroom with walls raised (Baer)

TURNBULL, *Tatum house, Monterey Bay, 1973* (Baer)

them in a spiral around a square central court open to the sky. Here this need to overlap the sheds to maintain continuous interior circulation fixes the roof heights, hence the widths of the rooms (based on a constant steepness of the roofs).

The Budge house, near Healdsburg on a knoll studded with oaks, adapts a regular plan to the classical rectangular format of the simple California farmhouse. An innovation here, in a vacation house for the long, hot, dry, and drowsy summers (which are in full contrast to the brisk summer months in San Francisco), is a set of overhead doors which turn three-quarters of the house. into a screened porch. Again, a simple notion is employed at a surprising scale, to reconnect with the diagram, while inside, as in a barn, the space expands into the reaches under the hipped roof, with a drawbridge across the center at the upper level to develop elements of mystery and remoteness (for the area beyond the bridge) in this simple finite box.

William Turnbull has designed in the years since 1965 a series of houses composed of rooms under sheds along a high, generally skylit circulation spine, which allows a freeing sense of continuous space. In

Tatum house, interior with stairway (Baer)

his Tatum beach house on Monterey Bay of 1973, he further expands the circulation into a three-story shanty with a baroque double staircase occupying the whole north shed of the house, while the living room occupies a south shed, and all the servant and sleeping spaces are piled up on three levels in the central spine. Here, the actual sense of one's own motion up the stairs activates the spatial drama.

Along the third route are a series of houses which sometimes bear a close resemblance to those along the second route: fairly smooth materials, trim and generally simple details, and surprising juxtapositions of rather spartan shapes are characteristic of both. But where the buildings of the second route surprise the inhabitant with exuberant verticality of space within some fairly simple collections of boxes, the buildings of the third route rely less on space and more on the animation of the volume with light, masterfully manipulated. The central figure on this third route is Joseph Esherick, whose earlier essays at "packing the box" and raising the California barn were discussed in Chapter 4. His work since 1960 has depended less and less on the renowned California easiness that has been treated through most of this book, in which indoors and outdoors join through walls of glass, as he has relied more and more on the careful choreographing of natural light, admitting it in sheets and shafts and moving pinpoints that dapple walls. His detailing, for instance, of the edges of skylights so that no shadow will edge the flowing brightness of

Skylight in a Joseph Esherick house

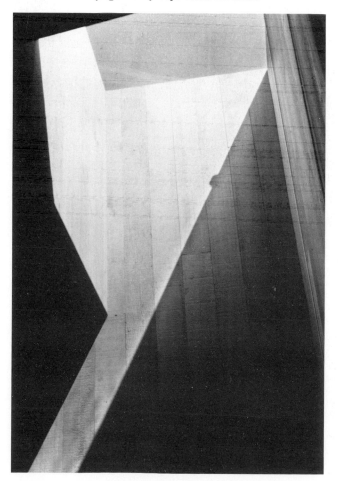

PETERS & DODGE, *Graham house, Berkeley, 1963 (Baer)*

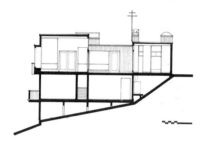

Graham house, section

Graham house, interior (Baer)

the wall which catches the light is at a level of care reminiscent of South German rococo churches rendered in white plaster by eighteenth-century genius stuccateurs.

Richard C. Peters has worked with Esherick and teaches lighting as well as architectural design at the University of California at Berkeley. He and Peter Dodge (of Esherick Homsey Dodge & Davis) designed the Graham house in the Berkeley hills in 1963. Under flat roofs, its spaces are much more contained than those in the works along the second route, but are animated by light, entering high and low and

through the ceiling, dappled by the shade of the neighboring eucalyptus.

A much more recent house, the Falk house in Berkeley, built for a family which had inhabited the Graham house but had grown too large for it, was designed in 1974 by Peters, Clayberg & Caulfield. Again the light plays on the white walls inside, while bleaching oil lightens the cedar walls outside to enhance the play of shadows on the cubic boxes.

At the Sea Ranch, Dmitri Vedensky, who had worked with Esherick, achieved in 1974 in his own house in the forest a smaller-scale, more animated

PETERS, *Falk house, Berkeley, 1974* (*Rob Super*)

Falk house, interior toward living room (Rob Super)

Falk house, plan

VEDENSKY, *Vedensky house, 1974 (Dmitri Vedensky)*

play of light and shade, depending on the contrast between rich wood surfaces and many bright-colored objects.

Almost fifteen years before, Joseph Esherick's Cary house of 1960 had begun to develop these concerns. It again is a fairly simple box, elaborated by the eyelashes and eyebrows of overhangs which soften the transition from the simple box to the bright light of the outside. There, I think, for the first time in several centuries, the windows came clearly to be seen not just as walls of glass as in earlier houses, nor as holes in solid walls, as in still earlier ones, but rather variously as chances to pick up light along a wall or floor or to look at a view through an opening shaded by trellises, each window responding to the special aspects of what lay beyond or the quality of entering light. The effects inside in three dimensions are far more complexly developed than they would have been in earlier Bay Area buildings, to get the pleasures of light on more surfaces. Not the extent of the space but the way the light falls in it is the key ennobling factor.

Twelve years later, the Romano house by Esherick Homsey Dodge & Davis, an elegantly understated but

Vedensky house, interior (Dmitri Vedensky)

Vedensky house, plan

ESHERICK, *Cary house, Mill Valley, 1960 (Roy Flamm)*

big fragment of a California barn, reflects pressures toward simplification and clarification, even as the light is fractured and sparkled through vertical railings and trellises over the windows. Inside, increasingly relaxed and increasingly nostalgic collections of furniture and juxtapositions of detail are by now allowed within the clear limits of this simple shape. On the shingled exterior the windows again are more than ever specific, not walls of glass but pieces of glass doing the one special thing they were set up to

do. They illuminate a highly controlled juxtaposition of dark woods (in the ceilings this time) and white walls, overlaid with a lush array of furniture and pillows and excitement in the bookshelves. There is now play between big and little spaces: main spaces and bays and special places to come to rest or be, very specific again and very softly comfortable in ways that nobody would have accused houses of the quarter century before of having been.

The routes that have brought Bay Area domestic

Cary house, interior showing window wall (Roy Flamm)

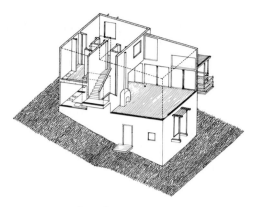

Cary house, axonometric

architecture from 1960 to the present dump us onto a muddled intersection of the present and the future, where finding enough mutually reinforcing signals to guess at what may happen seems almost hopeless. Construction of individually designed and built houses in the Bay Area is at a low ebb, with materials and labor very expensive (compared with multiply built condominia and townhouses), land almost absurdly costly, costs still rising, and volume way down. In addition, new laws reflect in frozen horror

Cary house, plan

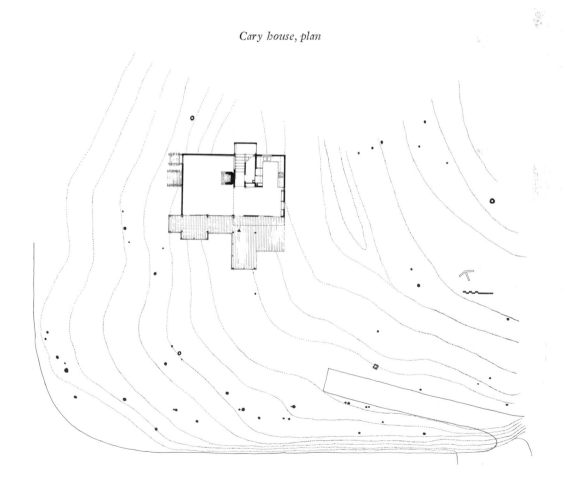

ESHERICK, HOMSEY, DODGE & DAVIS, *Romano house,
Kentwoodlands, 1972* (Baer)

Romano house (Baer)

Romano house, interior (Baer)

Romano house, plan

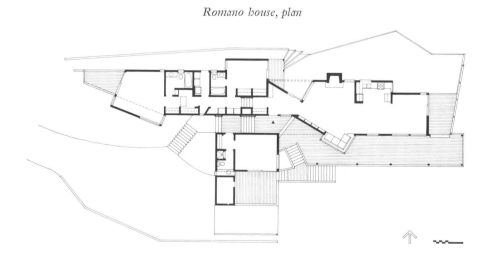

WURSTER, BERNARDI & EMMONS, *Baer house, Monterey, 1965* (Baer)

the energy crisis, and forbid the walls of glass which have allowed the close connections between indoors and out that were a central part of the Bay Area's arcadian drama. It seems a good time to signal the end of an era.

By way of a goodbye offering I proffer six houses I think indicate especially well where we've just been and even where we may be going:

The first (and oldest) of the six is Morley Baer's house in Monterey of 1965, one of the last works from William W. Wurster's own hand, powerful and simple inside its stone exterior, elegant at its fireplace wall, more unabashedly nostalgic than would have been possible in the decades before, but with a char-

acteristically Wurster twist: the Baers had liked the stone fireplace in Wurster Bernardi & Emmons' 1949 house in Woodside (illustrated on pp. 176-80) and wanted a fireplace like that, so Wurster made their house like that on the *out*side, then made the fireplace of three great pieces of granite on the wood wall. The details in this house of the great master of simplicity are taut in their refinement; the whole seems to be passing from the earlier more casual Bay Area idiom to a celebration of naturalness which would have brought delight to the heart of a Zen tea master.

The second house in the collection is the Hecht house of 1973 in San Francisco by Marquis Associates, Peter Winkelstein in charge. It is a large house,

304

Baer house, fireplace wall (Baer)

on many levels, which open up vertically to a skylit space and out to a dizzying steep hillside through walls of glass, making for constant surprises in the hills so close above the city. As the section shows, indoors are boxes within boxes, flooded with light, but then the light is played with and sparkled, divided by small-scaled elements like the close-together verticals of the railings. The space is not only developed, but made habitable and then inhabited by the stairs that slide up through it. Interior views as well look through windows into the high space, down through glass walls to the terrace, and down again, in leaps that would make the acrophobic blanch, to the city far below. The sophisticated manipulation of space

and light of this past decade is here, with power and elegance, at a great price.

Much more modestly, Ivan Poujiatine of the firm AGORA in 1973 developed a more rustic house in Mill Valley, with excitements of space and light but less precision in the details. They suggest economies (like the use of salvaged timbers) which the future may well mandate for those individual houses which are built.

The last three houses are altogether fringe to the Bay Area dwellings of these past seventy-five years, but they may well describe some avenues of the future. In 1965 John Campbell of AGORA made a houseboat for himself under some of the same pres-

MARQUIS ASSOCIATES, *Hecht house, San Francisco, 1973* (*Ezra Stoller*)

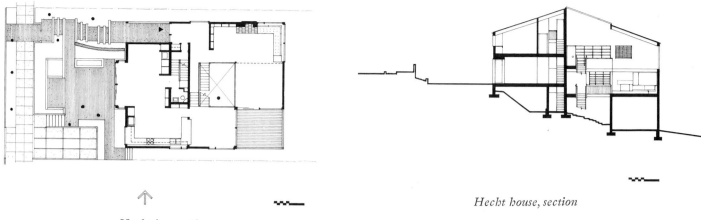

↑

Hecht house, plan

Hecht house, section

Hecht house, interior (Ezra Stoller)

POUJIATINE, *Poujiatine house, Marin County, 1972* (Peter Xiques)

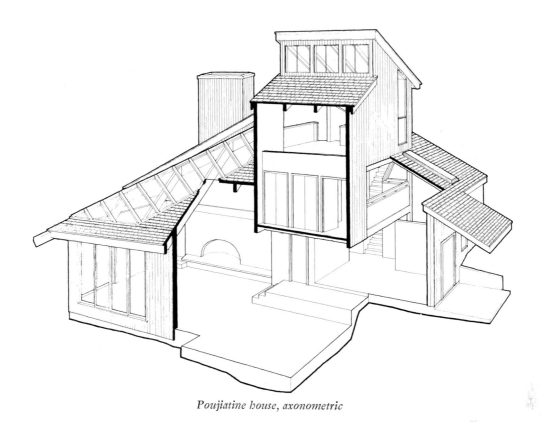

Poujiatine house, axonometric

sures that have forced residents of Asian cities off expensive land into the harbor. He bought a greenhouse and put it on a barge, then partitioned it and shaded it with plastic and slats.

Those who exercise the "wood-butchers' art," making their homes by hand with a pastiche of old parts and new at Canyon or on the Bolinas Mesa or at a number of other places, are continuing the participatory spirit that welled up in the sixties and perhaps finding a way for many to have a house that they feel a part of, and are willing to spend a great deal of time on, and can possibly even afford, if they are not too sorely beset by regulatory agencies. The owner/artists are generally in for some physical discomforts and must usually develop considerable tolerance for visual lacunae. But the do-it-yourself system does offer a chance for the future.

The main chance, though, I believe, is the chance to put new dwellings into old ones, to get the same excitement from the collision of old forms and new ones that earlier builders got from inserting themselves into the Bay Area's still-arcadian landscape. The Solomon house in San Francisco gets its excitement from the increasingly arduous requirements about holding houses up. Here steel bents do that for an old house, and their collision with the old frame provides the occasion for some high art. It's probably not the Third Phase of the Bay Area Tradition anymore, but it points the way to what we may hope will come next.

CAMPBELL, *Campbell houseboat, adrift, 1965 (Joshua Freiwald)*

ingled dome by Jamie and Tom Archer, window by Bruce Sherman,
Kim Hick, and Lou Galetti, 1973 (Bruce Sherman)

SOLOMON, *Solomon house, San Francisco, 1972, remodeled interior*
(*Joshua Freiwald*)

Solomon house, diagram

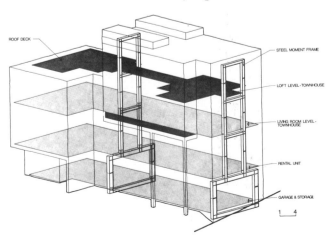

ROOF DECK

STEEL MOMENT FRAME

LOFT LEVEL - TOWNHOUSE

LIVING ROOM LEVEL -
TOWNHOUSE

RENTAL UNIT

GARAGE & STORAGE

1   4

7

Arcadia
Revisited

SALLY WOODBRIDGE

In the previous chapters, various authors have explored the ways in which an architectural tradition took root in the Bay Area in the 1890s and flourished, by means of permutation, through several generations of architects and clients into the 1970s. As David Gebhard explained in the Introduction, this tradition has not been the dominant way of building in terms of volume. But it has become a way of building frequently identified with this place. Now, as the twentieth century draws to a close and the acceleration of information exchange has created an ever-broadening market for architectural images, it is appropriate to bring our inquiry about tradition in the Bay Area up to date.

Cobbled from local and imported pieces of the past, the Bay Area Tradition has used the most plentiful, and therefore economical, materials in current methods of construction. Sustained by an emotional involvement with the land and the climate, its architects have shunned theory while making an ideological use of materials such as redwood. Previous chapters have shown how the tradition has fed on itself while being cannibalized in turn by the rest of the world. Roger Montgomery consigned the Bay Area's architectural legacy to the world, while Charles Moore wrote a tentative obituary for Arcadia.

But the decade from 1976 to the late eighties has shown — to paraphrase Mark Twain — that the reports of the tradition's death have been highly exaggerated. The regional strain in Bay Area design is alive and well; it continues to mutate in healthy ways.

Charles Moore's prediction of fewer and fewer single-family houses was shared by many. Certainly the diminishing number of sites and the rising costs of building have been no surprise. Among the more disagreeable surprises in the mid-1970s were the sky-rocketing interest rates and costs of energy. Since, for most architects, designing houses consumes more time and attention than their fees recover, these constraints indicated that the custom-designed house would become unaffordable for most designers and clients.

Yet, if the quantity of such houses has diminished, the quality has, on balance, held up. Moreover, with the expanding pride and interest in the Bay Area's architectural heritage, refurbishment of the existing houses has increased. Awareness and self-conscious emulation have strengthened the Tradition.

The dwellings presented here respond as before to urban and suburban contexts and to old and new challenges. Perhaps the major challenge today is finding a building site. Many communities which were the loci for the treasured houses presented in previous chapters have now adopted "no-growth" measures. Existing sites, be they steep hillsides formerly considered unbuildable, or patches of land in dense urban areas produced by demolition of other buildings or the subdivision of larger parcels, are affordable only to the very rich. Thus the Tradition's elitist quality, also noted by Gebhard, is increasingly based on wealth alone. An educated preference for the simple life rooted in the land is much less likely to influence current taste in the design of houses than it did in previous generations—never mind that apparently "simple houses" now take what was once a fortune to build.

Recent history did provide one unprecedented and influential turn of events in the world-wide energy crisis of the mid-1970s. The new building codes produced by this crisis affected the design of houses through new requirements for proper orientation and regulation of the amount of glazing permitted in a building. "Solar" became a household word. But if meritorious displays of energy-conserving strategies mark—even mar—the appearance of many houses designed in the late 1970s, the best designs strengthened the relationship between structure and climate without making a visual fuss about it.

The current taste for historical reference in design has produced adaptations—even direct quotations—of the stylistic hallmarks of Bernard Maybeck, Ernest Coxhead, and William W. Wurster, as well as the anonymous rural and urban buildings of the past.

Our first two houses evoke the barn and the ranch house

as though Arcadia still flourished. The house designed by William Turnbull and Associates for William and Jean Allewelt was completed in 1977. The Allewelts are from Sacramento and San Francisco respectively. After nearly ten years in the San Joaquin Valley, they moved to the San Francisco peninsula where they lived from 1963-1977. Their return to the Valley was by choice. The land they purchased is not far from the Pope Ranch on which William Wurster built the house discussed in Chapter Four. Though both the Pope and the Allewelt houses share the California barn/ranch image, they offer contrasting ways of evoking that image. Although they did not state a preference for a barnlike house, Bill Allewelt's position as President of the Tri-Valley Growers, a fruit and vegetable canning cooperative, and their plans to have a walnut grove beside the house called for a house that suited their ties to the land. Perusing Jean Allewelt's collection of houses clipped from magazines over the years, Turnbull sensed a preference for simplicity and light-filled interiors. The clients were also interested in combating the fierce valley summer heat by

WILLIAM TURNBULL & ASSOC., *Allewelt house, near Madera, 1977 (Rob Super)*

Allewelt house, view from garden (Rob Super)

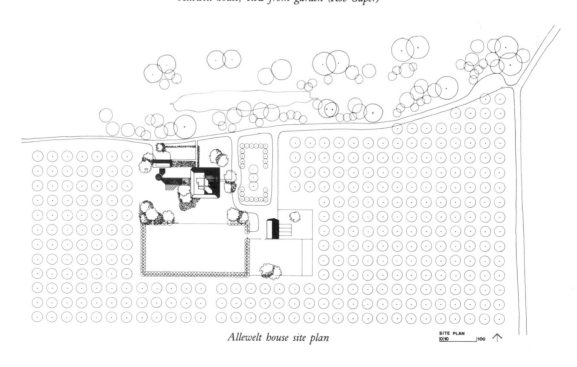

Allewelt house site plan

SITE PLAN
|0|10 |100

means other than air conditioning.

Standing beside the walnut grove, the completed house looks very like a barn. Upon closer inspection, it induces a feeling of nostalgia by appearing to be falling into ruin. Ragged incisions in the roof, revealing the rafters, suggest the onslaught of decay. In reality this is functional symbolism; the openings are vents which allow the house—and the occupants—to breathe during the torrid summers. To assist the air cooling process, a "street" was cut diagonally through the boxy volume of the house in the direction of the prevailing summer winds.

The street's other function is to separate the sleeping quarters of the parents from those of the children, which will one day be a guest wing. Enlivened by shadows cast by sunlight filtering through the roof rafters, the street is an ever-intriguing indoor-outdoor living room, with a fireplace and cooking area near the kitchen. Other areas—the more formal front living room and the encircling veranda—provide places for various social occasions.

Nineteenth century colonial settlement in California furnished twentieth century designers with building prototypes that have proved to be most adaptable not only in form but also in materials. From the Mediterranean via Mexico came the use of adobe brick walls, often combined with wood. Adobe was left the color of earth or, when lime could be extracted from sea shells and other sources, whitened with plaster. For several reasons the venerable stone buildings which enrich our perception of Mediterranean scenery are missing from the California landscape. In northern California, wood was plentiful and accessible while good building stone was not. (The granite wall of the Sierra was not ready-at-hand.) Wood buildings also withstood earthquakes better than unreinforced masonry. When the preferred redwood became less plentiful and more expensive, stuccoed wood frame buildings, often scorned in northern California as cheap and tacky, became respectable. The ability of stucco to mimic adobe and even stone suited a variety of purposes. Simple, stuccoed walls capped with tile roofs helped to recall California's Hispanic past. Stuccoed buildings could be given a strong geometry to mark the human presence in a landscape dominated by natural forms.

These and other thoughts were uppermost in the mind of Andrew Batey when he undertook the design of the John Leonards' house in a tributary of the Napa Valley. The clients had come to San Francisco from Chicago. They planned to live in the city and spend weekends tending a

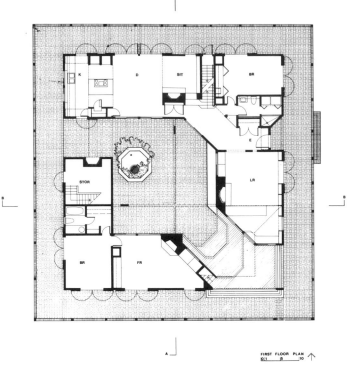

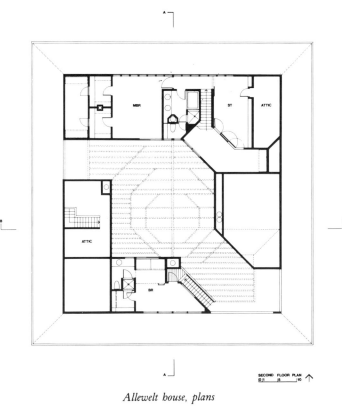

Allewelt house, plans

316

Allewelt house, interior of court (Rob Super)

BATEY, *Leonard house, Napa, 1977 (Henry Bowles)*

Leonard house drawing, plan

vineyard for which they had acquired 75 acres of an old cattle ranch. Soon, weekends were not enough; they felt compelled to make the whole enterprise part of their daily lives.

Their decision to build was accompanied, as it often is, by a search for the ideal house and architect. In a book on landscape architecture, they found their ideal expressed in the plan of a typical 1850s California ranch house. The plan showed three simple blocks of space set at right angles to each other to form a court open at one end. Covered passages connected the rooms; the whole was framed by a low wall. The materials were adobe brick, tile roofs, and wood framing members and posts. Having identified their ideal,

Leonard house, living room interior (Henry Bowles)

they chose their architect, Andrew Batey, because he lived in the Napa Valley and had designed houses there that they liked.

As completed in 1977, the house expresses its origins mainly in its general form and colors. The red, standing-seam metal roof hints at tile through its color, but also bows to the old barn on the property. The round *corredor* columns are of concrete, but the floors are terra cotta tile from Mexico. The plastered concrete block walls are white on the inside and go well with the wooden ceiling truss rubbed with white gesso. The plan permits a separation of parents' and children's bedrooms in two wings. Through a simple entrance door, the courtyard garden is partially visible at

the end of the *corredor*. The 3000 square feet of living space is distributed symetrically around the court.

A year after completion of the Leonard house, Andrew Batey formed a partnership with Mark Mack, a Viennese architect, who had come to California in 1976. Batey and Mack were committed to a purist approach to architecture—they called it Neo-Primitivism. Eschewing historical eclecticism as superficial, they preferred to look back to building traditions which integrated decor with construction and emphasized elemental forms and a limited palette of materials. Plans were worked out by testing clients' needs on a series of basic plan types: the square, rectangle, cross, "L", "U", and "H".

Leonard house courtyard (Henry Bowles)

Though the Kirlin house, designed by the partners and completed in 1981, has definite affinities with the Leonard House, it is developed more along the "rationalist" lines of Neo-Primitive philosophy. The controlled use of solar energy influenced the plan in several ways. Courtyards buffer the northeast and southwest sides of the house. The amount and availability of sunlight dictated the small openings on the north side and glazed walls of the southwest court. The use of broad overhangs creates a covered perimeter for the southwest court which prevents the sun's strong summer rays from reaching the interior. Tile floors and the massive concrete block fireplace and wine storage room store the sun's heat in winter.

The sense of ambient comfort experienced either sitting in the sun-warmed winter court (the house is bermed on three sides to increase this effect) or in the shaded summer court proves the efficacy of the plan. The strong earth color and stepped parapet around the metal roof remind us more of the traditional adobe buildings of the Southwest than

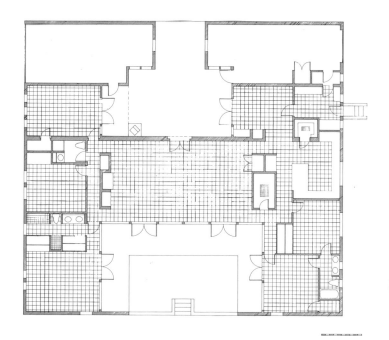

Kirlin house, plan

BATEY/MACK, *Approach to Kirlin house, Napa, 1981 (Henry Bowles)*

Kirlin house, living room and court (Henry Bowles)

those of California. But the designers have adhered to the Mediterranean ideal in their response to the critical factors of landscape and climate.

Although the house in the vineyard or the orchard stems naturally enough from the "ranch house" family tree, a functional association with rural pursuits ceased to influence the choice of this prototype long ago. As our next house demonstrates, continuity is as much a matter of the family tree of architects as of house types. Designed for southern Californians who moved to northern California, this Marin County house compounds references to place with tributes to previous architects whose work is strongly associated with California. Not only does its design bow to the Hispanic rancho, but it filters this prototype through the work of William W. Wurster and Cliff May, the two progenitors of the mod-

ern ranch house in northern and southern California, respectively. Wurster and May never collaborated and might well have resisted the idea. However, they proved to be most compatible when brought together, figuratively speaking, by architect Charles Moore and his clients, Lou and Miriam Licht.

For many years the Lichts owned a house in west Los Angeles designed by Cliff May for himself in 1939 and remodeled by him in 1949. The house used wood siding and adobe brick; it had broad overhanging roof eaves, and spread, low to the ground, in a U-shape on its three-acre site. After two of the four grown-up children moved to northern California and taxes on their property soared, the Lichts decided to move north. They bought a one-half acre corner lot in Marin County on a road winding up to Mt. Tamalpais.

MOORE, *Licht house, Mill Valley, 1980 (Alice Wingwall)*

Licht house entrance (Alice Wingwall)

A dozen or so scrub oaks and four great pine trees studded the sloping site.

They chose Charles Moore as their architect because as Miriam Licht put it, "We had read his books; we liked his outlook, and, although the one Moore house we saw did not suit us, it perfectly suited its client."

Moore and his clients worked through cardboard models, cutting them up this way and that, to reach a consensus about the design of the house. Although the Lichts did not necessarily want a recapitulation of their Cliff May house, they did want a modern farm house. For his part, Moore envisioned fusing influences from the southern and northern parts of the state through an architectural recall of William W. Wurster's early houses. He particularly favored the Gregory farm house, discussed in previous chapters. A May-Wurster-Moore house also seemed a fitting use of his own experience designing houses in both locales during his peripatetic career.

One of the study models was a two-part farmhouse connected by a stepped hall 32′ long, 20′ high and 8′ wide. At each end were two large dormer windows. The south-facing one framed a large Monterey pine. A subsequent meeting

Licht house, hallway and entrance to upper level (Sally Woodbridge)

involved further changes made by slicing up the model again. The Lichts worked out small scale needs and desires with Nicolas Pyle, Moore's associate in the office who managed the project. They found a young Danish contractor, Steen Moller, whose command of craftsmanship made the most of the materials.

Beyond a white grapestake gate and fence, the entrance court is framed by the downhill garage and workshop wing of the house, the upward slope of the hill opposite it, and the wall with the main entrance. A covered walkway, or exterior *corredor*, begins at the garage, runs past the kitchen door, and turns the corner to continue for two more bays, one of which has a sunken garden court. The last bay straddles a wooden bridge to the door. Inside, the stair landing affords an opportunity to sense the plan of the house from the midpoint of the north-south axis. To the north a short flight of steps leads up to the bedroom wing; to the south

Licht house, view from entrance to lower level (Alice Wingwall)

the stairs lead down to the living areas of the house. Trees and sky are framed in the tall dormer windows at each end. The upper wing has a tree house quality; the lower level spaces are joined by a few steps. Two sitting rooms, both small, occupy the southwest corner of the house. The lowest has one wall with shelves and another with glass doors opening into the greenhouse; it recalls the formal parlor with its showcase of household treasures, most of them ceramics by Miriam Licht. Up a few steps and offset from this space is a second, less formal sitting area, more like an inglenook, with a built-in couch and a fireplace. The lower landing of the *corredor* leads, through glass doors, to the generous deck raised above the downward slope of the site and pierced by the trunks of oak trees which partially shade it. Separated by a largely glass wall, deck and kitchen have a pleasant reciprocity. With a backdrop of resawn wooden cabinets painted white to reflect light from the skylights above, the kitchen is, appropriately, the main stage of this modern farmhouse.

The house fits so comfortably into the ranch tradition that the hand of its designer is scarcely noticeable. Elements such as the cut-out arches in the court and the vertical accent of the stair hall reveal that this is a Moore and not a May or Wurster creation. But the main effect is one of synthesis. What in the 1950s would have been a one-floor H-plan has become a subtle split-level design incorporating traditional elements of both the mid-19th and the mid-20th century ranch house.

Rarely are clients so anchored in the California tradition as the Lichts were. Still, there are other appropriate matches of people, tradition, and place. In another part of Marin County, architects Richard Fernau and Laura Hartman were given the challenge of designing a house for a newly arrived Italian family who wanted to recall the family's country villa near Rome where they were accustomed to spending their summers.

Their California landscape was a fair match for the old Italian one and, overall, well endowed with rolling oak-studded hills. But the actual building site for the house was restricted to a narrow strip of land defined by active slide areas. (Nature is rarely so permissive in California as appearances suggest.) The linear form and plan of the house, which runs parallel to the hillside in a north-south direction, uses this constraint to advantage.

To gain maximum southeast exposure for the house, the

FERNAU/HARTMAN, *Marin County villa, 1983 (Mark Citret)*

SITE PLAN

N 0 10 20 50

Marin County villa, site plan

architects worked out a plan in the shape of a key. The back of the house follows the hillside; the front steps in and out, multiplying the possibilities for sunlight from the south and making complementary indoor-outdoor spaces along a generous terrace.

The approach to the house from the drive at the south end leads up the steps and along the raised terrace to the main entrance. At intervals along the way, the path widens to include small spaces which complement interior rooms. Beyond the terrace a panorama of hills and valley stretches to the horizon. The narrow width of the house makes the view as accessible to the rooms inside the house as it is to the terrace.

Inside the entrance at the north end of the house, a stair hall leads to the living room as well as to the lower and upper halls. Set down a few steps, the living room is a full stop with the fireplace on axis with double glass doors. The room is a discreet space implying formal occasions and a comparable attitude for its occupants. This hierarchy of living spaces from informal to formal, from the familial to the adult world is echoed on the upper floor by the location of the master bedroom.

In contrast to the typical 3,000 square foot house of the previous two decades, this is a house with rooms. Space does not flow unimpeded along a horizontal plane. Rather, it is orchestrated as a sequence of separate spaces experienced

327

Marin County villa, view toward terrace from dining room (Mark Citret)

Marin County villa, view of terrace outside dining room (Mark Citret)

Marin County villa, view of terrace outside dining room (Mark Citret)

temporally not visually. This approach has the effect of expanding the house although the visual quality of "spaciousness," for which the open-plan house was noted, is absent. Instead of the flat or tilted single-plane roof of the postwar Modern house, a gabled roof with cross gables articulates the upper floor bedrooms and hallway.

Though there is no overt expression of energy conservation, Fernau and Hartman were very conscious of this aspect of the design. In addition to its southeast orientation, the house's narrow section with well-placed operable windows, awnings, and transoms offers the maximum opportunity for cross-ventilation. The top floor hall, which runs the length of the house, serves as a means of circulation for air as well as people. During the hot summer days, the hall windows can be opened to pull the prevailing southeast breezes

Upper hallway, Marin County villa (Mark Citret)

329

through the house. The hall color is, appropriately, an icy blue. In the traditional Mediterranean manner, the occupants regulate their interior environment by opening it up or closing it off.

This "villa" succeeds in capturing the familiar Mediterranean image of a strong, manmade form standing out against the hillside, yet wedded to it by earthen color. By contrast, another house Fernau and Hartman designed in Marin County in 1985 is likely to all but disappear into its landscaped setting in future years. The clients planned it largely for retirement when they would satisfy their passion for gardening. In 1904, Charles Keeler, an ardent publicist for the "simple life" lived in the north Berkeley hills and wrote a book, *The Simple Home.* In it he said, "Hillside architecture is landscape gardening around a few rooms for use in case of rain." Keeler might as well have been writing about this house.

As with the former house, this is a long, narrow, two-story, stuccoed house that forms a wall along the east property line. The kitchen, the most important room, is pulled out into the garden where it meets a trellis which, in turn, joins two other trellises to form an H-shaped plan of complementary inside and outside spaces. Surrounding this living area is an orchard interspersed with gardens. The house is walled and turns in upon itself; the elevation facing southwest is configured for views of the garden and Mt. Tamalpais beyond. In its isolation from its immediate surroundings and use of borrowed scenery, it creates a rural context for a very small parcel of land in a conventional suburb.

The Large-Small house, discussed in Chapter Four, continues to be a constituent element of the Bay Tradition. Maybeck was known for hand crafting his small houses. He personally laid floors, painted decorative motifs, and experimented with materials. Now that residential sites are

SITE PLAN

FERNAU/HARTMAN, *Marin County house site plan*

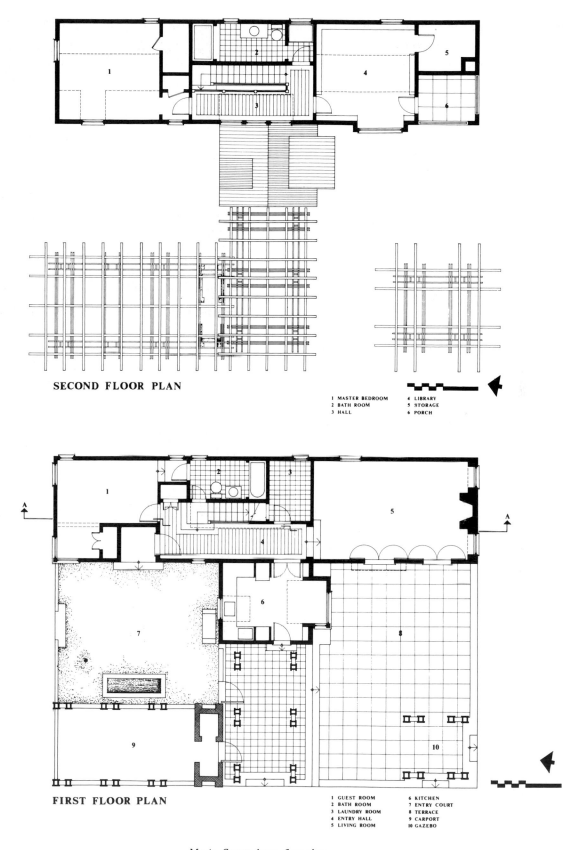

SECOND FLOOR PLAN

1 MASTER BEDROOM   4 LIBRARY
2 BATH ROOM   5 STORAGE
3 HALL   6 PORCH

FIRST FLOOR PLAN

1 GUEST ROOM   6 KITCHEN
2 BATH ROOM   7 ENTRY COURT
3 LAUNDRY ROOM   8 TERRACE
4 ENTRY HALL   9 CARPORT
5 LIVING ROOM   10 GAZEBO

Marin County house floor plans

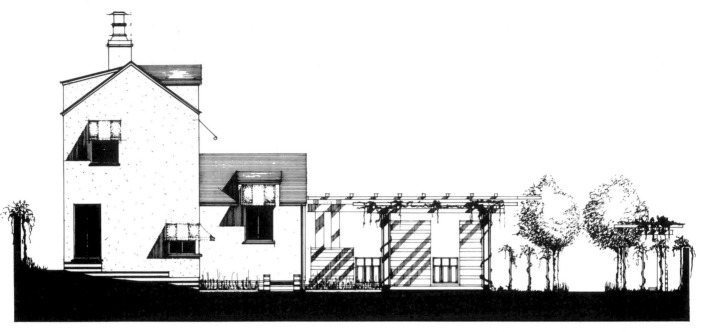

NORTH ELEVATION

Marin County house, north elevation

Marin County house, west elevation

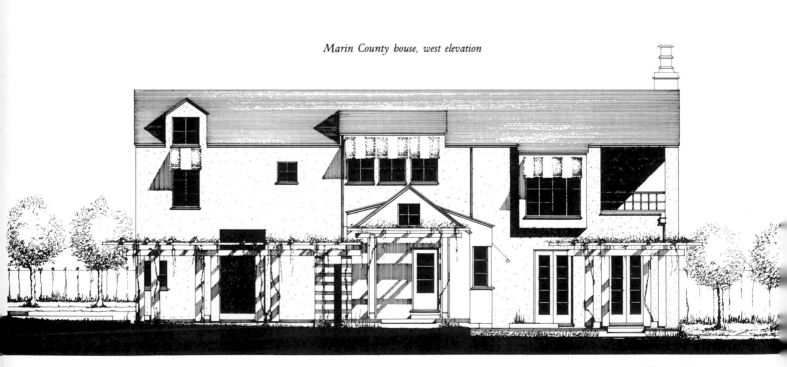

WEST ELEVATION

measured out in smaller and more expensive pieces, fledgling architects and clients are, more than ever, likely to reach for greatness in the small house. Young architects and clients often face the challenge of compressing dream houses into old and dense contexts and, to keep the price down, doing parts of the building with their own hands.

A good example of this phenomenon is the Tibbitts house, designed by Glenn Lym and built between 1976 and 1978. Paul and Leslie Tibbetts and Glenn Lym, Leslie's cousin, had grown up together. As children the cousins had planned houses; Leslie had grown up in a 1950s house designed in Berkeley for her parents by their uncle, who was an architect. Such things foster expectations not easily fulfilled, but fate was generous. Through family connections, they came by a sliver of land near downtown Berkeley with a tiny shingled cottage on it.

At first they wanted to save the cottage, which had been a real estate sales office. But its lack of foundations made the addition of a second story impossible. They decided to salvage the porch and the front gate, framed by a palm and a redwood tree, and to raze the rest. From the street nothing appears to have changed. A path made of bricks from parts of the old cottage leads to an entrance door on the side of a tall, narrow shingled box. The structure is only thirteen feet wide at the front and seventeen feet wide at the back where the trapezoidal plot of land broadens.

Since the house could not expand horizontally, Lym put the main living space in the center of the structure where it reaches up to the skylit roof. On either side of this light, airy room are two-story sections with loft-like bedrooms above that look into the living room. (Since the Tibbettses had once dreamed of remodeling a barn, the idea of sleeping lofts appealed to them.) On the ground floor at the front of the house is a tiny room with a bay window. This private space is introduced by an arched entrance with columns at the top of a few steps. A bit of architectural fanfare in the form of a stepped opening also introduces the kitchen.

Above the parlor is the master bedroom which gains a feeling of spaciousness by means of a sloping ceiling with a skylight and a tree house view of thick branches through the windows. Both the main bedroom and the children's room opposite it have windows opening into the living room which permit inter-communication on this level.

The stair has an unintended eccentricity which contributes to the spatial illusion of the house. Because the stair walls run parallel to the slanting west wall of the house while the stair treads run perpendicular to the straight wall, one has the feeling of mounting in a moving plane. Space is again distorted when, at the top of the stair, the diagonally-laid floor boards contradict the direction one's feet have been pursuing.

Since the Tibbetts' budget could not accommodate the

Tibbetts house living room, looking toward front of house (Rob Super

level of craftsmanship they admired and longed for, they had to supply it with their own hands. They learned to cut and lay shingles for the interior living room walls as well as finish the other wood surfaces. They even plugged the 2,000-odd nail holes in the floors.

If it is the exceptional client who performs the role of the craftsman on his house, it is an accepted way of build-

ing for architects. Still, the structurally integrated decorative program which architect Thomas Gordon Smith designed and executed for his large-small Richmond Hill house, in Richmond on the East Bay, was exceptionally ambitious. Though radically different from the Tibbetts' approach, Smith's house stands firmly in the Bay Area Tradition.

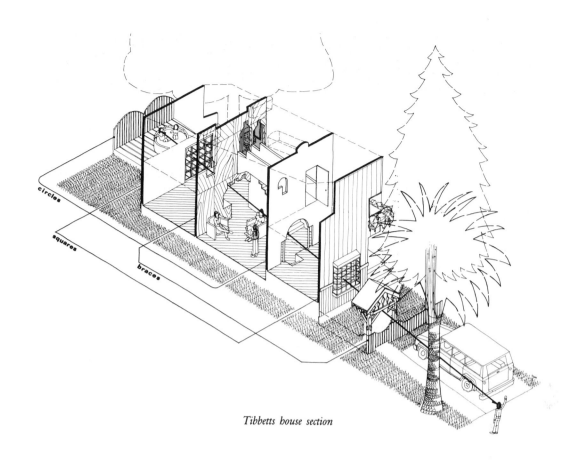

circles

squares

braces

Tibbetts house section

Tibbetts house, site and floorplans

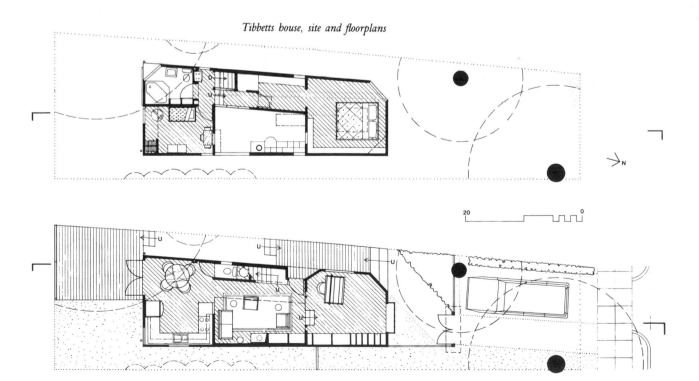

N

20   0

SMITH, *Richmond Hill house, Berkeley, 1983-84 (Henry Bowles)*

A native of Berkeley and a graduate of the University of California in painting and architecture, Smith had admired Bernard Maybeck's work since his student days. A Rome Prize took him to that city in 1979 where he spent the year versing himself in the architectural theories of Bernini and Borromini as well as academic treatises on Roman wall painting. From these sources, he developed a personal approach he called "literate Classicism." Upon his return home, he designed two small Classical villas on speculation to test his ideas. The family house was his second constructed commission.

Since he could not afford to replicate the Classical details of the buildings he admired, Smith took to haunting marble and stone yards, salvage companies, and even demolition sites. Nostalgia was not his motive. Later, after living with the re-used shards he had incorporated into his house, he concluded that he would have preferred designing the parts to fit the whole instead of doing it the other way around.

The house has a strong vertical emphasis. The approach, by means of a pergola on paired columns (salvaged from a tubercular sanatorium in Livermore), is formal and markedly different from the neighboring houses which turn their backs on the street. A wall revetment of reused marble and Texas limestone enriches the facade. The monumental effect of this combination of elements and materials is tempered by the intimate scale of the entrance porch.

The smaller paired columns of this porch (also salvaged from the sanatorium) support a tall, narrow, second-story bay proportioned to frame a large arched window. Three such windows came from the demolished St. Anne's Home in San Francisco.

Once inside the door, the airy openness of the upper floor beckons the visitor up the stairs rather than into the strictly functional ground floor dormitory. At the top of the stairs is the dining-kitchen space which extends across the stair well. Above this space is a play loft for the children.

The climactic moment is the living room at the back of

Richmond Hill house, dining room (Henry Bowles)

Richmond Hill house, living room (Henry Bowles)

the house on which Smith lavished much of his creative energy. Here, a square comprising about half the floor area frames a diagonal composition of two ovals. The northwest corner of the house, at one end of the axis, has a view of Mt. Tamalpais through arched window openings set in a shallow alcove. At the other end, an interior alcove with a balcony above it contains a virginal. Triangular alcoves in the other corners convolute the room without taking up precious space. The black concrete floor set with colored aggregate and fragments of marble in a terrazzo of geometric patterns also reflects the room plan in its design. Smith not only designed the floor but executed all but the final finishing.

The room is an integrated composition, a set piece, in which Smith worked out his ideas about synthesizing elements of historical Classicism in response to present needs and constraints. While the spatial concept comes from the Baroque, the decorative scheme follows the third style of Roman-Pompeian wall painting. The hallmark of this style is a black background. The colors of the painted vignettes are typical of this style. Smith executed the paintings in four straight days on the wet, integrally-colored plaster walls.

Though the black walls absorb a lot of light, the brightly colored paintings seem to replenish it. The room is far from gloomy.

The paintings' theme is the passage of time. Four scenes from the mythical life of Persephone symbolize the seasons. Below each scene, vignettes with flowers and birds also refer to the seasons. Around a painted oculus in the ceiling, small scenes in nine interlaced triangles depict the stages of life for man and woman. A final sequence marks the century's progress with impressionistic sketches of gas stations. This bit of whimsy was inspired by the area's chief landmark, a gigantic gas storage tank. A final touch which lifts the room into another time and place is a selection from a verse by Thomas D'Urfey, set to music in the late 17th century by Henry Purcell:

On the brow of Richmond Hill
Which Europe scarce can parallel
Every eye such wonders fill
To view the prospect round
Where the silver Thames doth glide
And stately courts are edified.

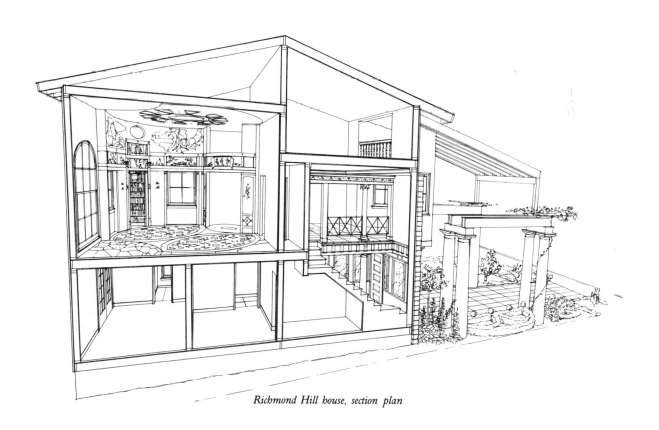

Richmond Hill house, section plan

Apparently, this heavy load of symbolism did not make the room intimidating. Early on, the Smiths noticed that their children had turned the floor into a board game, using its patterns for hopscotch or toy car tracks. Another benefit of the concrete floor is its capacity to store the sun's heat on cold days.

Although the architect earnestly wished to give Classicism an everyday reality, when viewed from the world that is real for most of us, his house expresses one of our enduring fantasies: the one in which we escape from ground floor reality into an Arcadian realm.

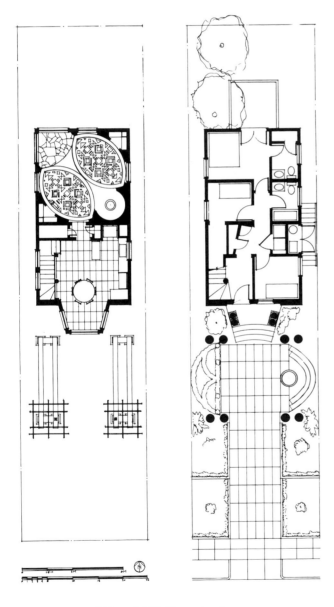

Richmond Hill House, site plan

Jeremy Kotas is another architect who relishes the spirited and often irreverent manipulations of stylistic vocabularies that animate the work of Coxhead, Polk, and Maybeck. In designing a house for himself in San Francisco's Mission district, Kotas decided to invoke the past selectively. Since he had very limited means to do this, he had to substitute allusion for three-dimensional reality. For example, a Classical arched parapet capping the facade has been reduced to a steel hoop embedded in the roof.

A flagpole gives a vertical staccato accent to the low-lying mass visible from the street. Mediterranean California is expressed in the simple, white stuccoed geometry and the tiled entrance steps. Passers-by have been astonished to see a standard, overhead garage door opening off the raised entrance terrace where no car can get. This relatively inexpensive means of opening up a wall of the house to permit inside and outside to flow together also reminds us that California is as wedded to the car as to nature. The house steps back from the street in a series of planes and descends a story and a half down the hill. Kotas worked out the geometry of the house by rotating the diagonal of a 16′ square to form a Golden Mean rectangle the width of the house. The main space is 12′ high and 24′ square. Since the sub-spaces are alcoves partially visible from the main space, movement from front to back is necessary to reveal the spatial geometry. Light from a three-story stairwell illuminates the mid-section of the house.

Like many of the houses on this street, Laidley Castle, as Kotas dubbed it, gives the impression that a smaller older house has been extended over time by a series of additions.

Kotas has planned to endow his street with yet another amalgam of Bay region architecture. This was to take the form of a small house set in a niche in the hillside opposite Laidley Castle. As designed, a stacked sequence of openings and projecting bays takes up most of the facade. The entrance is in the side of the house at the top of a flight of steps. The historical allusions mostly consist of overscaled balusters on a split-level balcony which expresses, as do the stepped windows, the rise of the interior stairway. Coxhead had used this kind of architectural punning on his otherwise blank facade at 3234 Pacific Ave. Kotas thought to pay tribute to this inspired economy of expressive means. Alas, the house has not been built, but it may yet be; and when it is, architectural historians will rejoice in the discovery on faraway Laidley Street, of two examples of the kind of self-conscious continuity a tradition needs to remain supple.

KOTAS, *Laidley Castle, San Francisco, 1980, 1984-85 (Larry Harrel)*

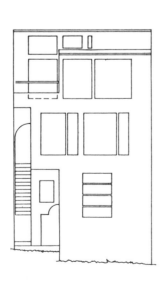
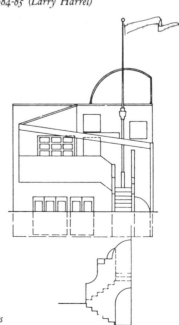

Laidley Castle, elevations

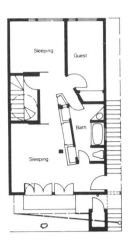
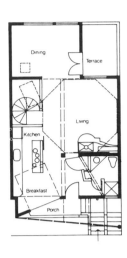

Laidley Castle, floorplans

Laidley Castle interior (Mark Citret)

Laidley Castle, drawing

KOTAS, *Laidley Street project (unbuilt)*

343

To build in an historic Bay Tradition context is a rare opportunity these days. The Hermitage, a 7-unit condominium on the top of Russian Hill, resulted from a lengthy battle over zoning for the hill which, among other things, demonstrated that San Franciscans had become conscious of their city's architectural heritage.

The generally modest character of the hilltop's residential development made it refreshingly different from Nob Hill, its complement to the south, where residential towers and hotels are the norm. In the postwar lull of the 1950s when most prospective home builders went to the suburbs, development of the quiet hilltop seemed unlikely. The only contemporary building was a house built on its Taylor Street slope.

Still, the growing market for in-town dwellings with views made Russian Hill an obvious target for new towers. In 1959, when the zoning for the hill was reviewed, residents lost their appeal for single residence zoning. Instead, the hill was zoned for highrise residential structures for which there were several building applications. Battles followed between the hilltop community and a developer who acquired the property on which two of the hilltop's earliest buildings stood. These were one of the three simple shingled houses built by a Mrs. Marshall in 1888 and the cottage at the end on the brow of the hill where Joseph Worcester had lived. These and other neighboring buildings (discussed in Chapter Two), such as the Polk-Williams house, testified to the hill's fame as a turn-of-the-century gathering place for Bay Bohemians. In one day, without any notice to the neighbors, the two humble buildings were demolished.

This act aroused the community to action. Organized as the Old Russian Hill Association, residents launched a series of appeals which lasted until 1962, when the developer tired of waiting and offered the group the opportunity to purchase the site, which they did. The Association also acquired the site across the street in front of the original Livermore farmhouse and a site on Green Street which backed up to the Vallejo Street site. There the matter rested, for no developers came forward to build what the group wanted: 18 units on the north side of Vallejo and 8 on the south side, instead of the 120 originally planned.

In 1970, a 40-foot height limit was applied to the hill. By then the group had reduced its program to 18 units with a two-and-one half to one ratio of parking to residential unit. The design was to be in the tradition of the two best known architects represented by houses on the hill: Willis Polk and Julia Morgan, and also compatible with the two remaining Marshall houses next door. Esherick Homsey Dodge and Davis were hired to design a building for the north site.

The work of this local firm threads its way through the second and third phases of the Bay Tradition. Joseph Esherick, whose work of the late 1940s and 1950s imbued postwar Modernism with a regional character, founded the firm. In the 1970s, George Homsey, Peter Dodge, and Charles Davis became partners. The firm continues an approach to design that is relatively resistant to fashion. In designing the Russian Hill condominiums, George Homsey, principal designer on the project, studied houses by the first generation of Bay Tradition designers. Although the building's massing appears to have been freely derived from historical precedent, it was almost wholly determined by restrictions on the site. The legal constraints generally concerned the view rights of the neighboring buildings. Easements and air rights held by apartment houses fronting on Green Street modeled the north and east sides of the structure, while consideration for the scale of the Marshall houses next door influenced the west side. Although no legal restrictions existed on the Vallejo Street facade, the clients and the designer agreed that it would be an affront to the character of the street to have a wall rising abruptly from it when the adjacent houses were set back from the roadway in a traditional suburban pattern. The schematic model the architects built to demonstrate the effect of the restrictions on the building's mass conformed almost exactly to the final design.

The building materials—wood shingles and painted wood trim—and architectural features: gable roofs and balustrades patterned after Polk's design for the Vallejo Street balustrades, relate the building to its context and persuade the viewer that the tradition is still lively.

The condominium structure is significantly larger than its neighbors. At about 3,200 square feet, each unit is comparable in size to the houses Esherick was designing for individual sites in the city in the 1950s. Seven houses are packed into one envelope—a jump in density which hardly responds to current market demands. Since many of the older houses on the hill are by now multi-unit dwellings, the pressures for increasing the density of the hill's population have, in a modest way, been accommodated through internal adjustments. Though not the rural enclave it once was, Russian Hill has preserved its distinctive character and

ESHERICK/HOMSEY/DODGE/DAVIS, *The Hermitage, San Francisco, 1984*

The Hermitage from end of Vallejo Street

its continuity with the past.

Existing buildings are not the only reference for new design. Topography and street patterns frame the picture of a place. One born-and-bred San Francisco architect who has worked with evangelical zeal to promote an appreciation of the city's grid pattern as a design element is Daniel Solomon. A resident of Telegraph Hill (the Solomon house is discussed on p. 311), Solomon has been studying San Francisco's block patterns and housing types since the 1970s, both in design studios at U. C. Berkeley and as a consultant for the San Francisco City Planning Department.

Like most American cities, San Francisco was laid out on a grid plan to facilitate the sale of land. Since a Mexican mayor, Francisco de Haro, commissioned the first city survey, the unit of measurement was the Spanish vara, which was about 2'9". In the subsequent American surveys, the standard lot size worked out to be 25' wide by 100' or 125' deep. For the streetcar suburbs that covered hills during the second half of the 19th century, a residential building type evolved quite rapidly. Two and three-unit buildings, two bays wide, were set on raised basements of varying height, depending on the slope of the site. Entrances were sometimes in the center but more often on the side. Facade styles changed, but plans remained more or less the same, as they

SOLOMON & ASSOC., *Pacific Heights Townhouses, San Francisco, 1979 (Joshua Freiwald)*

have in row houses everywhere. The persistent use of bay windows, no matter what the style, enlivens the buildings' profiles, while the topography of hills works the tiers of houses into fine-grain tapestries.

Solomon is not just concerned with the streetscape. He considers the buildings to be a "permeable screen between a public world of streets and a private world of courtyards and gardens." While consulting with the city on a new zoning ordinance in the late 1970s, Solomon got a chance to practice what he was preaching in a housing project at Sacramento and Lyon streets. Called the Pacific Heights Townhouses, the project consisted of a continuous band

of buildings on a 112' x 127' corner lot. The facade pattern reflected the 25' grid in a composition of bay windows stacked above garages with entrances on one side. Cornice lines and setbacks matched those of older housing. This "screen" was indeed permeable; entrances opened into a back garden court where there were two more units. Since much of the city's older housing stock has mid-block housing—cottages that were often slipped into back lots—this pattern is also typical.

These shingled townhouses were completed in 1979. In 1982, Solomon designed a two-unit building for a single lot on Russian Hill. The approach was the same: the facade

Pacific Heights Townhouses, site plan

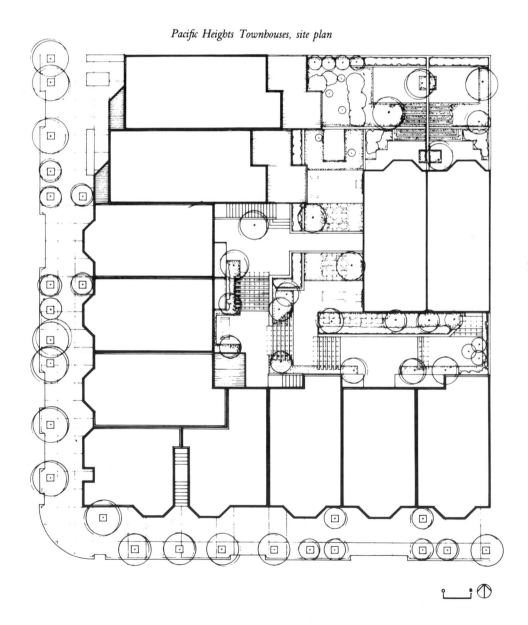

uses contemporary window sash and other detail in a variation on the vernacular styles found throughout the city's older neighborhoods.

The latest in the series of modest housing projects from this office is Amancio Ergina Village, completed in 1986. The project occupies one of the last unbuilt sites in the second phase of the Western Addition Redevelopment area. A previous design had been taken all the way through the approval process, but was mired in financial difficulties. When it halted, the mayor's office asked a housing expert, James San Jule, to assume the development responsibilities, which he did on a *pro bono* basis. He then asked Solomon to redesign the project.

The Amancio Ergina project offered non-profit, cooperative housing to people whose income limited down payments to 5 and 10 percent. No federal financing was involved. Seven other kinds of subsidies were needed to make it possible for low income people to live there. By the time Solomon got the project, the budget was fixed.

While the opportunity to rebuild a piece of the former

SOLOMON & ASSOC., *Glover Street Condominiums, San Francisco, 1982 (Henry Bowles)*

Glover Street Condominiums, floor plans

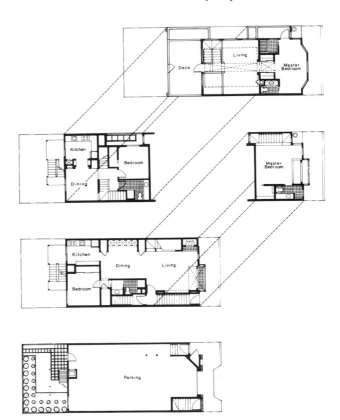

SOLOMON & ASSOC., *Amancio Ergina housing, San Francisco, 1985 (Henry Bowles)*

streetcar suburb was exhilarating, the reality of having to redesign the project and have it completed in five short months was appalling. The legacy of the earlier design was not altogether negative. Because the Redevelopment Agency had approved it and the three-quarter block site had been cleared, parking was permitted on the surface in the middle of the site instead of having to be put underground. This meant that both parking and security measures fit within the budget.

The completed project fits so smoothly into the neigh-borhood that it hardly seems new. The architects achieved an impression of 25-foot-wide building fronts by visually dividing the 50-foot fronts with stacked, projecting bays and staggered cornices. An A-B-A pattern of windows in the upper part of the bays strengthens the row house image. All but four of the 72 units have entrances from both the street and the court. A stoop precedes the security gate; behind it, more steps lead to a landing with the unit entrances. Back porches and stairs are boldly composed to create a strong visual interest for the buildings' back sides.

Amancio Ergina housing (Henry Bowles)

The court itself suggests the right mix of neighborliness and privacy, of openness and security.

The last building in this selection of current work by Bay Area architects takes us back to the hills. It is a four-story, two condominium building shoe-horned onto what must be the last patch of buildable land on Telegraph Hill's east side. ACE Architects, David Weingarten and Lucia Howard, the building's designers, have a reverence for Bay Tradition architects of earlier generations. Like others of this generation of Bay Area architects, they received their architectural degrees from U. C. Berkeley and were influenced by architects such as Joseph Esherick, who taught there.

The condominium site is on Darrell Place, a narrow pedestrian lane about one block long. Darrell starts at the Filbert Street right-of-way, which features a discontinuous wooden

Amancio Ergina housing, courtyard side of buildings (Henry Bowles)

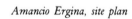

Amancio Ergina, site plan

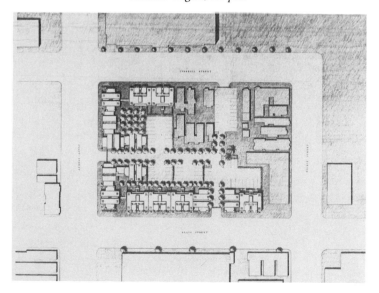

stair (the grade was too steep for a street) leading downhill through a garden maintained by the residents. Downhill from Darrell is Napier Lane, a Gold Rush vintage boardwalk with houses to match in character if not dates. Houses on Darrell are less homogeneous, but the general ambience of the hill pulls everything together.

The architects intended the design as an archaeology of the Bay Tradition, an homage to Maybeck, Wurster, Esherick, and Moore. They described the design as a collision of three emblematic buildings. The pseudo-masonry of scored and rough-cast stucco on the ground floor contains a vaulted undercroft or cave, the place of origins. Inside, Baroque overtones in the wall treatment and in the plan of the oval study combine with the monumental red fireplace and cast steel kitchen serving island to evoke the spirit of Maybeck. The wooden upper stories, which incorporate a two-story atrium, stand for the evolution from the open, horizontal plan of the 1940s and 1950s to the tight, vertical

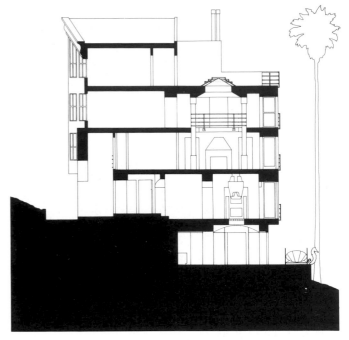

ACE ARCHITECTS, *Darrell Place Condominiums, section*

Darrell Place Condominiums, floor plan

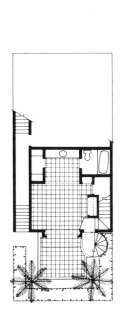  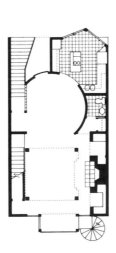 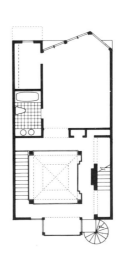 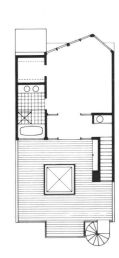

Darrell Place Condominiums, San Francisco, 1986 (Christopher Irion)

Darrell Place Condominiums, living room in upper unit (Christopher Irion)

Darrell Place Condominiums, view to study in lower unit (Christopher Irion)

one of the 1960s and 1970s. The layers are blended rather than neatly sorted out. Maybeck is again recalled in the two-sided bay window, while a section of bold cornice molding on the roof also speaks of Coxhead and Polk.

This symbolism is well integrated into the design of the whole. Appreciations and enjoyment of the building do not depend on deciphering a cleverly contrived historic code.

We hope that the Bay Tradition will have many more chapters. One of the reasons for this hope is that the work which we consider to be in the tradition does not represent a comeback of has-beens. Indeed, the strength of this vaguely structured tradition lies in its susceptibility to personal interpretation. And, although limits to building opportunities loom larger than ever, as long as people manage to build dwellings in an increasingly crowded environment, the tradition will continue to inspire lively solutions.

Darrell Place Condominiums, rear view (Christopher Irion)

Notes

FOREWORD TO THE NEW EDITION

1. David Gebhard, Harriette Von Breton and Robert Winter, *Samuel and Joseph Cather Newsom, Victorian Architectural Imagery in California* 1878-1908 (Santa Barbara: University Art Museum, U.C.S.B., 1979).

2. David Gebhard, "Architectural Imagery, The Missions and California," *The Harvard Architectural Review*, Vol. 1, Spring 1980, pp. 137-145; David Gebhard, "Some Additional Observations on California's Monterey Tradition," *Journal of the Society of Architectural Historians*, 46:1 (June 1987):157-170;Karen J. Weitz, *California's Mission Revival* (Los Angeles: Hennesey and Ingalls, 1984); David Gebhard, "The Monterey Tradition: History Reordered," *New Mexico Studies in the Fine Arts*, Vol. 7, 1982, pp. 14-19; David Paul Bricker, *Built for Sale: Cliff May and the Low Cost California Ranch House*, unpublished M.A. thesis, University of California, Santa Barbara, 1983.

INTRODUCTION

1. Lewis Mumford, "The Skyline," *The New Yorker* 23 (Oct. 11, 1947), 94-96, 99; *The Museum of Modern Art* 15:3 (1948), 4-21.

2. "Is There a Bay Region Style? Symposium," *Architectural Record* 105 (May 1949), 92-97.

3. *Ibid.*, p. 95.

4. *Domestic Architecture of the San Francisco Bay Region* (San Francisco: San Francisco Museum of Art, 1949), p. 5; see also: "Domestic Architecture of the San Francisco Bay Area—An Exhibition of the San Francisco Museum of Art," *Architectural Record* 108 (Sept. 1949), 119-26; "San Francisco Exhibition: Bay Region Architecture," *Art News* 48 (Feb. 1950), 52.

5. *Domestic Architecture of the San Francisco Bay Region*, p. 6.

6. Herbert D. Croly, "The California Country House," *Sunset* 18 (Nov. 1906), 50-65.

7. *Ibid.*, pp. 51-52.

8. Kenneth Reid, "The Architect and the House, No. 3: William Wilson Wurster," *Pencil Points* 19 (Aug. 1938), 472.

9. Henry-Russell Hitchcock, "An Eastern Critic Looks at Western Architecture," *California Arts and Architecture* 57 (Dec. 1940), 22, 23.

10. *Ibid.*, p. 22.

11. Talbot F. Hamlin, "What Makes It American: Architecture in the Southwest and West," *Pencil Points* 20 (Dec. 1939), 762-76; "California Whys and Wherefores," *Pencil Points* 22 (May 1941), 339-44.

12. Talbot F. Hamlin, "California Fair Houses," *Pencil Points* 20 (May 1939), 293-96.

13. *Ibid.*, p. 296.

14. See: "Residential Architecture of the San Francisco Fair," *Architectural Forum* 71 (Sept. 1939), 179-94; "Architecture Around San Francisco Bay," *Architect and Engineer* 145 (June 1941), 16-55. In the exhibition "40 Architects Under 40," held at the Architectural League of New York, the following Bay area architects were represented: Hervey P. Clark, John E. Dinwiddie, Albert H. Hill, Phillip E. Joseph, and John Funk.

15. Ernest Born, "Exhibition of Residential Architecture," *California Arts and Architecture* 58 (June 1941), 24-25.

16. "More Sources in Western Living," *Sunset* 86 (March 1941), 14-15.

17. William W. Wurster, "San Francisco Bay Portfolio," *Magazine of Art* 37 (Dec. 1944), 301-05.
18. *Ibid.*, pp. 301, 303.
19. Elizabeth Mock (ed.), *Built in USA: A Survey of Contemporary American Architecture Since 1932* (New York: Museum of Modern Art, Simon & Schuster, 1945).
20. *Ibid.*, p. 14.
21. Henry-Russell Hitchcock and Arthur Drexler (eds.), *Built in USA: Post-War Architecture* (New York: Museum of Modern Art, 1952).
22. Walter Landor, "West Coast U.S.A.–Post War," *Architects' Yearbook*, No. 3 (1949), pp. 130-33.
23. The post–World War II California Ranch House represented a mixture of elements gathered from both northern and southern California. Basically though, it was a Los Angeles product, and its major popularizer both before and after the war was the Los Angeles designer Cliff May.
24. For an early article on the then-developing Third Phase see David Gebhard, "The Bay Tradition in Architecture," *Art in America* 52 (1964), 60-63; also see the "Introduction" to *A Guide to Architecture in San Francisco and Northern California* (pp. 11-27), by David Gebhard, Roger Montgomery, Robert Winter, John Woodbridge, and Sally Woodbridge (Santa Barbara and Salt Lake City: Peregrine Smith, 1973).

2. LIFE IN THE DOLLHOUSE

1. Advertisement of Gladding, McBean & Co., in *Architect and Engineer* 99 (November 1929), p. A.
2. Eugene Neuhaus, "Unique Store Building in Berkeley," *Architect and Engineer* 83 (November 1925), 57.
3. *Ibid.*, 56.
4. The work of Thomas, Jones, and Comstock was never extensively published during the 1920's. A drawing of the Hume house in Berkeley by Thomas appeared in an advertisement for Ariston Steel Windows in *Architect and Engineer* 39 (April 1931), 18. Hugh W. Comstock's work of the twenties has recently been published in *The Fairy Tale Houses of Carmel*, by Joanne Mathewson (Carmel, 1974). W. R. Yelland's work was better published: see "Work of W. R. Yelland, Architect," *Architect and Engineer* 75 (December 1923), 52-62; M. E. Goss house, Piedmont, *Architect and Engineer* 85 (May 1926), 106; Dr. D. Richards house, Berkeley, *Pacific Coast Architect* 31 (June 1927), 31-32; Thornberg Village, *Architect and Engineer* 90 (August 1927), 34, 65, 66; Harry E. Miller, Jr., house, Atherton, *Architect and Engineer* 106 (August 1931), 38; "Some Recent Work of W. R. Yelland," *Architect and Engineer* 118 (August 1934), 10-17.

5. For additional illustrations of the twenties work of Henry A. Gutterson see: William McDuffie House, Berkeley, *Architect and Engineer* 73 (April 1923), 79-82; Raymond T. Farmer house, *Architect and Engineer* 96 (January 1929), 41-42; J. E. Rich house, Berkeley, *Architect and Engineer* 97 (April 1929), 113; Dr. Herbert M. Evans house, Berkeley, *Architect and Engineer* 98 (August 1929), 71-73. For examples of the twenties work of Walter H. Ratcliff, see: "Portfolio of Recent Work of W. H. Ratcliff, Jr.," *Architect and Engineer* 84 (February 1926), 88-103; Dr. Hubert Heitman house, Berkeley, *Architect and Engineer* 91 (October 1927), 97-98; house of F. L. Naylor, Berkeley, *Architect and Engineer* 96 (January 1929), 93.
6. W. R. Yelland, "The Auvergne Village," *Architect and Engineer* 66 (August 1921), 66.

3. WILLIAM WILSON WURSTER:
AN ARCHITECT OF HOUSES

1. William Wurster, "Competition for U.S. Chancery Building, London," *Architectural Record* 119 (April 1956), 222.
2. William Wurster, "Architectural Education," *AIA Journal* 9:1 (January 1948), 36.
3. William Wurster, "College of Environmental Design, University of California. Campus Planning, and Architectural Practice," Regional Cultural History Project, General Library, University of California, Berkeley, 1964, p. 270 (in the Bancroft Library). Quoted by permission of the Director of the Bancroft Library.
4. William Wurster, letter to *California Engineer* 14 (November 1936), 52-53.
5. William Wurster, "The Outdoors in Residential Design," *Architectural Forum* 91 (September 1949), 68-69.
6. William Wurster, "College of Environmental Design, University of California Campus Planning and Architectural Practice," Regional Cultural History Project, General Library, University of California, Berkeley, 1964, p. 269 (in the Bancroft Library). Quoted by permission of the Director of the Bancroft Library.
7. William Wurster, letter to Mr. Arthur McK. Stires, Architectural Editor, *House & Garden*, January 24, 1940 (never published).
8. William Wurster, "A Home in the Hills," *Sunset* 65 (July 1930), 23.
9. William Wurster, "From Log Cabin to Modern House," *New York Times Magazine*, January 20, 1946, pp. 10-11.
10. William Wurster, "Four Houses in California," *Architectural Record* 64 (May 1936), 35.

11. William Wurster, letter to William Adams Delano, May 15, 1933 (never published).
12. William Wurster, "San Francisco Bay Portfolio" *Magazine of Art* 37:8 (December 1944), 300-5.
13. William Wurster, "Is Imagination a Liability or an Asset?" *House & Garden* 120:1 (July 1961), 4, 112.

4. FROM THE LARGE-SMALL HOUSE TO THE LARGE-LARGE HOUSE

1. Mel Scott, *The San Francisco Bay Area: A Metropolis in Perspective* (Berkeley and Los Angeles: University of California Press, 1959), p. 271.
2. *Domestic Architecture of the San Francisco Bay Region* (San Francisco: San Francisco Museum of Art, 1949). (unnumbered).
3. Walter Gropius and Marcel Breuer taught their first Harvard Graduate School studio in 1937. Henry Hill was a graduate student in the course, which he remembers as fundamental to the development of his architectural attitudes. The work of Gropius and Breuer, who were much more articulate than their West Coast counterparts, provided Modern architecture in the United States with a powerful dogma. The West Coast architects in the San Francisco Bay Area were viewed as a "soft sell" by comparison.
4. Gardner Dailey and Joseph Esherick, "House D-2, Magic Carpet Series," *Architectural Forum* (September 1942), pp. 132-34.
5. The symposium, titled "What's Happening in Modern Architecture?," attempted to focus on the issues of functionalism and humanism. Several hundred invited architects attended; twenty spoke, and the museum catalogued the proceedings. A witty and incisive review appeared in *The Architectural Forum* for March 1948, pp. 12-13, which closed with the following paragraph:
   While the Museum meeting did not provoke any ringing new credo of American architectural theory, it was useful as a platform for reflecting the trend of European architectural thinking. It would undoubtedly give some extra confidence to the large number of American architects who have never considered coziness the equivalent of original sin. It possibly offered some secondary conclusions: One thing the architectural participants took away was the unshakable conviction that nobody knows anything about architecture but architects. Others walked out muttering that architects are good architects, confused talkers. One thing Mumford took away was a badly bruised Bay Region.
6. Because of space limitations several architects active in the residential field at the time, such as Hervey Parke Clark, Clarence Mayhew, Anshen & Allen, Francis Joseph McCarthy, Eldridge Spencer, Joseph Stein, Bolton White and Jack Hermann, Kitchen & Hunt, and Frederick Confer are not represented by illustrations of buildings in this chapter.
7. All these architects are now established in their own firms.
8. Both Henry Hill and James Ekin Dinwiddie were deeply interested in developments in the European Modern Movement. Hill was personally convinced that with a "world class" architect in residence the Bay Area would become a major center of architectural theory and practice. In pursuit of this goal he persuaded Eric Mendelsohn to join him and Dinwiddie in 1948 in practice in San Francisco. The firm only lasted a short time, but in 1952 Mendelsohn designed a house in Pacific Heights in San Francisco which clearly shows the marriage of the Bay Region with the International Style.

5. MASS-PRODUCING BAY AREA ARCHITECTURE

1. Roger Montgomery, "Comment on Lee Rainwater's 'Fear and the House as Haven in the Lower Class,'" *Journal of the American Institute of Planners* 32:1 (January 1966), 31-37.
2. Taped interview with Francis Violich, April 29, 1975.
3. Taped interview with Vernon DeMars, April 18, 1972.
4. Violich interview.
5. DeMars interview.
6. Elizabeth Mock (ed.), *Built in USA: A Survey of Contemporary American Architecture Since 1932* (New York: Museum of Modern Art, Simon & Schuster, 1945), pp. 60-63.
7. CIAM: Congrès internationaux d'architecture moderne, international rallies of contemporary architects which took place irregularly beginning in 1928 at La Sarraz, Switzerland.
8. Quoted in Mel Scott, *The San Francisco Bay Area* (Berkeley and Los Angeles: University of Calif. Press, 1959), p. 253.
9. DeMars interview.
10. Ibid.
11. Taped interview with Joseph Eichler, July 1972.
12. Charles Moore et al., *The Place of Houses* (Holt, Rinehart and Winston, Inc.; New York, 1974), pp. 41, 34, 31, 34.
13. Violich interview.

6. THE END OF ARCADIA

1. My lists do not pretend to completeness, and do not mean to judge excellence; some important (and very handsome) houses by McCue, Boone, and Tomsik, for example, and some Donald Olsen houses for which I have a profound personal admiration are not included, because they seem to me to have more important connections with other movements elsewhere than with the three routes described here.

Architectural Biographies

WILLIAM STEPHEN ALLEN

Born in 1910, Allen received the degree of Bachelor of Architecture in 1935 and Master of Architecture in 1936 from the University of Pennsylvania. After working as a designer for the San Francisco firm of Masten & Hurd from 1937 to 1940, he formed a partnership with Robert Anshen. The firm was active principally in the field of housing in the postwar period, producing, with Jones & Emmons, the designs for Eichler Homes.

ROBERT ANSHEN

Anshen was born in 1910 and died in 1964. After receiving a Bachelor's in architecture in 1935 and a Master's in 1936 from the University of Pennsylvania, he worked as a designer for the San Francisco architect Clarence Tantau from 1937 to 1939. In 1940, he joined William Allen in partnership (see above).

ANDREW BATEY

Born in 1944 in Merced, California, Batey received a B.A. from Occidental College in Los Angeles in 1966; a Diploma in the History of Art from Oxford University in 1968; and an M.A. from Cambridge University in England in 1971. The following year he worked for Norman Foster Assoc. in London. After his return to the United States in 1973, Batey combined his own practice in Texas with work for Luis Barragan in Mexico City. In 1978, he formed a partnership with Mark Mack which was dissolved in 1986. Batey has also taught architectural design in various departments, including U.C. Berkeley, U.C.L.A., Princeton University, and the University of Pennsylvania. In 1987, he became Dean of the School of Architectural Studies of the California College of Arts and Crafts in San Francisco. He also maintains an architectural office in San Francisco.

THEODORE C. BERNARDI

He was born in 1903 and received the degree of Bachelor of Architecture from the University of California, Berkeley, in 1924. After working as a designer for William W. Wurster from 1934 to 1942, he practiced independently from 1942 to 1944 before becoming a partner in the firm of Wurster, Bernardi & Emmons in 1945.

HENRIK BULL

Born in 1929, Bull received the degree of Bachelor of Architecture from the Massachusetts Institute of Technology in 1952. He practiced independently from 1956 to 1967, principally in the field of residential design. In 1968 he became a partner in the firm of Bull/Field/Volkman/Stockwell.

CHARLES WARREN CALLISTER

Callister was born in 1918 and attended the University of Texas from 1935 to 1941. He came to California in 1946 and practiced with Jack Hillmer for a year. From 1947 to 1954, he practiced independently in the field of residential design; from 1955 to 1968 the firm was Callister, Payne & Rosse; from 1969 to 1971, Callister & Payne; from 1972 to date, Callister, Payne & Bischoff.

JOHN CARDEN CAMPBELL

Born in 1914, he received a degree from Sacramento College in 1937. From 1937 to 1940 he attended the Rudolph Schaeffer School of Design. From 1946 to 1968, he was a partner in the firm of Campbell & Wong, one of the Bay Area's major firms in the residential field. In 1970, he formed the firm of Campbell & Rocchia, and since 1971 has practiced independently.

THOMAS D. CHURCH

Church was born in 1902 and graduated from the University of California, Berkeley, in 1921. In 1925, he received the degree of Master of Arts in Landscape Architecture from Harvard University. Since 1928, he has practiced in the San Francisco Bay Area and has made a major contribution to the field of modern landscape design, principally in the decades 1930-1960.

HERVEY PARKE CLARK

The architect was born in 1899 and received the degree of Bachelor of Architecture from the University of Pennsylvania in 1921. After working in Philadelphia for Hood, Godley & Fouilhoux, he came to San Francisco, where he practiced independently in the field of residential design from 1933 to about 1970.

HUGH W. COMSTOCK

The designer was born in 1894; he spent most of his adult life in Carmel. It was during the 1920's that he designed and constructed the many small medieval fairy-tale doll-like houses which came to characterize the community. He died in Santa Barbara in 1950.

MARIO CORBETT

Born in 1900, Corbett studied design at the California School of Fine Arts. After further study of architecture in offices and through European travel, Corbett was admitted to the profession in 1932. From 1932 to the early 1960's he maintained a private practice in San Francisco which was most influential in residential design in the postwar decade.

ERNEST COXHEAD

The architect was born in 1883 in England. He was apprenticed to the architect George A. Wallis and later worked for Frederic C. Chancellor. He attended the Royal Academy of Art, and also classes at the RIBA. In 1884-85 he won the Silver Medal for drawing of the Royal Institute of British Architects. He came to Los Angeles c. 1887 and practiced there until he removed his office to San Francisco in 1890. Alone, or in partnership with his brother Almeric, he practiced in San Francisco until his death in 1933. His most productive period was between 1890 and 1905.

GARDNER A. DAILEY

Dailey was born in 1895 and was educated at the University of California, Berkeley, Stanford University, and Heald's College of Engineering. He gained further architectural training in architects' offices in the San Francisco Bay Area and also studied landscape design. He opened a San Francisco office in 1926 which had great influence in the residential field in the pre- and postwar decades. The firm had a diversified practice after 1950. Gardner Dailey died in 1967.

VERNON A. DeMARS

Born in 1908, DeMars received the degree of Bachelor of Arts in Architecture from the University of California, Berkeley, in 1931. From 1936 to 1942, he was District Architect for the Farm Security Administration's regional office located in San Francisco, where he contributed significantly to the field of low-cost housing design. In 1943 and 1944, he was Chief of Housing Standards for the National Housing Agency in Washington, D.C. From 1945 to 1949, he was in private practice; from 1953 to 1967 in partnership with Donald Reay. Since then the firm has been DeMars & Wells. In the post–World War II period he was associated with Donald Hardison in several social housing projects. In 1953 he joined the faculty of the Department of Architecture, University of California, Berkeley; he retired in 1975.

JOHN E. DINWIDDIE

Dinwiddie was born in Chicago in 1902. He attended the University of Michigan, where he did his graduate work in architecture under Eliel Saarinen. He worked in New York for York and Sawyer, and in San Francisco for Bliss and Fairweather and for Lewis Hobart. In the late 1930's he formed a partnership with Henry Hill and Philip Joseph; it was during this period that he produced his most widely known houses. He died in 1959.

PETER DODGE

Born in 1929 and recipient of a Bachelor of Arts in Architecture from the University of California, Berkeley, in 1956, he worked thereafter in the office of Joseph Esherick, becoming an Associate in 1963 and a partner in the firm of Esherick, Homsey, Dodge & Davis in 1972.

GARRETT ECKBO

Eckbo was born in 1910. He received the degree of Bachelor of Science in Landscape Architecture in 1935 and a Master of Arts in the field in 1938 from the University of California, Berkeley. As one of the chief contributors to the field in the postwar period, he has been a partner in the following firms: Eckbo & Williams, 1942-57; Eckbo, Dean & Williams, 1958-67; Eckbo, Dean, Austin & Williams, 1968-72; Garrett Eckbo, 1973-.

DONN EMMONS

Born in 1910, Emmons received the degree of Bachelor of Architecture from Cornell University in 1935. After a few years of working in Southern California architectural offices, he came to San Francisco, where he worked from 1938 to 1942 for William W. Wurster. In 1945, after serving in the Navy, he became a partner in the firm of Wurster, Bernardi & Emmons.

JOSEPH ESHERICK

Born in 1914 and recipient of the degree of Bachelor of Architecture from the University of Pennsylvania in

1937, he came to San Francisco shortly thereafter and worked in Gardner Dailey's office from 1939 to 1941. In 1946, he opened his own office, which has been a major influence in the field of residential design, although the practice became diversified in the late 1950's. The firm was Joseph Esherick & Associates in 1963, and became Esherick, Homsey, Dodge & Davis in 1972. Esherick has also served on the faculty of the Department of Architecture, University of California, Berkeley, since the 1960's.

ALBERT FARR
The architect was born in Omaha, Nebraska, in 1871. He spent most of his childhood with his parents in Japan. In his late teens he returned to the United States and worked as a draftsman for Clinton Day and for the Reid Brothers in San Francisco. In the early 1900's he established his own office in San Francisco. During the 1920's he was associated with J. Francis Ward, and the firm became widely known for its Period houses, most of which were Tudor. Farr died in 1945.

RICHARD FERNAU
Fernau was born in Chicago in 1946. After receiving a B.A. in Philosophy from U.C. Berkeley, he went on to earn an M.Arch. from U.C.B.'s College of Environmental Design in 1974. Following work with Buchanan Architects in Berkeley, New World Pictures in Hollywood, and Steiger Partner Architekten in Zurich, Switzerland, Fernau opened his own practice in the Bay Area in 1978. In 1980, he joined with Laura Hartman to form the firm, Fernau & Hartman. Fernau has also taught in the Department of Architecture at U.C. Berkeley since 1981.

ROBERT A. FISHER
Born in 1929, Fisher received a Bachelor of Arts degree in Architecture in 1952, and a Master of Arts in Architecture in 1953 from the University of California, Berkeley. After a year of private practice in 1962, he formed a partnership with Rodney Friedman in 1964, which has been principally involved in the field of housing.

RODNEY FRIEDMAN
Born in 1933 and recipient of a Bachelor of Arts in Architecture from the University of California, Berkeley, in 1956, he has been since 1964 a partner in the firm of Fisher-Friedman.

JOHN FUNK
Funk was born in 1908, and received the degree of Bachelor of Arts in Architecture from the University of California, Berkeley, in 1931, and a Master of Arts in Architecture in 1932. From about 1935 to 1938 he worked in William W. Wurster's office. Since 1939 he has practiced independently, contributing significantly to the field of residential design until 1955.

CARL GROMME
Born in 1898, Gromme attended the University of Pennsylvania, receiving a Bachelor of Architecture degree in 1923. In 1926 he moved to California, where he worked in the office of Arthur Brown, Jr. In 1934 he opened his own practice in San Rafael from which he retired in 1968.

HENRY H. GUTTERSON
The architect was born at Owatonna, Minnesota, in 1884. He was educated at the University of California and later at the Ecole des Beaux-Arts in Paris. He worked in the offices of D. H. Burnham, Willis Polk, and John Galen Howard; he also taught briefly at the University of California, Berkeley. Though he designed independently as early as 1909, he did not establish his own office until 1913. His most productive years were from 1910 through 1930. He died in 1954.

LAWRENCE HALPRIN
Born in 1916, Halprin received a Bachelor of Science degree in Plant Science from Cornell University in 1939, a Master of Science from the University of Wisconsin in 1941, and a Bachelor of Science in Landscape Architecture from Harvard University in 1943. From 1946 to 1948 he worked as a designer for Thomas Church. He opened his own office in 1949, which became Lawrence Halprin & Associates in 1972. His practice shifted from residential landscape design to corporate and civic projects in the 1960's.

DONALD HARDISON
Born in 1916, Hardison received a Bachelor of Arts degree in Architecture in 1938 from the University of California, Berkeley. He has been most active in the field of social housing and has been in private practice since 1948; the firm became Hardison and Komatsu in 1958. During the 1950's Hardison associated in several projects with Vernon DeMars.

LAURA HARTMAN
Laura Hartman was born in Charleston, West Virginia, in 1952. She received a B.A. in Art from Smith College and an M.Arch from U.C. Berkeley in 1978. Before forming the firm of Fernau & Hartman, she worked with Esherick Homsey Dodge and Davis, and as a designer with Dolf Schneiblie e Associatti, Architetti in Agno, Switzerland. She is a lecturer in the Department of Architecture at U.C. Berkeley.

ALBERT HENRY HILL
Henry Hill was born in 1913. In 1935 he received a Bachelor of Arts in Architecture from the University of California, Berkeley. He received a Master of Architecture degree from Harvard in 1937. From 1938 to 1946 he worked in association with John Ekin Dinwiddie in San

Francisco. From 1947 to 1948 he was in partnership with Eric Mendelsohn, and since then has practiced independently in San Francisco and Carmel (in association with Jack Kruse since 1970). He has been most active in the field of residential design.

JACK HILLMER
Born in 1918, Hillmer received his architectural education at the University of Texas. He came to the San Francisco Bay Area during the war and in 1946 formed a partnership with Charles Warren Callister. Since 1947 he has practiced independently.

GEORGE HOMSEY
Born in 1926, Homsey received the degree of Bachelor of Arts in Architecture in 1951. Thereafter he worked in the office of Joseph Esherick, joining the firm as an associate in 1963 and becoming a partner in Esherick, Homsey, Dodge & Davis in 1972.

JOHN GALEN HOWARD
Howard was born near Boston in 1864. He attended MIT and later the Ecole des Beaux-Arts in Paris. He worked in the offices of H. H. Richardson, of Sheply, Rutan and Coolidge, and of McKim, Mead and White. In 1894 he established a partnership with Samuel M. Cauldwell in New York. In 1901 he came to the Bay Area to open his own practice, to supervise the construction of the University of California, and to teach architecture at the university. He remained as Supervising Architect of the University of California from 1901 through 1924, and as Director of the School of Architecture from 1913 through 1928. His major work was in the Beaux-Arts mode, though a number of his domestic commissions of the early years were Craftsman and woodsy. He died in 1931.

LUCIA HOWARD
Born in Fort Sill, Oklahoma, in 1951, Howard received a B.A. in English from Wellesley College in 1973 and an M.Arch. from U.C. Berkeley in 1977. Howard and David Weingarten formed Acme Plan Preparers which was changed to ACE Architects in 1982. The office is in Berkeley. Both Howard and Weingarten have taught in the Department of Architecture at U.C. Berkeley.

CARR JONES
Born about 1880 in Berkeley, Carr Jones attended the University of California there and took a degree in electrical engineering. While enrolled at the university he studied informally with Bernard Maybeck at his home. Architecture became his avocation. He built about a dozen houses from the mid-teens to the mid-thirties, contributing much of the hand labor himself. None of them was ever published. He died in 1965.

WILLIAM F. KNOWLES
The architect was born c. 1875 and was educated at Stanford University, where he took a degree in Engineering. Between 1893 and 1895 he was a draftsman in the San Francisco office of Clinton Day. In 1897 he established his own independent practice, though he did work from time to time with other architects. His earliest work was in the shingle mode, but by the mid-1900's he was established as a major exponent of the Craftsman bungalow. He continued to practice in San Francisco as late as the 1950's.

JEREMY KOTAS
Kotas was born in Tripp, South Dakota, in 1943. He received both his B.Arch. and M.Arch. from U.C. Berkeley, in 1969 and 1971. Following graduation, Kotas worked for Frank O. Gehry Assoc. in Los Angeles from 1972 to 1974. From 1976 to 1980, Kotas managed his own office; he also worked as a staff Architect with the San Francisco Department of City Planning in Urban Design from 1978 to 1981. Since 1981, he has had a partnership with Anthony A. Pantaleoni.

FREDERICK LANGHORST
Born about 1908, Langhorst was a member of the Taliesin Fellowship from 1931 to 1936. From 1937 to 1941 he worked in the office of William W. Wurster; thereafter he practiced privately and in association with Lois Langhorst and Roger Lee. He was most active in the residential field in the 1940's.

LOIS W. W. LANGHORST
Ms. Langhorst was born in 1914. She received a Bachelor of Architecture degree from the University of Oklahoma in 1938, and a Bachelor of Science in Architectural Engineering in the same year. In 1940 she received a Master of Architecture degree from the Massachusetts Institute of Technology, and in 1966 a Master of Fine Arts from Harvard University. She practiced in association with Fred Langhorst from about 1948 to 1950, and formed a partnership with Roger Lee and Ward Higgins from 1960 to 1964. Her major work in the Bay Area was in the field of residential design in the 1940's.

ROGER LEE
Born in 1920, Lee received the degree of Bachelor of Arts in Architecture from the University of California, Berkeley, in 1941. He was associated with Fred Langhorst from 1948 to 1959, and in partnership with Lois Langhorst and Ward Higgins from 1960 to 1964. He was most actively involved in the field of residential design in the Bay Area in the 1940's and 1950's. In 1964 he moved his practice to Hawaii.

FRANCIS E. LLOYD

Born in 1900, Lloyd received his training at the University of Pennsylvania, after which he worked in the offices of Bertram G. Goodhue and Charles A. Platt. He came to practice in California about 1933 and died c. 1939.

GLENN LYM

Glenn Lym was born in June 1944, in Berkeley. After he received a B.Arch. from U.C. Berkeley in 1967, he went to Harvard University where he got a Ph.D. in Social Psychology in 1975. Upon his return to the Bay Area, he spent short periods in several architectural offices before working for Esherick Homsey Dodge and Davis from 1978 to 1986. Since 1986, he has maintained his own office in San Francisco.

DONLYN LYNDON

Lyndon was born in Detroit in 1936, the son of Southern California architect Maynard Lyndon. He received his architectural education at Princeton University and a Master of Fine Arts in Architecture in 1959. In 1960 he came to California and joined the faculty of the Architecture Department of the University of California, Berkeley, and the firm of Moore/Lyndon/Turnbull/Whitaker. He left the firm in 1965 and returned to the East, where he was Head of the Department of Architecture of the Massachusetts Institute of Technology from 1967 to 1975.

MARK MACK

Mack was born in 1949 in Judenburg, Austria. He attended Technical High School in Graz and later entered the Academy of Fine arts in Vienna, graduating in 1973 with the degree Magister Architecturae. While attending school, he worked for Steiger & Partners in Zurich and Atelier Hans Hollein in Vienna. After graduation, he came to America to work with Hausrucker, Inc. in New York until 1976. He later moved to the San Francisco Bay Area and worked as a free-lance architect and renderer. In 1978, Mack formed a partnership with Andrew Batey, and in 1985, he founded his own firm, MACK. Since 1986, he has been an Associate Professor of Architecture at the University of California.

ROBERT MARQUIS

He was born in 1927 and received his architectural education at the University of Southern California and the Accademia delle Belle Arti in Florence, Italy. In partnership with Claude Stoller from 1956 to 1973, his major work in the Bay Area in the residential field occurred in the late 1950's, after which the practice became diversified, as did many others, to include educational and larger-scale housing projects. After 1974 the firm became Marquis & Associates.

EDGAR MATHEWS

He was born in 1866 in Oakland, California. His father, Julius Mathews, was a pioneer architect in the East Bay area. Edgar Mathews attended the Van Der Naillen School of Engineering in San Francisco and then worked in several architectural firms in the Bay area. In 1897 he opened his own office in San Francisco. By the early 1900's he had established himself as an important designer of town residences.

BERNARD MAYBECK

Maybeck was born in 1862 in New York City. He studied at the Ecole des Beaux-Arts in Paris until 1886, when he returned to New York and joined the office of Carrère and Hastings. In 1888 Maybeck formed a partnership with James Russell in Kansas City. In 1889 he came to the Bay Area and commenced to design both for himself and for others, including A. Page Brown. In 1894 he began to teach at the University of California, and it was there that he met Phoebe Apperson Hearst. He prevailed upon her to sponsor a competition for a site plan for the University of California and served as the principal advisor for the competition through 1901. From 1900 through 1920 Maybeck designed in a number of modes, including the Craftsman and the classical Beaux-Arts. During the 1920's he produced a number of important designs in the Spanish Colonial revival style. He continued to design small houses through the 1930's; he died in 1957.

CLARENCE W. W. MAYHEW

He was born in 1907 and was educated at the University of California, Berkeley. He worked in the San Francisco office of Miller and Pflueger before opening his own private practice in 1934. He continued to practice architecture until his retirement in 1955. His most significant designs were accomplished between 1934 and 1942.

FRANCIS JOSEPH McCARTHY

McCarthy was born in 1910 and took his degree in Engineering at Stanford University. He worked as a draftsman in the office of William W. Wurster before he established his own independent practice in 1938. His most important work belongs to the pre-1942 Bay Area Tradition. He died in 1965.

CHARLES W. MOORE

Born in 1925, Moore received the degree of Bachelor of Architecture in 1947 from the University of Michigan, a Master of Fine Arts from Princeton University in 1956, and a doctorate in Architecture from Princeton in 1957. From 1947 to 1949 he worked in the San Francisco Bay Area in the offices of Mario Corbett, Joseph Allen Stein, and Hervey Clark. From 1962 to 1965, he was Chairman of the Department of Architecture at the College of Environmental Design, University of California, Berkeley. During this period the firm of Moore/Lyndon/Turnbull/Whitaker was also formed. The firm contributed significantly to the field of residential design in the Bay Area at this time. From 1965 to 1969 Moore was Chairman of the Department of Architecture and Dean of the Faculty of Design at Yale University. In 1970 the firm became Charles Moore Associates; in 1975, Moore/Grover/Harper.

JULIA MORGAN
The architect was born in San Francisco in 1872. She grew up in Oakland and attended the University of California between 1890 and 1894, taking her degree in Engineering. She studied and worked with Bernard Maybeck, then went to Paris to attend the Ecole des Beaux-Arts. She left the Beaux-Arts in 1900 and worked in France for two years with the architect Chaussemiche. In 1902 she returned to San Francisco and worked in the office of John Galen Howard. She started her own practice in 1904 and continued until she closed her office in 1950. Most of her major work was accomplished between 1910 and 1930. She died in 1957.

LOUIS CHRISTIAN MULLGARDT
The architect was born in Washington, Missouri, in 1866. He obtained his architectural education through working in several offices in St. Louis; later he worked as a draftsman in the office of Shepley, Rutan and Coolidge in Boston, and of Henry Ives Cobb in Chicago. He opened his own practice in St. Louis in 1894. He later worked for two years in England, and in 1905 he came to San Francisco and worked in the office of George Alexander Wright and Willis Polk. In 1906 he again returned to private practice, which continued through the early 1920's. His major buildings were designed during the decade 1908-18. He died in 1942.

CLAUDE OAKLAND
Born in 1919, the architect received a B.S. in Architecture from Tulane University in 1941. He worked as a designer in the San Francisco firm of Anshen & Allen from 1950 to 1960, contributing substantially to the design of housing for the developer Joseph Eichler. In 1963 the firm became Claude Oakland & Associates.

RICHARD C. PETERS
Born in 1928, Peters received Bachelor of Architecture and Bachelor of Science degrees from Georgia Institute of Technology in 1956, and a Master of Fine Arts in Architecture degree from Princeton University in 1958. He has been most active in the field of residential design in the Bay Area, as a lighting consultant in private practice from 1958 to 1964, and in the firm of Peters, Clayberg &

Caulfield since 1965. From 1972 to 1975 he served as Chairman of the Department of Architecture, College of Environmental Design, University of California, Berkeley.

WILLIS POLK
Polk was born in Jacksonville, Illinois, in 1867. He grew up in St. Louis, and in 1880 he was apprenticed to the St. Louis architect Jerome B. Legg. By the mid-1880's he was in partnership with his father, and at the end of the decade he worked in the St. Louis office of Van Brunt and Howe. In 1888 he worked briefly in Los Angeles for Ernest Coxhead. He then entered the New York office of A. Page Brown and accompanied Brown when the office was moved to San Francisco (in 1889). In 1890 he established a partnership with F. M. Gamble; later he worked for and with several firms including that of Daniel Burnham. His major works occurred from 1893 through the early 1900's. He continued to practice actively until his death in 1924.

WALTER H. RATCLIFF
Ratcliff was born in London in 1881 and came with his parents to California in 1897. He attended the University of California at Berkeley and studied under Bernard Maybeck and John Galen Howard. After his graduation in 1903 he worked in the Howard office along with William Gray Purcell. He went to Europe in 1906-7 to study architecture on his own, and when he returned late in 1907 he set up his own private practice in San Francisco. Between 1914 and 1920 he was the City Architect of Berkeley. He died in 1973 in Berkeley.

GEORGE ROCKRISE
Rockrise was born in 1916 and educated at Syracuse University in New York. He received the degree of Master of Architecture from Columbia University in 1941. He came to San Francisco and worked in the office of Thomas Church as a designer of pool houses and other garden structures. In private practice from 1949 to 1959, he was most active in the field of residential design. After 1960 his work turned increasingly to other fields, including urban design. His firm was Rockrise & Watson from 1960 to 1967 and Rockrise and Associates in 1968, and has been Rockrise/Odermatt/Mountjoy/Amis since 1971.

ROBERT ROYSTEN
Born in 1918, Roysten was educated at the University of California, Berkeley, where he received the degree of Bachelor of Science in Plant Science in 1940. He has been a major contributor to the field of landscape design since 1945 as a principal partner in the following firms: Eckbo, Roysten & Williams, 1945-1957; Roysten, Hanamoto & Mays, 1958; Roysten, Hanamoto, Mays & Beck, 1960, and Roysten, Hanamoto, Beck & Abey since 1967.

THOMAS GORDON SMITH

Thomas Gordon Smith was born in Oakland, California, in 1948. After receiving a B.A. in Art and Modern Dance in 1970, followed by an M.Arch. in 1975 from the University of California, Berkeley, he worked in several Bay Area architectural offices. A Rome Prize in architecture enabled him to spend the year 1979-80 in Rome at the American Academy. Returning to the Bay Area, Smith opened his own office which he maintained from 1981 to 1986, when he joined the faculty of the School of Architecture at the University of Illinois in Chicago (where he also has an office). Smith has received two Graham Foundation grants. The first (1983) funded work on his book, *Classical Architecture: Rule and Invention,* (Peregrine Smith Books, 1988). The second (1987), supplemented by grants from the American Philosophical Society and the University of Illinois Campus Research Board, is being used to document Hellenistic buildings in Turkey with the goal of illustrating Vitruvius' *Ten Books.*

DANIEL SOLOMON

Born in 1939, Solomon received the degrees of Bachelor of Architecture in 1963 and Master of Architecture in 1966 from the University of California, Berkeley. He has been in private practice in San Francisco since 1967. He is on the faculty of the Department of Architecture, College of Environmental Design, University of California, Berkeley.

CLAUDE STOLLER

Stoller was born in 1921 and educated at Black Mountain College and Harvard University, where he received the degree of Master of Architecture from the Graduate School of Design in 1949. He was in partnership with Robert Marquis from 1956 to 1973 and active in the field of residential design in private practice since 1973. He also served during those years on the faculty of the Department of Architecture, University of California, Berkeley.

HUGO W. STORCH

Born in San Dimas, Mexico, in 1873, Storch attended school in Mazatlán and San Francisco. Little is known of his career except that he worked in the office of the San Francisco architect John Gash, in the 1890's. He was apparently more in demand as an engineer than as an architect and was an expert at integrating elevator structures into existing buildings. He died in 1917.

JOHN HUDSON THOMAS

The architect was born in Ward, Nevada, in 1878. His younger years were spent in the Bay Area until he went east to Yale University, from which he graduated in 1902. In the fall of 1902 he entered the Department of Architecture at the University of California, Berkeley, and studied under Bernard Maybeck and John Galen Howard. After receiving his degree in architecture he worked for two years in the Berkeley office of Howard. In 1906 he entered into partnership with George T. Plowman. In 1910 he established his own independent practice which continued until his death in 1945. His work was not frequently published, but examples can be found in the *Architect and Engineer* and in the *Western Architect.*

WILLIAM TURNBULL

Turnbull was born in 1935 and was educated at Princeton University, where he received the degrees of Bachelor of Arts in 1956 and Master of Fine Arts in Architecture in 1959. From 1960 to 1963 he worked in the San Francisco office of Skidmore, Owings & Merrill and also joined the firm of Moore/Lyndon/Turnbull/Whitaker from 1962 to 1965. In 1965 the firm became M/L/T W–Moore/Turnbull, and in 1970, M/L/T/W–Turnbull Associates. Turnbull's work has been mainly in the residential field.

DMITRI VEDENSKY

Born in 1930, Vedensky received the degrees of Bachelor of Art in Architecture in 1952 and Master of Arts in Architecture in 1955. From 1955 to 1963 he worked as a designer in the office of Joseph Esherick and since 1964 has practiced privately in residential design.

FRANCIS VIOLICH

Born in 1911, Violich received a Bachelor of Science in Landscape Architecture in 1934. From then until 1936 he worked for the Rural Resettlement Administration. After a year of graduate work at Harvard he worked for the Farm Security Administration from 1937 to 1939. In 1943, after extensive travel in Latin America and work for the Pan-American Union, he joined the faculty of the City and Regional Planning Department of the University of California. In 1951 he assumed a joint appointment in Planning and Landscape Architecture, from which he retired in 1976.

DAVID WEINGARTEN

Weingarten was born at Fort Ord, California, in 1952 and grew up in Monterey. In 1973, he received a B.A. in Political Science from Yale University; in 1977, he received an M. Arch. from U.C. Berkeley. Weingarten formed a partnership with classmate Lucia Howard following their graduation. First called Acme Plan Preparers, the office has been called ACE Architects since 1982. Weingarten has also taught in the Department of Architecture at U.C. Berkeley.

WILLIAM W. WURSTER

The architect was born in 1895 in Stockton, California. He studied architecture at the University of California, Berkeley, under John Galen Howard, and graduated in 1919. He then worked in the New York office of Delano and Aldrich, and in the San Francisco office of John Reid. He established his own practice in 1926; in 1944 Theodore C. Bernardi became a partner, and in 1945 Donn Emmons became a third partner. Wurster taught at MIT in the early 1940's and became Dean of its School of Architecture in 1944. In 1951 he returned to the West to be Dean of the School of Architecture of the University of California, Berkeley (later the College of Environmental Design). His most provocative work was accomplished during the 1930's and early 1940's. He died in 1973.

WALTER RAYMOND YELLAND

He was born in Los Gatos, California, c. 1890. He went east to study at the University of Pennsylvania and then returned to California to study architecture at the University of California, Berkeley. He began his own private practice in 1917 and continued to be very active until World War II. In the early 1950's he moved to Milan, Italy, and he died there in 1966.

Index

Aalto, Alvar, 20
ACE Architects, 350-55
  Darrell Place Condominiums, San
    Francisco (1986), 350-55
AGORA, 305
Alameda, Calif., 27, 252
Allen, William S., 361
American Institute of Architects Journal, 358
Anshen, Robert, 250, 361
Anshen & Allen, 171, 250, 359
  Eichler home, Terra Linda (1955), 251
  Greenmeadow, Palo Alto (c. 1950), 250
Architect and Engineer, 7, 101, 37, 358
Architect's Yearbook, 8, 357
Architectural Forum, 156, 165, 313, 358, 359
Architectural League of New York, 357
Architectural News, (San Francisco), 80
Architectural Record, 3, 170, 313, 358
Ariston Standardized Casement Window, 101
Art in America, 358
Art News, 357
l'Art Nouveau, 14, 68
Arts and Architecture, 7
Arts and Crafts. *See* Craftsman
  Movement
Atchison Village, Richmond, Calif.,
  (1941-42), 237, 246
Atherton, Calif., 80, 81, 110, 358

Baroque architecture, 40
Bates, Congressman George W., 238
Batey, Andrew, 316-22, 361
  Leonard house, Napa Valley (1977),
    316-19
Batey & Mack, 319-22
  Kirlin house, Napa (1981), 320-22
Bauer, Catherine, 147, 232, 234, 281

Baylis, Douglas, 175
Beaux-Arts. *See* Ecole des Beaux-Arts
Bechtel Marinship, 238
Belvedere Lagoon, 211
Belvedere Peninsula, 10, 60, 63, 64, 65,
  67, 70, 71, 80, 211, 221, 227
Bénard, Emile, 76
Berkeley, Calif., 4, 5, 12-19, 38-41, 43-55,
  71, 73-79, 81-83, 86, 87, 89, 92, 94, 95,
  100-12, 114, 133, 206, 231, 254, 257, 333,
  337, 358
Bernardi, Theodore, 147, 197, 238, 239,
  254, 257, 361
  Bernardi house, Sausalito (1950), 197,
    198
Big Sur, Calif., 126, 281
Bohannson, David, 243
Bolinas, Calif., 309
Born, Ernest, 7, 170, 171, 357
  Born house, San Francisco (1950-51),
    170, 171
Boston, Mass., 8, 10
Breuer, Marcel, 140, 155, 170, 171, 172, 185,
  358, 359
Brown, A. Page, 23, 24, 36-39, 80, 81, 82
  California Building, World Columbian
    Exposition, Chicago (1893), 80
  Church of the New Jerusalem (Sweden-
    borgian), San Francisco (1899), 36, 37,
    38, 39
  Mary Ann Crocker Old People's
    Home, San Francisco (1890), 36
Brown, E. B., 122
Built in U.S.A., 171
Bull, Henrik, 177, 183, 266, 275, 277, 280,
  361
  house, San Rafael (1966), 276, 277, 278,
    279

Sims house, San Francisco Peninsula
  (1961), 274, 275
Bungalow, 7, 8, 87. *See also* Craftsman
  Movement
Burlingame, Calif., 198
Byzantine architecture, 10, 50

Cairns, Burton, 231, 234
California Engineer, 358
Callister, Charles W., 10, 20, 214, 220,
  254, 257, 259, 266, 361
  Heritage Woods, Avon, Conn., 254
  house, Berkeley (1948), 217
  house, Berkeley (1952), 218, 219
  house, Berkeley (1958), 220, 221, 222
Callister & Payne, 254, 257
  Hiller Highlands, Berkeley (1967-72),
    254, 257
Campbell, John, houseboat (1965), 305,
  310
Campbell, John C., 171, 183, 206, 211, 361.
  See also Campbell & Wong
Campbell, R. N., 243
Campbell & Wong, 171, 183, 206, 211
  house, Belvedere Lagoon (1958), 213, 214
  house, San Francisco Peninsula (c.
    1960), 182
  house, Saratoga (1963), 211, 212
Canyon, Calif., 309
Carmel, Calif., 102, 114, 119
Castlewood Country Club, 110
Chicago, 80
Church, Thomas, 126, 133, 142, 163, 169,
  172, 174, 198, 214, 238, 362
  Donnell garden, Sonoma County
    (1947-48), 175
  garden, Burlingame (1954), 199, 201
  small garden, San Francisco, 167

Cincinnati, Ohio, 64
City Beautiful Movement, 8, 12. *See also* Ecole des Beaux-Arts
Clark, Hervey Parke, 17, 159, 238, 243, 357, 359, 362
Clark & Beuttler, 171
Classicism, 337, 339
Clients (architectural), 8, 76, 80, 99, 100, 125, 129, 183
Colonial Revival (U.S.), 4, 10, 16, 36, 57, 99. *See also* Federal Revival
Comstock, Hugh W., 102, 114, 119, 358, 362
  cottage, Carmel (1925), 119
Tuck Box Shop, Carmel (1926), 114, 118
Confer, Frederick, 359
Confer & Ostwald, 171
Congrés Internationaux d'Architecture Moderne, 215, 232
Contra Costa County, Calif., 155, 251
Corbett, Mario, 10, 20, 159, 170, 171, 177, 183, 362
  house, Wolfback Ridge, Marin County (1948), 20, 180, 181
Cotswold cottage architecture, 16
Coxhead, Ernest, 6, 9-14, 16, 22-34, 36-38, 40, 47, 57, 60, 62, 63, 66, 69, 73, 76, 80, 87, 97, 98, 100, 102, 314, 340, 354, 362
  Coxhead house, San Francisco (1893), 24-27
  Coxhead house, San Mateo (1903), 27, 28, 29
  Earl house, Los Angeles (1895), 24
  Greenlease house, Alameda (1892-94), 27, 30, 31
  Holy Innocents Church, San Francisco (1890), 11
  Murdoch house, San Francisco (1892), 57, 60, 62, 66, 67
  Pacific Avenue house, San Francisco (1902), 32-34
  Porter house, San Francisco (1902), 32-34, 69
  St. John's Episcopal Church, Petaluma (c. 1890), 10, 11
  St. John's Episcopal Church, San Francisco (1890), 10, 24
  St. John's Episcopal Church, Monterey (1891), 10, 11
  Waybur house, San Francisco (1902), 32, 33, 34, 69
Craftsman Movement (Arts and Crafts), 3, 8, 9, 12, 13, 14, 38, 68, 73, 83, 87, 90, 92, 102, 183, 197
Cramm, Ralph Adams, 10
Croly, Herbert D., 3, 4, 357

Dailey, Gardner, 5-10, 17, 20, 156-59, 161, 163, 165, 166, 169, 171, 183, 202, 359, 362
  Coyote Point Training School, San Mateo County (1942-43), 183
  house, Woodside (1940), 5, 158

Flats on Telegraph Hill, San Francisco (1941), 166
  house, Ross (1940), 159
  Owens house, Sausalito (1939), 183, 184
Daly City, Calif., 229
Davis, Charles, 344
Delano, William Adams, 358
Delano & Aldrich, 122
DeMars, Vernon, 231, 232, 238, 246, 248, 359, 362
  Firebaugh Farmworkers' Camp, 233
  Visalia Farmworkers' Camp (c. 1937), 233
  Woodville Farmworkers Camp 232, 235
  Yuba City Farmworkers' Camp 232, 235
DeMars & Hardison, 246, 247, 248, 249
  Easter Hill Village, Richmond (1954), 246, 247, 248
  Plaza Project, Richmond (1957), 249
Depression of the 1930s, 4, 124, 155, 163, 165, 231
Dinwiddie, John Ekin, 6, 7, 17, 159, 171, 357, 359, 362
  Roos house, San Francisco, (1938), 6, 161, 162
Dodge, Peter, 295, 344, 362
Doelger, Henry, 229
Drexler, Arthur, 357
Duchamp, Marcel, 31

Earthquake of 1906 (San Francisco), 80
East Bay, 334
Easter Hill Village. *See* DeMars & Hardison
Eckbo, Garrett, 231, 244, 362
Eckbo, Roysten & Williams, 171, 172, 205, 206, 207, 214, 215
  garden, Atherton (1957), 215
Ecole des Beaux-Arts, 12, 38, 76, 80, 156, 183. *See also* City Beautiful Movement
Eichler, Joseph, 230, 244, 248, 250, 251, 252, 253
  Eichler home, Sunnyvale (1960), 250, 252
  Greenmeadows, Palo Alto (1953), 250
Ellis, Mrs. Ralph, 122, 125
Emmons, Donn, 148, 197, 238, 239, 254, 257, 362
  Emmons, house, Mill Valley (1948), 197, 198
Esherick & Esherick, 194-96
  Esherick house, Kentfield (1950), 194-96
Esherick, Homsey, Dodge & Davis, 266, 291, 344-45
  The Hermitage, San Francisco (1984), 344-45
  Romano house, Kentwoodlands (1972), 298, 302, 303
Esherick, Joseph, 10, 17, 20, 22, 165, 171, 183, 184, 198, 266, 277, 291, 344, 350, 352, 359, 362-63
  Cary house, Mill Valley (1960), 298-301
  Esherick house, Ross (1946), 193

  house, Kentwoodlands (1957), 202, 203
  townhouse, San Francisco (1951), 185-88
Esherick, Rebecca Woods, 195
Esherick, Wharton, 183

Farm Security Administration, 231-38, 247, 248, 261, 263
Farr, Albert, 60, 63, 69, 70, 71, 363
  Belvedere Land Company building, Belvedere (1905), 70, 71
  London house, Sonoma County (1911), 69
  townhouse, San Francisco (c. 1900), 69
Federal Revival in architecture, 4, 99. *See also* Regency Revival
Federal Terrace, 237
Fernau & Hartman, 325-32
  Marin County house, Marin County (1985), 330-32
  Marin County villa, Marin County (1983), 325-30
Fernau, Richard, 325-32, 363
Filtration Division of the City of Sacramento, 122
Firebaugh, Calif., 233
Fisher, Robert A., 363
Fisher-Friedman, 259, 260
  Islandia, Alameda (1966-69), 260
Fitzgibbon, James, 267
Foster City, Calif., 251
French Norman architecture, 16, 40. *See also* Norman Revival
Friedman, Rodney, 363
Fuller, Buckminster, 261
Funk, John, 6, 8, 10, 17, 171, 172, 185, 206, 244, 251, 357, 363
  Funk house, Lafayette, (1948), 171, 172
  house, Los Altos Hills (1955), 207, 208
  townhouse, San Francisco (1948), 191
  Woerner house, Marin County (1948), 173, 176, 177

Gebhard, David, 313, 358
Georgian architecture (English), 40, 69, 71, 99
German architecture, 14, 40
Gilbert, Cass, 10
Gill, Irving, 92, 170
Gladding McBean & Co., 100, 358
Golden Gate International Exposition, San Francisco (1939), 7, 357
Goodman, Michael, 6, 17, 163
Gothic architecture, 43, 50, 72, 95
Gothic Revival, 8, 99, 100
Great Society, 258, 259
Greek Revival, 4, 99
Green, Aaron, 238, 243
Greene, Charles, 170
Greene & Greene, 170
Greene, Henry, 170
Greenwood Common, 244-46
Gregory, Frances, 76
Gregory, Mr. and Mrs. Warren, 76, 122, 123, 145

Gromme, Carl, 363
Gropius, Walter, 156, 170, l85, 358, 359
Gutterson, Henry, 9, 10, 14, 16, 102, 104, 108, 358, 363
   Evans house, Berkeley, 358
   Farmer house, Berkeley (1918), 104, 108, 314
   McDuffie house, Berkeley, 358
   Rich house, Berkeley, 358

Halprin, Lawrence, 171, 172, 174, 175, 195, 227, 238, 246, 247, 254, 363
   Esherick garden, Kentfield (1950), 194-96
   garden, Belvedere (1957), 226
   garden, Woodside (1949), 176, 177-80
   Woerner garden, Marin County (1948), 173, 174, 176, 177
Hamlin, Talbot F., 7, 357
Hardison, Donald, 246, 363
   Potrero Project, Richmond (1960), 249
Hartman, Laura, 325-32, 363
Harvard University, 152, 163, 170, 231, 358
Hearst, Phoebe Apperson, 81
Hearst, William Randolph, 92
Heims, Richard, 202
   garden, Kentwoodlands (1957), 202
Herman, Jack, 359
Hill, Albert Henry, 10, 20, 170, 185, 203, 205, 357, 358-59, 363
   house, Orinda (1951-53), 203-6
   townhouse, San Francisco (1952-53), 192
Hillmer, Jack, 20, 214, 217, 220, 221, 222, 364
   house, Belvedere (1950), 223-25
Hillmer & Callister, 214
   house, Kentwoodlands (1946-47), 215, 216
Hillsborough, Calif., 248
Hirshen, Sanford, 261, 263, 264
   housing, Indio, Riverside County, 261, 262
   housing, Watsonville, Calif., 262-64
Hirshen & van der Ryn, 261, 263
Hitchcock, Henry-Russell, 6, 7, 357
Hollins, Marion, 125, 126
Homsey, George, 10, 20, 267, 269, 344, 364
   Rubin house, Albany (1960), 267, 269
Hopi style, 92
Howard, Henry, 123
Howard, John Galen, 9, 76-80, 123, 245, 364
   Howard house, Berkeley (1912), 76-80
Howard, Lucia, 350-55, 364
Howe, George, 183
Hyde, Charles, 122

Indian art (American), 14, 92
International (Modern) Style, 7, 16, 22, 161, 170, 185, 230, 232, 247, 261, 359

Japanese influence, 158, 159, 214, 217, 219

Jones, A. Quincy, 250
Jones, Carr, 10, 16, 114-18, 358, 364
   house, Piedmont (c. 1930), 117
   house, Palo Alto (1934), 114, 116
Jones & Emmons, 250
Joseph, Phillip E., 357
Journal of the American Institute of Planners, 359

Kahn, Louis I., 20, 261, 266, 267, 280
   bath house, Trenton, N.J. (1955), 267, 268
Kaiser, Henry, 236
Kansas City, Mo., 64
Kaplan, Ellis, 183
Keeler, Charles, 73, 98, 99, 229, 330
Keith, William, 38
Kensington, Calif., 104, 107
Kitchen & Hunt, 359
Klimt, Gustav, 267
Knowles, William F., 30-33, 60, 63, 364
Kotas, Jeremy, 340-43, 364
   Laidley Castle, San Francisco (1980, 1984-85), 340-43
   Laidley Street project (unbuilt), 340, 34
Kump, Ernest, 170, 258

Ladera, Calif., 244
Lafayette, Calif., 168, 169, 171
Lake Tahoe, Calif., 102
Landor, Walter, 8, 357
Langhorst, Frederick, 170, 238, 364
Langhorst & Langhorst, 168, 169, 238
Langhorst, Lois, 169, 170, 238, 364
   house, Lafayette (1947-49), 168, 169
Lanier, Albert, 183
Leafe, James, 183
Le Corbusier, 156, 183, 232, 234
Lee, Roger, 20, 206, 364
   house, Berkeley (1955), 209
   house, Mill Valley (1956), 210
Life Magazine, 156
Livermore Valley, Calif., 252
Lloyd, Francis, 238, 243, 365
London, Jack, 69
Long Island, N.Y., 122
Los Angeles, Calif., 24, 57, 76, 244, 263, 357
Lucas Valley, Calif., 251
Lym, Glenn, 333-34, 365
   Tibbetts house, Berkeley (1978), 333-34
Lyndon, Donlyn, 10, 20, 254, 256, 257, 268, 280-88, 289, 365. *See also* Moore/Lyndon/Turnbull/Whitaker

Macintosh, Charles R., 14
Mack, Mark, 316-22, 365
Madera, Calif., 202
Magazine of Art, 7, 357, 358
Marin County, Calif., 8, 43, 102, 158, 172, 238, 241, 242, 243, 263, 322, 325
Marquis, Robert, 365

Marquis & Stoller, 258, 266
   Green-Johnston house, Sausalito (1960), 267, 270, 271
   Hecht house, San Francisco (1973), 304, 306, 307
   Pence House, Mill Valley (1965), 267, 272, 273
   St. Francis Square, San Francisco (1961), 258
Massachusetts Institute of Technology, 76, 147, 152, 246
Mathews, Arthur, 68
Mathews, Edgar, 60, 63, 64, 68, 365
   apartment house, San Francisco (c. 1900), 68
Mathewson, Joanne, 314
May, Cliff, 322, 323, 325, 357
Maybeck, Bernard, 5-9, 12-14, 16, 20, 22, 23, 30, 34, 35, 36, 38-53, 60, 63, 71, 73, 76, 82, 97, 98, 100-05, 170, 183, 229, 264, 276, 314, 330, 337, 340, 352, 365
   Anthony house, Los Angeles (1927), 102
   Boke house, Berkeley (1902), 5, 38-40
   Chick house, Berkeley (1913), 13, 46, 48, 49
   Christian Science Church, Berkeley (1910), 48, 50-53, 82
   Faculty Club, University of California, Berkeley (1902; 1903-4), 13
   Goslinsky house, San Francisco (1909), 14, 34, 35
   house in Forest Hill, San Francisco (1916), 104
   Keeler house, Berkeley (1894), 13
   Kellog house, Palo Alto (1899), 13
   Kennedy house, Berkeley (1923), 102, 103
   Mathewson house, Berkeley (1916), 40, 41
   Palace of Fine Arts, Panama Pacific Exposition, San Francisco (1915), 13, 14
   Roos house, San Francisco (1909; 1926), 40, 42, 43
   Senger house, Berkeley (1907), 43, 44, 45, 57
Mayhew, Clarence, 17, 231, 315, 365
McCarthy, Francis Joseph, 6, 10, 17, 159, 170, 359, 365
McCue, Boone, & Tomsick, 359
McKim, Mead & White, 76
Medieval architecture (English), 16, 24, 63, 99
Mediterranean Revival. *See* Spanish Colonial Revival
Mendelson, Eric, 359
Mexican architecture, 10, 12
Mills, C. Wright, 251
Mill Valley, Calif., 197, 198, 206, 210, 267, 272, 273
Minneapolis, Minn., 8
Mission Revival, 3, 10, 12, 14, 38, 51, 80, 81, 82, 83, 84, 86, 90, 94, 95, 156
Mock, Elizabeth, 8, 357, 359

Modern Movement, 49, 97, 156, 157, 161, 169, 171, 183, 230, 243, 359
Modesto, Calif., 171
Moler, Steen, 325
Monterey, Calif., 10, 11
Monterey Colonial Style, 156, 157
Monterey Revival Style, 4, 16
Montgomery, Roger, 313, 358, 359
Moore, Charles W., 10, 20, 22, 114, 177, 183, 231, 246, 253, 254, 259, 263, 264, 313, 322-25, 352, 359, 365. *See also* Moore/Lyndon/Turnbull/Whitaker
    Licht house, Mill Valley (1980), 322-25
    Moore house, Orinda (1962), 254-56, 267, 268, 280-85, 288-91
Moore/Lyndon/Turnbull/Whitaker, 254-56, 267, 268, 280-85, 288-89
    Bonham house, Big Sur (1961), 280-83
    Jenkins house, (1962), 267-69
    Jobson house, Big Sur (1961), 281, 285
    Sea Ranch Condominiums, Sea Ranch, (1965), 230, 246, 253-56, 258
    Talbert House, Oakland (1962), 21, 280, 281, 284
Moore & Turnbull:
    Budge house, Healdsburg (1966), 290, 291
Morgan, Julia, 9, 14, 71, 72-80, 83, 183, 344, 366
    William Randolph Hearst house, San Simeon (1919-37), 72-73
    house, Berkeley, 71
    Howard house, library addition, Berkeley (1927), 79, 80
    Livermore house, San Francisco (1917), 72, 73
    St. John's Presbyterian Church, Berkeley (1910), 73-76, 83
Mt. Diablo, Calif., 134
Mt. Tamalpais, Calif., 159
Mullgardt, Louis C., 9, 84-89, 366
    Evans house, Mill Valley (1907), 84-88
    Taylor house, Berkeley (1908), 86, 89
Mumford, Lewis, 3, 170, 232, 357, 359
Museum of Modern Art (New York), 3, 7, 8, 171, 232, 357, 359

Napa Valley, 319
Neo-Primitivism, 319, 320
Neuhaus, Eugene, 100, 358
Neutra, Richard, 156, 172, 237
    Channel Heights, San Pedro (1942), 237
New Brutalist architecture, 8
New Deal, 229, 230-32, 243, 248, 259
Newsom, Samuel & Joseph C., 229, 264
New Yorker, 357
New York Times Magazine, 358
Norman (French) architecture, 16
Norman Revival, 99, 100, 110

Oakland, Claude, 250, 366
Oakland, Calif., 8, 14, 21, 43, 90-94, 118, 155, 169

Office of Economic Opportunity, 261
Old Russian Hill Assn., 344
Olsen, Donald, 359
Oriental architecture, 50, 95

Palo Alto, Calif., 7, 13, 114-17, 147
Panama Pacific International Exposition of 1915, San Francisco, 83
Pasatiempo, Calif., 126, 148
Pencil Points (Progressive Architecture), 6, 7, 357
Petaluma, Calif., 10, 11, 202
Peters, Richard, 10, 20, 291, 366
Peters, Clayberg & Caulfield, 266, 295, 296, 297
    Falk house, Berkeley, (1974), 295, 296, 297
Peters & Dodge, 294, 295
    Graham house, Berkeley (1963), 294, 295
Philadelphia, Pa., 183, 266
Piedmont, Calif., 110, 113, 358
Pilot Project (Hardison & DeMars), 248
Planned Unit Developments, 245
Plowman, George, 87
Point Richmond, Calif., 145
Polk, Willis, 6, 7, 9, 10, 12, 14, 16, 22, 23, 24, 27, 30, 36, 37, 38, 40, 56, 57-61, 63-65, 67, 72, 73, 80, 81, 82, 87, 97, 98, 183, 340, 344, 354, 366
    Batten house, San Francisco (1891), 56, 57
    gatehouse, Coryell estate, Atherton, (c. 1912), 80, 81
    Polk-Williams house, Russian Hill, San Francisco (1892), 10, 11, 57-61, 344
    Rey house, Belvedere Peninsula (1893), 10, 60, 63, 67, 80
Porter, Bruce, 31, 36, 38
Portland, Ore., 64, 183
Poujiatine, Ivan, 305, 308, 309
    Poujiatine house, Marin County (1972), 305, 308, 309
Prairie School of architecture, 14, 90, 95
Pre-fabrication, 169
Pueblo art, 14. *See also* Indian Art
Pyle, Nicholas, 325

Queen Anne Revival, 10, 27, 57, 78, 90. *See also* Colonial Revival; Shingle Style

Rainwater, Lee, 359
Ranch house (California), 7, 8, 125, 157, 206, 318, 322, 357
Ransom, Harry, 231
Ratcliff, W. H., Jr., 10, 14, 16, 102, 104, 109, 358, 366
    Heitman house, Berkeley (1927), 358
    Naylor house, Berkeley (1927), 104, 109, 358
Reed, John, Jr., 122

Regency Revival, 16, 157
Reid, Kenneth, 357
Richardson, Henry Hobson, 76
Richmond, Calif., 230, 236, 237, 246, 248, 249, 334
Rockrise, George, 174, 211, 227, 366
    house, Atherton (1957), 215
    house, Belvedere (1957), 226
Romanesque architecture, 10
Roysten, Robert, 171, 175, 366
    garden, Funk house, Lafayette (1948), 171, 172
    garden, Los Altos Hills (1955), 207
    garden, Orinda (1951-55), 205
Roysten, Hanamoto & Beck, 254, 257
    Hiller Highlands (landscape architects), Berkeley (1967-72), 254, 257
Rural Resettlement Admin., 231
Russian Hill, 344, 347

Sandburg, Carl, 6
San Diego, Calif., 156
Sandy & Babcock, 259
    Pajaro Dunes, Santa Cruz (1974), 259
San Francisco Museum of Art, 3, 169, 170, 357, 358
San Jose, Calif., 252
San Leandro, Calif., 155
San Mateo, Calif., 27, 28, 29, 155
San Rafael, Calif., 277
San Simeon, Calif., 72
Santa Clara Valley, Calif., 155, 248, 251
Santa Cruz, Calif., 6, 17, 19, 123, 125, 134
Sausalito, Calif., 237, 238
Schindler, R. N., 156
Schweinfurth, A. C., 9, 10, 36, 51-55, 80, 81, 82
    Hacienda del Pozo de Verona, Pleasanton, 81
    Moody house, Berkeley (1898), 51, 52, 53
    Unitarian Church, Berkeley (1899), 54, 55
Scott, Mel, 155, 237, 238, 358, 359
Secessionist architecture, 14, 92, 95
Shepley, Rutan & Coolidge, 76
Shingle Style, 10, 12, 13, 27, 36
Smith, Thomas Gordon, 334, 336-40, 367
    Richmond Hill house, Richmond (1983-84), 334, 336-40
Solano, Calif., 155
Solar energy, 314, 320
Solomon, Daniel (Solomon & Assoc.), 309, 311, 346-50
    Amancio Ergina Village, San Francisco (1985), 348-50
    Glover Street Condominiums, San Francisco (1982), 347-48
    Pacific Heights Townhouses, San Francisco (1979), 347
    Solomon house, San Francisco (1972), 309, 311
Sonoma County, Calif., 68, 174
South African architecture, 51
Spanish architecture, 12
Spanish Colonial Revival, 16, 99, 156, 229, 316, 322, 330, 340

Spanish Medieval architecture, 102
Spencer, Eldridge, 359
Stanford University, 157
Steilberg, Walter, 72, 74, 183
Stein, Joseph, 244, 359
Stick Style, 38
Stickley, Gustave, 38
Stockton, Calif., 122
Stoller, Claude, 367
Storch, Hugo, 82, 83, 84, 367
  Park Congregational Church, Berkeley
    (1916), 82, 83, 84
Summerson, Sir John, 281
Sunnyvale, Calif., 248, 250
Sunset Magazine, 7, 357, 358
Swiss architecture, 14, 38
Syosset, N.Y., 122

Tantau, Clarence, 10, 14, 126
Telegraph Hill, 346, 350
Thomas, John Hudson, 9, 10, 14, 15, 16,
    17, 18, 22, 84, 87, 89, 90-97, 102,
    104-7, 358, 367
  Bell (Wintermute) house, Berkeley
    (1913), 94-97
  Dungan house, Berkeley (1915), 14, 15,
    105-7
  Hume house, Berkeley (1928), 16, 17, 18,
    358
  Locke house, Oakland (1911), 14, 90-91
  Peters house, Berkeley (1915), 14, 15, 92,
    94
  Randolph house, Berkeley (1913), 87, 89,
    90
  Thomas house, Kensington (1928), 104,
    107
Thompson, Elizabeth Kendall, 170
Tudor Revival, 94, 100
Turnbull, William (Wm. Turnbull &
    Assoc.), 10, 20, 22, 254-56, 267, 268,
    280-85, 289-93, 314-17, 367
  Allewelt house, near Madera (1977),
    314-17
  Tatum house, Monterey Bay (1973), 291

United States Bureau of Labor Statistics,
    169
University of California, Berkeley, 9, 13,
    76, 100, 122, 148, 163, 171, 231, 232, 337,
    346, 350, 358
University of Pennsylvania, 183
Usonian houses, 277

Vallejo, General Mariano, 202
Vallejo, Calif., 237, 238
Van der Rohe, Mies, 50, 156

Van der Ryn, Sim, 261, 263
Vedensky, Dmitri, 10, 266, 295, 367
  Vedensky house, Sea Ranch (1974), 295,
    297, 298
Veterans Administration, 156
Violich, Francis, 231, 263, 359, 367
Visalia, Calif., 233
Vitruvius, 71
Voysey, Charles F. A., 13, 14, 102

Walnut Creek, Calif., 251
War housing, 236-43
Warnecke, John Carl, 238, 243
Warner, Daniel, 183
Waybur, Julian, 31
Weingarten, David, 350-55, 367
Western Architect and Engineer, 220
White, Bolton, 359
Winter, Robert, 358
Wöfflin, Heinrich, 266
Wolfback Ridge, Calif., 20
Wong, Worley, 171, 183, 206, 211
Woodbridge, John, 358
Woodbridge, Sally, 358
"Wood-Butchers," 9, 114, 309
Worcester, Joseph, 36, 37, 38, 99, 344
World Columbian Exposition of 1893,
    Chicago, 80
World War II, 17, 148, 152, 155, 243, 245,
    265, 266
Wright, Frank Lloyd, 14, 170, 217, 221,
    238, 248, 250, 266, 267, 275, 277, 280
Wurster, Catherine Bauer. *See* Bauer,
    Catherine
Wurster, William W., 4, 6, 7, 8, 10 16,
    17, 19, 20, 22, 121-53 154-59, 161, 163,
    170, 177, 183, 197, 202, 217, 232, 234,
    235, 238, 245, 250, 265, 266, 314, 323,
    352, 357, 359, 368
  Benner house, Berkeley (1934), 133
  Butler house, Pasatiempo (1931-32), 126,
    129
  Carquinez Heights, Vallejo (c. 1941), 238
  Chabot Terrace, Vallejo (c. 1941),
    238-40
  Chickering house, Woodside (1941),
    140, 141
  Church house, Pasatiempo (1931) 126, 131
  Clark house, Aptos (1937), 134, 135
  Corbus house, Palo Alto (1941), 147
  Doble house, San Francisco (1939), 142
  Dondo house, Point Richmond (1935),
    145, 146
  Green house, Mt. Diablo (1938), 134,
    136
  Gregory farmhouse, Santa Cruz
    (1926-27), 6, 17, 19, 123-25, 202, 252,
    257, 323

Grover house, San Francisco (1939), 4,
    165, 192, 193
Hammill house, San Francisco (1937),
    134, 135
Harley-Stevens house, San Francisco
    (1940), 163, 164
Hollins house, Pasatiempo (1931), 126,
    127
Jensen house, Berkeley (1937), 143, 144
Kaplansky-Howes house, Pasatiempo
    (1931), 126, 128
Le Hane house, Palo Alto (1937), 7, 137
MacKenzie house, Pasatiempo (1931),
    126, 130
Pasatiempo Country Club and Estates,
    Santa Cruz (1931-32), 125-26
Pope house, Orinda (1940), 137, 139, 314
San Leandro Filtration Plant, San
    Leandro (1924), 122
Turner house, Central Valley (1941),
    137, 138
Voss house, Big Sur (1931), 126, 132
Wurster house, Stinson beach (1962),
    148, 152-53
Van Duesen house, Berkeley (1938), 17
Wurster, Bernardi & Emmons, 10, 148-52,
    171, 175, 184, 198, 238, 254, 257
  Coleman house, San Francisco
    (1961-62), 148, 150
  Heller house, Lake Tahoe (1951), 148,
    149
  Henderson house, Burlingame (1954),
    148
  house, Burlingame (1959), 199, 200, 201
  house, Woodside (1949), 176-80
  Pope ranch house, Madera (1958), 149,
    202, 204
  Salz house, San Francisco (1954), 148,
    151
  townhouse, San Francisco (1951), 189,
    190
  Woodlake, San Mateo (1965), 254, 257

Yelland, W. R., 10, 16, 19, 100, 101, 102,
    110-13, 358, 368
  Garthwaite house, Castlewood Country
    Club (1927), 110
  Goss house, Piedmont (1925), 110, 113,
    358
  Miller house, Atherton (1929), 110, 358
  Richards house, Berkeley (1927), 358
  Thornberg Village, Berkeley (1928), 16,
    17, 19, 110-12, 358
  Tupper and Reed Music Store, Ber-
    keley (1926), 100, 101
Yeon, John, 183
Yuba City, Calif., 232, 234, 248
Yuill-Thornton, Alec 183